THE *Sex* DEVOTIONAL

365 DAYS OF PASSION, POSITIONS,
AND PURE PLEASURE

OLIVIA ST. CLAIRE

Adamsmedia
AVON, MASSACHUSETTS

Published by
Adams Media, a division of F+W Media, Inc.
57 Littlefield Street, Avon, MA 02322. U.S.A.
www.adamsmedia.com

ISBN 10: 1-60550-354-1
ISBN 13: 978-1-60550-354-7

Printed in the United States of America.

10 9 8 7 6 5 4 3 2 1

Library of Congress Cataloging-in-Publication Data
is available from the publisher.

This publication is designed to provide accurate and authoritative information with
regard to the subject matter covered. It is sold with the understanding that the
publisher is not engaged in rendering legal, accounting, or other professional advice.
If legal advice or other expert assistance is required, the services of a competent
professional person should be sought.
—From a *Declaration of Principles* jointly adopted by a Committee of the American
Bar Association and a Committee of Publishers and Associations

Many of the designations used by manufacturers and sellers to distinguish their
product are claimed as trademarks. Where those designations appear in this book
and Adams Media was aware of a trademark claim, the designations have been
printed with initial capital letters.

This book is available at quantity discounts for bulk purchases.
For information, please call 1-800-289-0963.

This book has been written to provide information and inspiration. The author is
not engaged in rendering medical, psychological, or other professional services. If
medical or other expert assistance is required, or if persistent physical and/or emotional conditions exist, the services of a competent professional should be sought.
The author is not responsible for any adverse effects or unforeseen consequences
resulting from the use of the information and techniques contained in this book.

Certain sections of this book deal with activities that may be potentially hazardous,
dangerous, or illegal. The author, Adams Media, and F+W Media, Inc. do not
accept liability for any injury, loss, legal consequence, or incidental or consequential
damage incurred by reliance on the information or advice provided in this book.

My heartfelt gratitude goes out to the people who have contributed to the realization of this book:

To my agent, for her brilliant guidance in the book's development, her unwavering support and wise counsel in matters both technical and personal, and her unflagging efforts to find the perfect home for me and my work.

To my friends Deborah, Claudia, and Karen Marie for listening, advising, and opining—brilliantly and generously.

To all the people at Adams Media, especially Paula Munier and Matt Glazer, for being so responsive, supportive, and professional, and for making the book look and feel even better than I hoped.

To my beloved husband, for bringing me tea, hugs, and flashes of insight when I needed them most, charitably staying away when creative sparks needed room to fly, and loving me truly, madly, and deeply, every single day.

Contents

Introduction

With silk, I walk differently.

— KATHARINE HEPBURN

WHEN YOU WEAR silk next to your skin, or feel the beat of a samba, or hear poetry read by a lover, something happens. An inner spark ignites that makes you glow. Your curves get curvier, your thoughts drift over to the wild side, and you burn with a hot, new fire. Suddenly, you've got mystery, edge, and wicked sex appeal.

This alchemy is in a woman's nature. We are never more alive than when in the grip of passion, never more passionate than when caught up in a fever of creation — birthing new life, new ideas, new sensations. We are creatures of transformation, new in every moment, constantly turning the world into magic. No wonder men are enchanted and mystified. When at our dazzling best, we are simply beyond their powers of comprehension.

And yet we forget. Too many meetings, carpools, and evilly constructed swimsuits can drain us of the life-sap we need to branch out and flower. We may get worn down by last year's shoes, lovers who don't worship us as they should, and bosses who make us adhere to schedules instead of our own natural rhythms.

But it doesn't take much to help us remember who we are. A few words, a touch, or an exciting new idea can instantly reconnect us to that hot, incandescent feeling that is the source of our sensual power.

Designed to help you feel that power every day of the year, this little book dishes up something sassy and inspiring for each one of your days and every one of your nights — because when you feel beautiful, smart, and sexy, you make connections you never thought of before. What was once an ordinary spatula becomes a tool for mixing your watercolors or a kinky implement for fun love spankings. Maybe you smell a lilac, and suddenly understand that an armful of heady blossoms would fill your home with sensual bounty and your life with lush, dizzying sex. You begin to see that your sexuality can operate *outside* the bedroom, energizing every part of your life—from the way you dance to the way you write a business proposal or plan a dinner party.

And when you make passion a *daily habit*—as important as exercise, moisturizing, or a healthy breakfast—you change the very fabric of your being. According to studies at the University of Pennsylvania, passionate sensations create feelings of well-being, slow the aging process, boost the immune system, tone muscles and skin, and even build brain power. On top of it all, passion floods your body with endorphins—the chemical agents that promote happiness and peak performance. So when you feel hot and sexy, you are literally zestier, smarter, healthier, and more radiant. You shimmer.

Through the ages, daily devotionals have been the steady companion of women like you, who seek inspiration. But this one provides something new—the brain food and emotional juice that feed your *passion*. Grounded in ideas as ancient as the stars but as modern as your BlackBerry, the days in this book offer a treasure trove of facts that stimulate, practices that pamper, and sex techniques that sizzle. And each weekly theme opens a doorway to places inside passion you probably never thought of before. Whether you consult these pages every day, skip a few now and then, or dip in at your sexy whim, a cornucopia of mind- and body-invigorating images awaits you. If you explore them, they will turn you into an inspired lover who can bring any man to his knees.

It's easy. Just take a moment to give each day's page your full attention. Let the poetry sing to your soul—or tickle your funny bone. Allow the erotic facts and sexy mythology to fire your imagination. Open your heart to the girlfriend-to-girl-friend secrets meant only for You. And if you desire, use your body (and the steamy techniques designed for You Two), to feast in the pleasures of the bedroom.

If, for even a few moments a day, you let these ideas work on you, if you try a tip or two—if you let passion become your habit—you will find that you walk, talk, and think differently. Your every move will breathe the hot perfume of sex. You will charm strangers and astonish lovers. You will discover a power you never knew you had. And, just by being your delicious self, you will cut a sexy—and brilliant—new path through everybody's world. Are you ready?

All of You

Body

We touch Heaven when we lay our hands on a human body.

— NOVALIS

DID YOU KNOW there are forty-five miles of nerves in your skin? Or that, by taking the same pose you had during yesterday's conversation, your body helps you remember it faster? Much more than window dressing, your body is a boundless source of knowledge and pleasure. With one twinge, it can tell you which path to avoid. It can dazzle your senses with sunsets, sonatas, gardenias, and caresses. Your woman's body can create new life, have endless orgasms, and kindle the ecstasy that changes men's lives. All you have to do is be *in* it.

You Instead of giving a kiss, try receiving it with your body. Let the textures of your lover's skin sink into yours. Drink in the moisture of his lips, his wet passion. Your lips will tell you who he is and how to love him. Your body will be awash with new sensations—and more alive and sexier than you knew it could be.

You Two Lay your whole body atop your lover. Tickle his groin with your pubic hair, then insert him. Lift your chest as if doing the Cobra, and rub your nipples against his. Grind circles against his pelvis. This pressurized, whole-body massage awakens every inch of his skin, engorges his genitals, and provides extra clitoral sensation for you.

Mind

An improper mind is a perpetual feast.

—LOGAN PEARSALL SMITH

DURING SEX, YOUR brain works hard, sending out the testosterone that keeps you hot and the oxytocin that makes you want to bond. When you *imagine* sex, it uses nearly the same nerve pathways and triggers the same arousing chemicals. So with one saucy thought, your pulse quickens, your breasts tingle, and you feel like a ripe fruit waiting to be tasted.

You Your "improper mind" can come in handy. Warm up for a quickie by picturing his bare chest five minutes before the event. Soothe menstrual cramps by sending mental heat to the area. Write a juicy love poem—sex hormones stimulate creativity. Attract any man by thinking sultry thoughts as you walk by—your pheromones will be flying.

You Two Although 54 percent of men think about sex every day, you want to make sure his mind is on you. Text him the following messages, about an hour apart. "2nite." "I want." "2 lick." "Your." "(fill in the blank)." The mental imagery and the delayed gratification will put his brain and other vital organs into all-day overdrive. (Just make sure you don't mind that the text trail leads back to you.)

By the way, women's brains contain about 11 percent more brain cells than men's *and* a larger corpus callosum (the tissue connecting left and right sides). So be gentle with him.

Heart

It is only with the heart that one can see rightly;
what is essential is invisible to the eye.

—ANTOINE DE SAINT-EXUPÉRY

ACCORDING TO THE Institute of HeartMath, more than half the cells in your heart are similar to brain cells, capable of feeling, remembering, and learning on their own. When you come from your heart, you know things your brain doesn't—like whether someone is telling the truth, how to access your deepest passion, and exactly which touch will soothe your man or rock his world.

You If you focus your attention in your chest and breathe deeply, your heart produces an electromagnetic field 5,000 times stronger than the brain's. When facing your man, this field begins to synchronize his heart with yours—opening an unspoken dialogue of affection. Try it when you want to change his feelings or overwhelm him with love.

You Two Lick the pad of flesh just under his index, middle, and ring fingers. This is the hand reflexology area for the heart. Slide your tongue between the fingers (representing eyes and ears) and up to his fingertips (head), where you give him a mini "blow job." This integrates his heart and mind, while suggesting what sexy deeds you could be doing elsewhere.

Radiant Well-Being

WE ALREADY KNOW sex makes us feel good, but now science reveals it also helps us be healthier, lovelier, and even smarter. Just *thinking about* sex can produce these results:

- Medical studies at Wilkes University in Pennsylvania found that regular sex increases levels of immunoglobulin A, which boosts the immune system. Kissing, if you make it deep and long, lowers blood pressure and cholesterol levels.
- Making love releases estrogen, which makes hair shinier and skin smoother.
- "Orgasm triggers oxytocin release, causing you to feel more relaxed yet energized with a clear mind," says Jacob Teitelbaum, MD. That means you'll be more focused and creative.
- The Annapolis Fibromyalgia and Fatigue Centers reveal that sex releases a growth hormone that helps you lose weight, relieve pain, and look up to ten years younger.
- According to Derek Noble, host of FIT TV's *Urban Fitness*, sex works your pelvic core, glutes, abs, and legs, helping you tone and sculpt your entire body.
- Once-a-week sex can lead to more regular menstrual cycles and shorter menses, according to studies at Stanford University. It also lessens the severity of PMS.
- Brain-imaging studies at UCLA show that the estrogen released during sex improves memory and brain power.

Soul

*For lovers do not so much make love as they are remade by love —
dipped into the fire, melted down, reshaped.*

— SCOTT RUSSELL SANDERS, *A PRIVATE HISTORY OF AWE*

WHEN SEX IS good, your body trembles, your heart melts, your mind slides into a hot haze — and then something else happens. Your whole body seems to open, as if being taken out of your everyday self into something much brighter and bigger. You're no longer aware of who's doing what to whom, only of the delicious flow of energy between you. Except there is no longer a "between you." There is only a rapturous "one."

You The ancient Tantricas designed peak, soulful moments by viewing themselves as flesh-and-blood goddesses and their mates as gods. Try it. When you do, skin looks softer, more luminescent. Kisses feel satiny and sink deeper into your body. His entry seems to fill you with honey. Together, you create an ecstasy that heals the soul.

You Two Tell him you want to try something from *Playboy*. After several moments of thrusting in missionary, ask him to stop, breathe with you, and gaze into your eyes. (*Playboy* really did recommend eye-gazing.) You gaze back while doing the heart technique described on Day 3. Resume thrusting and repeat the whole cycle several times. The breathing synchronizes rhythms; the eye-gazing deepens intimacy; and the stop-start builds tension — all resulting in a soul-stirring orgasm.

All of You

To give of oneself—fully—is not merely a duty prescribed by an outmoded superstition, it is a beautiful and thrilling privilege.

—TERRY SOUTHERN AND MASON HOFFENBERG, *CANDY*

PHYSICISTS TELL US that when billions of molecules are enclosed in a container, their random movements suddenly synchronize and begin acting as one. That new "one" is more than the sum of its parts. So it is when you engage *all* of yourself in the act of making love. More than just your body, mind, heart, and soul, you become some new Essence of Woman, overflowing with a pleasure and radiance that alters the molecules of every nearby man.

You Every day, do something that stimulates all the parts of you. Imagine yourself as Aphrodite and caress your lover with her silken chemise. Wear perfume that reminds you of tropical nights. This synergy will spark all kinds of womanly possibilities.

You Two Get on top and insert him. Undulate your hips, then stop and squeeze one of his nipples till you feel his erection twitch. Thrust again. After a few minutes of alternating, lean forward to kiss him—arousing his lips, nipples, and genitals, and imagining a cord of energy between them. Lay your heart on his. You'll be setting off a string of explosives in body, mind, and heart that ignites his soul.

A Day Off

Remember that feeling sensual produces almost the same sensations — and the same glow — as an actual roll in the hay. So wear something silky, smell a gardenia, walk to the beat of a samba. Whatever brings out the sexy in you.

DAY

7

The Sensual Body

Body as Instrument

Your body is the harp of your soul,
And it is yours to bring forth sweet music from it or confused
sounds.

—KAHLIL GIBRAN, *THE PROPHET*

DAY
8

THINK OF YOUR body as an instrument of love. If you were a cello, you might regard your size 42 hips as the perfect shape for making the full, rich tones of passion. You might show your man a different fingering for your most sensitive "strings." If his penis were a flute, perhaps you'd hold it in your mouth and tap your fingers lightly across the fleshy pipe. If together you were cymbals, would you touch edges to ring like a bell or make exciting crash-bang-wallops?

You If you want to be a virtuoso lover, you have to become the master of your own instrument. Close the curtains, put on inspiring music (Ravel's *Bolero*? Roxy Music's *Avalon*?), and pluck your own strings. Find out how firmly you like your knobs turned, what makes your G-spot hum, and when your main love organ wants to *accelerando*. Teach him how to play the *Ode to Joy* on your finely tuned body.

You Two Make music on *his* body. Place your lips on his inner thigh, belly, neck, or genitals, and moan, as if rhapsodizing over hot butterscotch sauce. Growls and moans make your lips vibrate like a sex toy, but in a softer, warmer way, and with more varied sensations—high pitches creating fast, shallow pulsations and lower sounds making for slow, penetrating throbs.

Nipple Teasing

Men still don't understand about breasts . . . a woman's have a direct hot line to her clitoris. A man who can dial this correctly and will only take the time can do anything.

—ALEX COMFORT, MD, DSC, *THE NEW JOY OF SEX*

DID YOU KNOW that your nipples contain *genital* corpuscles? With the same kind of trigger-happy nerves that fill your clitoris, no wonder they reach out for more when stroked or kissed. But your ultrasensitive nipples can be used to *give* as well as *receive* pleasure. When erect, they make a provocative set of massage tools, combining the firm, focused pressure of a knuckle with the silky softness of a baby's fingertip.

You Just as exercise tones muscles, stimulation of nipple tissues tones your libido. Expose your nipples to a gentle breeze, a shower massager, or cool smooth sheets. Admire them in a mirror and learn from the way they rise, darken, and intensify when stroked. Your responsive nipples are the stuff of every man's wet dreams.

You Two Caress his mouth with your breast tips and allow him to lick you. Press your nipples against his and roll them together with your fingertips. Trail one rosy bud into his navel, the hollow of his neck, the space between his toes. He gets titillating views and sensations—while you fire up the clitoral nerves that reside in your own breast tissues.

DAY

9

Juices of Love

In the Hindu way of thinking, the fluids that the woman secretes as she becomes aroused . . . are considered the nectar of the Goddess . . . [and] highly beneficial to male well-being.

—DAVID AND ELLEN RAMSDALE, *SEXUAL ENERGY ECSTASY*

FOR A MAN, the smell, taste, and feel of a woman's love juices are a fierce, visceral turn-on. If you are producing lubrication, he knows you're ready and willing and he's done something very right. Plus, the thought of plunging his member into your hot wetness is like your imagining dipping your tongue into a vat of warm caramel sauce. Who knew that something so natural, and so ordinary that it's almost invisible, is one of your most devastating weapons?

You In research at the University of Texas, three out of four men preferred the most fertile-smelling woman. Try dabbing your seductive natural lubricant behind your ears or between your breasts. Demure but deadly, savor your wicked little secret while sitting in a meeting. And when evening rolls around, leave your guy wondering why he can't keep his hands off you.

You Two 1) Tell him how wet you are. Just before you climb into bed, allow him to touch-test for himself. 2) Look him in the eye, slip your finger into your own nectars and smooth some onto your tongue or across his lips. 3) Invite him to lick your fingers while you pleasure yourself.

5 Unusual Perspectives on the Female Body

1. Ears—In medieval Europe, gentlemen were so aroused by the female ear that women were forced to wear large caps that kept these tempting appendages safely covered.
2. Derrière—Some historians claim the Valentine heart shape we use as a symbol of love originated in a primal and picturesque view—a woman seen from behind, bent over and presenting an invitation to some randy fun.
3. Hair—While considering a woman's locks her most beautiful asset, some Hindus also believe that dangerously provocative hormones lie at the base of the hair shaft. So when her husband dies, a good Hindu woman must shave her head—thereby securing her chastity.
4. Breasts—In Mongolia, large breasts are considered pitiable deformities.
5. Foot—Freud claimed that a woman's foot was similar to the phallus, and when she slipped it into a shoe, sexual union was symbolically complete. For a foot fetishist, aroma is often the major attraction—headier than a woman's perfume or the distinctive fragrance of sex.

Hips

She's a big-hearted girl with hips to match.

— HENNY YOUNGMAN

IN MANY AFRICAN cultures, girls reaching puberty are trained in the art of hip-swinging—to attract men while walking and to bring on orgasm during sex. Intuitively, these women understand the mesmerizing spell cast by the rhythmic sway of a pelvis. Without benefit of push-up balconet bras or smoky eyeshadow, their bodies proclaim, "I've got magic between my legs, baby, and I know ways of moving it that'll melt your knees."

You A study published in the *Journal of Sexual Medicine* found that the women who walk with greater hip rotation are the ones who have vaginal orgasms. Improve your hip rotation (and trigger primal feelings) by undulating like a belly dancer. Add PC squeezes by clenching and releasing the muscles you use to stop urination. Breathe in as you rock forward, releasing and breathing out as you tilt back, and sexual energy will shoot from your pelvis to your head—literally making you dizzy with desire.

You Two During doggie-style, have him stay still while you control the action with your hips. Circle to create extra friction, or tilt your rear end up to place his penis on your G-spot. Undulate slowly; then punctuate with wild, wanton thrusting. He'll love being under your power—and getting great views of your succulent hindquarters.

The Hair Down There

Blue hair, vault of shadows, be for me
the canopy of overarching sky;
here at the downy roots of every strand
I stupefy myself on the mingled scent
of musk and tar and coconut oil for hours . . .

—CHARLES BAUDELAIRE (TRANS. RICHARD HOWARD)

DAY 13

TO A MAN, a woman's pubic hair is like a secret forest—earthy, dark, and rich with the promise of undiscovered treasure. Even if a man knows you well, he may spend hours fantasizing about how this familiar thatch would look trimmed differently, or shaved, or peeking out from behind a Brazilian bikini. Your pubic hairstyle says a lot about who you are—Earth Mother au naturel, stripped and clipped *Playboy* centerfold, naked but demure Venus.

You Get a bikini wax with a difference. Ask the cosmetician to dye your hair with a stencil in the shape of a heart, or star, or lightning bolt. Don't worry; it will fade away in about a month. Or weave in tiny flowers or rhinestones. Or simply perfume the top of your mound. It will make you feel beautiful, naughty, and outrageous.

You Two 1) Give him a private viewing of your newly ornamented pelvic coif. 2) Invite *him* to do the decorating. 3) Ask him to shave you. (See Day 87.) The fact that you are giving your pubis this kind of attention will rearrange all his brain cells—even the ones *above* his waist.

A Day Off

Stand in front of a full-length mirror and find a sexy body part. What makes it alluring? Curves? Translucent skin? Ripeness? Wear clothes that play it up. Dot it with perfume. Move in ways that show it off. Ask your lover to kiss it. With your loving attention, you have created a potent sexual weapon.

DAY

14

Indulgence

More

Too much of a good thing is wonderful.

— MAE WEST

IN MUCH OF our lives, we remain imprisoned by the stingy, censorious attitudes of the Victorian era, afraid to allow ourselves too much pleasure. But in matters of love and sex, if something is good, more is usually better. That's part of the point, really. Give, give, and give some more; then soak it all in till your body explodes with delight. This sort of indulgence nurtures the soul.

DAY
15

You Buy not just one but an entire armload of hyacinth sprays and place the fragrant bouquets everywhere—even the bathroom, hallway, and laundry room. Got cashmere? Cocoon in all your sweaters, pashmina shawls, and faux fur throws. Treat yourself to a bottle of French wine, Italian shoes, or a Brazilian tango lesson. Expand your capacity for pleasure, and more pleasure will come your way.

You Two Make your sex lives lush. Lavish him with *more* genital kisses, and you'll get *more* back. Make him wait for intercourse until he gives you *more* breast play, *more* inner thigh stroking, *more* toe nibbling—and when he complies, moan *more*, shiver *more*, compliment him *more*. And most important, when he's inside you, make his thrusts even more vigorous by gasping, *"More, more!"*

Honey

Your lips, O my spouse,
Drip as the honeycomb.

—SONG OF SONGS 4:11

SWEET, GOLDEN, AND gooey, honey has been associated with sensuality since Middle Eastern women began using it 5,000 years ago to bless a new bride's home and to make an intoxicating beer called mead. Today, we know honey helps metabolize estrogen and increase the level of libido-enhancing testosterone in your blood. But this food of the gods is tastiest on your skin—smooth as a lover's caress and creamy thick as the nectars of love-making.

You According to l'Occitane, a French-based cosmetics firm, honey and brown sugar (in equal proportions) make a superb exfoliating paste. Add a drop of milk for moisturizing or a dash of jasmine essential oil for the hedonistic aroma. Either way, you'll emerge from your homemade facial feeling like an exotic and pampered sex goddess.

You Two 1) Blindfold your man. Drizzle honey from your breasts to your belly button, then onto your thighs. Tell him to find the sweet stuff using only his tongue. 2) Smear the amber liquid around the entrance to your love tunnel. It's candy for him and an invitation his lips can't refuse. 3) Anoint *him* with the golden elixir (use fingers, tongue, or pour directly from the jar) and have a scrumptious time lapping it off.

Nature

At times sudden, deep-reaching sensations would stir my blood.
A strange ardour would seize my imagination; the colours of nature
would seem more sparkling.

—GEORGE SAND, *LÉLIA*

NATURE IS EROTIC. Consider a forest—full of trees oozing sap, whispering winds, and wild, mating animals. Or an ocean—surging and mysterious, with waves crashing and spray flying. There's a power in nature that often teeters on the edge between beauty and danger, something that excites you, opens up all your senses, and makes you feel as juicy as a mango and primal as a wolf in mating season.

DAY

17

You Turn off your computer and go taste the world with your animal senses. Prowl. Sniff. Burrow. Press yourself against the rough bark of a tree. Bury your nose in a gardenia. Gorge on wild berries. Crack open a leaf and smell its scent. Marvel at the iridescence of light and shadow between the birches. When your senses come alive, you transform into something ripe and wild.

You Two Take your man to the woods or the backyard. Picnic on strawberries, fresh bread, kalamata olives, pungent cheese, and a bottle of full-bodied wine. Feed each other. Roll in the leaves. Stand him against a tree for some alfresco oral sex. The increased blood flow makes him extra swollen, and he gets a spectacular view of his savage mate. Finish making love on the blanket, covered in moss and tingling in the cool breeze.

The Master of Seductive Pampering

DESPITE THE LARGE bump on his nose, an unfortunate lack of hair, and his relatively short stature, Giovanni Jacopo Casanova was one of history's most successful lovers. His secret was lavish indulgence. To seduce a young nun in eighteenth-century Venice, he prepared:

- A flotilla of lanterns to light the maiden's path from gondola to opulently appointed apartment
- Hundreds of candles and mirrors, so her beauty would be "reflected a thousand times"
- Champagne, oysters, rich cheeses, and truffles—which he lapped up from the lady's modestly covered bosom
- Armloads of fragrant tuberoses
- A suite of secret alcoves, ablaze with candlelight
- The daring gift of a silk lace nightcap

Casanova understood that when a woman is immersed in voluptuous luxury, her senses come alive and her body blooms. She feels free at last to be all woman—sexy, lusty, and charmingly dangerous.

Chocolate

It's not that chocolates are a substitute for love. Love is a substitute for chocolate. Chocolate is, let's face it, far more reliable than a man.

—MIRANDA INGRAM

YOU CAN TRUST chocolate. It's always there to deliver a jolt of dark, creamy, sense-bludgeoning ecstasy when you need it. The Aztecs, who considered chocolate the sacred "blood of the earth," depended on its value as a currency and an aphrodisiac. Today, we know that much of chocolate's potency comes from the serotonin and phenylethylamine it contains—endorphins released when we fall in love.

You As far as I'm concerned, eating a little chocolate every day is necessary therapy. It even contains antioxidants. But to enjoy chocolate's divine decadence guilt-free, bathe in it. Mix together 1 cup powdered milk, ⅛ cup cocoa powder, 1 tablespoon cornstarch, and ½ teaspoon cinnamon. Pour this into bathwater as the tub is filling. If you nibble on a bonbon while you're soaking, who will know?

You Two Sucking on soft chocolate just before you meet his lips will make kissing all the sweeter. But to really rock his world, place a chocolate-covered doughnut around his erect member and try to lick off the frosting. Because the pastry won't be able to slide down much beyond the bulbous head, your tongue will be concentrating on a spot with more nerve endings than anywhere else on his body.

Hair

Beware of her fair hair, for she excels
All women in the magic of her locks;
And when she winds them round a young man's neck,
She will not ever set him free again.

—JOHANN WOLFGANG VON GOETHE, *FAUST*
(TRANS. PERCY BYSSHE SHELLEY)

DAY
20

FONDLING SOMEONE'S HAIR can be more intimate than a kiss. Our hair is tied up with our sense of self—masquerading in plain sight as the most visible yet vulnerable part of our sexual psyches. A bad hair day can be devastating. But when your tresses behave, you feel radiant, unbeatable, ready for the red carpet. Rethink your hair—because healthy, glistening strands can do a lot more than reflect sunlight.

You Brush until your scalp tingles. Then pull a fragrant treatment oil through your hair, tugging firmly enough to stretch the scalp. Blow-dry briefly to make the oil penetrate. Bask. Then massage in shampoo *before* wetting your hair, concentrating on the aromas, tingles, and cool creamy sensations. Rinse by pouring cupfuls of warm water, like mini waterfalls, over your crowning glory.

You Two Tickle him where it counts. That little bump just below his coronal rim (where the foreskin may have been snipped at circumcision) is extra sensitive. Skim your hair across this tender spot, lightly and slowly at first, and then with more gusto as he gets used to the shivery sensation. Eventually, you may want to hold your tresses in a ponytail and "whip" his thighs with them.

A Day Off

Sprinkle jasmine-scented sachets into your pillow-case. Dream humid, intoxicating dreams, and waft through tomorrow with the aroma of the tropics on your mind and in your hair.

DAY

21

The Elements

The Fires of Love

Some day, after we have mastered the winds, the waves, the tides and gravity, we shall harness for God the energies of love, and then, for the second time in the history of the world, man will have discovered fire.

—TEILHARD DE CHARDIN

DAY

22

FEW THINGS IGNITE passion more than letting your lover know you're aflame for his body and his loving. In fact, the editors of *Men's Health* report that what every man craves most in bed is hearing he's good. This is not as egotistical as it sounds. A guy wants to know he's effective. When he's making his woman feel good, he senses that all's right with the world. He's inspired. Generous even. If this is what *you* crave, be bold and let your passion blaze.

You Here's the secret. Your moans will inflame not only your lover, but you too. Wriggling wildly, screaming his name, and bucking like a bronco convinces your brain you actually *feel* what these exaggerated moves show. Further, your actions build heat and bring it to the surface of your skin. Sooner than you can shout "F**k me, your majesty!" (remember Annette Bening in *American Beauty*?), you will *both* be raging with white-hot desire.

You Two "Hot" is wiggling your hips during missionary. "Fire-y" is burying your fingers in his rump to drive him hard inside you. As he nears orgasm, squeeze his cheeks hard enough to leave a real impression. The combination of deep impact, exquisite pressure on his backside, and your animal lust will fan embers into outright flames.

The Waters of Love

I will sing of stately Aphrodite, gold-crowned and beautiful, whose dominion is the walled cities of all sea-set Cyprus. There the moist breath of the western wind wafted her over the waves of the loud-moaning sea in soft foam.

—HOMERIC HYMN TO APHRODITE

SOFT, SLIPPERY, AND oozing with the primal stuff of life, water is just plain sexy. Because its molecules actually squeeze together to form surface tension (that's what allows leaves, dragonflies, and boats to float), water literally "embraces" you as it glides across your skin. Could that be why we love to skinny-dip in a tropical lagoon, squish the morning dew between our toes, or have a lover lick us all over?

You Enhance the decadence of a solitary bath: 1) Turn off all the lights so you feel the invisible water, sponge, and bubbles even more. 2) With only about three inches of water in the tub, switch the incoming flow to the shower nozzle. Adjust it to the most concentrated spray and place your nipples and/or nether regions directly underneath.

You Two Make like dolphins—the only other animals who have sex for pleasure—and do it in the pool. Hang onto the rim and float, tummy down. He stands behind and enters. Move one of his hands around to hold open your labia. As you glide weightlessly back and forth, the water makes waves over your exposed clit and his testicles—a slick caress that adds indescribable sensation.

The Air of Love

The gentle breezes of the Summer night,
Blow o'er my love's fine form and face of light,
And from his breath I quaff draughts of delight,
Oh God! Oh God! why comes the dawn so soon?

—ANONYMOUS WOMAN TROUBADOUR OF PROVENÇAL (TRANS. FRANÇOIS
JUSTE MARIE RAYNOUARD), QUOTED IN *BLACKWOOD'S MAGAZINE*

DAY
24

ARISING FROM DEEP inside the body, your breath contains the most intimate parts of you—your warmth, your desire, your sexual fever, your unique pheromones. When you are aroused, the air from your lungs is even hotter and more velvety than usual, so it can blaze a musky, slow-burning trail across a lover's skin or simply transmit the spirit of love into his mouth as you kiss.

You Breathing controls the rhythms of the sympathetic nervous system. To calm and soothe, breathe slowly through your nose and into your belly. To charge things up, breathe rapidly through the mouth and into your chest. Panting brings on or intensifies a climax and reduces the hypersensitivity of your clitoris—so you can go on to multiple orgasms.

You Two To intensify a kiss, back away, look into his eyes, and breathe each other's breath. This "penetration" of the lungs helps synchronize his faster arousal with yours and creates the sensation of melting into one another's souls.

Elemental Beauty

THE HAWAIIAN KAHUNAS have a practice called *nalu*, which means "to form waves." By contemplating (or forming mental waves with) any natural object, you discover its hidden beauty—and therefore, your own. It's simple. Just look and listen with happy expectation, as if about to eat a piece of chocolate made by the new candy store in town. You know it'll be good but different, maybe even revealing. Like you on a good day.

DAY
25

Earth Nalu—For one minute, regard an ordinary rock. Notice its cracks, bulges, and varying colors. Is it similar to your body? Find something beautiful about it.

Air Nalu—For one minute, listen to the wind. Have you ever heard the way it sighs, then whispers, then howls? Does it sound like you when you make love?

Fire Nalu—For one minute, watch a flame. Can you learn something about dancing from its movements? What about the way it puts yellow, red, and blue together? Find something new about its shape.

Water Nalu—For one minute, immerse your hand in water. Notice the way the liquid moves and envelops your skin, the way it changes your temperature. How is it different from milk, tears, or love juices?

Space Nalu—For one minute, look at an empty sky. Besides the million shades of blue and gray, can you make out the multicolored molecules that make up space? Can you see how far it stretches into the unknown? Find something you never noticed before.

The Earthiness of Love

A garden enclosed is my sister, my spouse.

— SONG OF SONGS 4:12

YOUR BODY IS like the earth—made of long valleys and curvy peaks, smelling of flowers and musk, fecund as the rich, wet soil. For most men, the definition of sexy is a woman who is *in* her body and revels in its earthy appetites and wild joys. Men sense a raw truth, a compelling charm, about a lady who is not afraid to sweat, or be ten pounds overweight, or get twigs in her hair while she is being ravaged against a tree.

You Your body is sexy when it's *doing* things. According to research from Marquette University, when a woman focuses on function rather than appearance, she feels more positive about herself. Completing a 10K footrace, tilling a new garden, or learning a belly-dance routine gives you confidence about what your body can *do*—much sexier, earthier, and more empowering than fretting about how it *looks*.

You Two Don't waste the pumped-up libido and dewy skin that follows a good workout. Most men *love* the smell and feel of a fresh-from-the-gym female and fantasize about being over-powered by her. After your next power walk, grab his lapels and let him whiff your earthy self. Then throw him to the floor and have your way with him.

Space—
The Final Frontier of Love

*Thou demandest what is love? It is that powerful attraction towards
all that we conceive, or fear, or hope beyond ourselves.*

—PERCY BYSSHE SHELLEY

AT ITS BEST, sex propels you to the fierce edges of life, where
excitement collects like water against a dam, pushing against
your familiar boundaries. In ancient Sumerian rituals, lovers
deliberately violated that border, abandoning themselves to a
torrent of passion that left them stammering "Who am I?" Is
there, in fact, anything holier or more exhilarating than crossing—even with only one toe—that wild frontier where danger,
love, and ecstasy are perfectly balanced?

You Make sure you're with a lover you can trust; then drop
your inhibitions like snagged pantyhose and leap into the sexual unknown. Try some light S & M, semi-public sex, or crème
de menthe in your love tunnel. When you dare to sample things
outside your usual safe zone, you get the sizzle of unexpected
sensations and a boost to your self-confidence.

You Two There are as many ways to experiment with wild,
crazy sex as there are stars in space. Be brave. Videotape yourself applying olive oil to *every inch* of your body. Secretly tape
the two of you making love. Do something extra-naughty for
the camera—perhaps inserting one finger into your vagina and
licking off the juices. Invite him to watch film at eleven.

A Day Off

When I get off the plane in Hawaii, the first thing I notice is the air — velvety soft and dripping with the aromatic scent of plumeria, tuberose, and white ginger. So different from the thin, crackly air in the Rockies, where I live. Today, smell, taste, and feel the air in your neck of the woods.

DAY
28

Soft

The Underbelly

When he sees me in heat he quickly comes to me,
Then he opens my thighs and kisses my belly.

— THE PERFUMED GARDEN

THERE'S SOMETHING INTENSELY intimate about the belly. Within teasing distance of the genitals, it's one of our most ticklish and vulnerable spots. But it's strong too. With a fire in the belly, we're full of passion and a fierce desire to fight for our beliefs. Could it be here, at the center of our bodies, that we find out just how beautiful and spirited we truly are?

DAY

29

You In her latest play, *The Good Body*, Eve Ensler has liberated her belly (the thing that's "protruded through her clothes, her confidence, and her ability to work") by baring it to thousands. Celebrate yours by surrounding your navel with a temporary flower tattoo, donning a jeweled navel ring, or simply dancing in a low-slung sarong. Remember, round is beautiful.

You Two According to sex therapist Dr. Howard Devore, there's an erogenous connection between the hairline running south from a guy's navel and his brain. Plant little butterfly kisses there. Then slide your tongue firmly down from belly button to base of penis. Repeat until something else "comes up."

Fur

And laughter-loving Aphrodite, with face turned away and lovely eyes downcast, crept to the well-spread couch . . . and upon it lay skins of bears and deep-roaring lions.

—*HOMERIC HYMN TO APHRODITE*

DAY

30

AFTER FIG LEAVES, fur was our first clothing. Shivering in damp caves and drafty castles, we hung stag-hide curtains, slept under wolf-skin spreads, and lined nearly every garment with warm rabbit or beaver. By the Middle Ages, fur had become a symbol of power, reserved for the robes of kings. Fur will always have the "yum" factor, but today it may be classier to go faux.

You Whether natural or man-made, fur makes you feel like a million bucks. Why? Because it's beautiful and luxurious, yes. But also because the brush of fur against skin—our largest organ—"pets" the entire body and creates a bioelectric charge that makes you glimmer. So, in that mink-collared bomber, you not only *feel* dazzling, you actually *are*.

You Two A massage with a chinchilla mitt, soft and light as a cloud, will transport your man to heaven. Trail the mitt lightly over his entire body before skimming his face and massaging his temples. Circle your furry thumbs in his palms, the soles of his feet, and finally around his nipples. Stroke long and slow over his genitals until he purrs. For extra zing, cover his face with a fur-lined mask so he'll shiver with every unanticipated move.

Yum Yum

Oh, you man of all man, who fillest me with pleasure.
Oh, you soul of my soul . . .
you must not yet withdraw it from me; leave it there,
and this day will then be free of all sorrow.

— THE PERFUMED GARDEN

THE BASIC POSITION in Tantra is the Yab Yum—he sits
cross-legged; you sit in his lap with legs crossed behind his
back and hands on his shoulders. You can't move too much, so
the goal is not hot-and-heavy thrusting but blissed-out intimacy. In this pose, you can kiss passionately, whisper ador-
ingly, and fondle each other lovingly until you melt into a
puddle of love.

DAY

31

You Like four-hour foreplay, this pose is made to please a
woman. You get very deep (but not stabbing) penetration,
exquisite G-spot stimulation, and soulful eye contact. It's like
soft but intense sex for the right brain. You might even feel as
if your whole body becomes a vulva—quivering all the way up
to your forehead.

You Two Make this tranquil position sizzle by: 1) squeezing
your PCs to keep him tingling; 2) occasionally draping your
legs over his elbows so you can "rock" his world; 3) gazing
deeply into his eyes. According to Dr. Harrison Voigt of the
California Institute of Integral Studies, "sustained, steady eye
contact has an almost unlimited potential for generating pro-
found change in sexual experiencing."

The "Soft" Break

WHEN YOU'RE TRYING to close a business deal, run errands in traffic, or go for the burn at the gym, the idea of "soft" can get lost in the shuffle. But furry-purry things activate the brain's pleasure center, making you feel relaxed and sensual. Here are ten ways to take a rejuvenating "soft" break.

1. Wrap yourself in a towel fresh from the dryer.
2. Rub your tummy in slow, gentle circles for five minutes.
3. Pet a kitten, a fur collar, or a teddy bear. It even lowers blood pressure.
4. Nuke body lotion and smooth it over your neck, feet, and inner thighs.
5. Surround yourself with a luxurious blanket and go outside in the cold.
6. Read the poems of Mary Oliver.
7. Slather on lip balm. Try applying it to your nipples too — similar skin.
8. Listen to Kenny G.
9. Look at a picture of a koala bear.
10. Dab clary sage or lavender oil on a cotton ball and snuggle it in your cleavage.

Eyelids

Drink at his eyes,
Forgetting the purple scent of the vine.
Drink at his cheeks,
Forgetting the life of roses poured in crystal.
Drink at his heart,
Forgetting everything.

—THE THOUSAND AND ONE NIGHTS

DAY

33

IF THE EYES are the windows to our soul, then our eyelids are all we have to protect our most tender selves. When open, they allow us to reveal our love, our dreams, our vulnerabilities. When closed, they guard us from intrusion and hurt. Yet these vital shields are made of the thinnest skin on our bodies. How fragile, yet how dynamic, are the doorways to our passions!

You An eyelid mist can energize your entire body. Blend twelve drops of lavender oil (refreshes the mind and lessens hot flashes) and six drops neroli oil (relieves anxiety and lifts the spirits) in two ounces of distilled water. Pour into a spray bottle and spritz eyelids when you need a lift.

You Two Eyelid skin is similar to that of a man's scrotum — ultra thin, with hardly any cushioning fat, and full of lubricants and nerve endings. To awaken it, softly lick the area between his eyes and then his eyelids. Moisten your lower lip and pat it against his lids, then skim your tongue along the lashes and into the outer corners of his closed eyes. So intimate. So mesmerizing. So breathlessly erotic.

The Pillow

"If you're alone, I'll be your shadow. If you want to cry, I'll be your shoulder. If you want a hug, I'll be your pillow."

—AUTHOR UNKNOWN

A PILLOW IS more than a place to rest your head. It's a safe haven. A respite from reality. A dream cloud. Sweet with the smell and shape of your beloved, a pillow can be a personal love talisman. Encased in velvet, it can make you think languorous—or naughty—thoughts. And on a dark and stormy night, the right pillow can even protect you from the hairy monster under the bed.

You Pamper yourself shamelessly with a new bed pillow made of Pyrenees mountain duck down (super cuddly); a five-foot-long body pillow (eliminates the fear of sleeping alone); a silk pillowcase (won't tangle your hair); an herbal pillow (induces sweet dreams); or, for your bedmate, an anti-snore pillow (yup, it really works).

You Two To elevate missionary sex, wedge three firm pillows under your bum. At this angle, your hips do three things: 1) present a visual invitation that will make him moan; 2) angle your vaginal canal so he can go deeper than ever; 3) position your clitoris for maximum contact with his thrusts. These are more amazing tricks performed by the ordinary pillow.

A Day Off

Stroke the face of someone you love — a paramour, a child, a pet, yourself.

DAY

35

Lust Around the World

The Feet of Bali

What spirit is so empty and blind, that it cannot recognize the fact that the foot is more noble than the shoe, and skin more beautiful than the garment with which it is clothed?

—MICHELANGELO

DAY 36

THE BALINESE CONSIDER their feet a work of divine art. Guests in a home are often treated to a foot bath and massage on arrival. Woodcarvers cradle statues in their bare feet, leaving both hands free to sculpt. Dancers spend years learning to tell a story with gracefully curled toes and arched feet. And lovers touch each others' toes as a sign of deep intimacy.

You Pamper your feet Bali-style. Drizzle honey on your tootsies to heal and soothe the skin. Then soak them, honey and all, in a pan of warm water scented with jasmine oil—a natural moisturizer. Afterward, accessorize with the exotic swirls and loops of a Balinese toe ring.

You Two The Balinese seem to intuit that the nerves of the big toe are connected to the penis. When you're on top, facing his feet (or when loving him orally), squeeze and pull on his big toe as he starts to climax. This Balinese Toe-Tug Orgasm will send ripples of pleasure up and down his legs—and literally curl his toes.

French Champagne

Champagne is the only wine that leaves a woman beautiful after drinking it.

— MADAME POMPADOUR

ACCORDING TO LEGEND, the monk Dom Pérignon and his blind brother Pierre tried hard to *prevent* bubbles in their "mad wine," wanting to design a smooth, white brew the French court would prefer over burgundy. Unwittingly, they succeeded—by creating a quaff the royal mistresses called the "food of Aphrodite." Soon, Louis XV and his retinue were not only drinking the bubbly stuff but also bathing in it.

You Although Madame Pompadour, the king's chief mistress, used a whole tubful, you need very little champagne to enjoy what was once reserved for royalty. Pour one inexpensive bottle into your slightly-cooler-than-usual bathwater and soak. The hundreds of little "pops" revitalize your skin and delight your soul.

You Two Give him a champagne *shower*. Stand in the tub, hugging him, and pour bubbly between your bodies. Take small sips and spurt fizzes all over his chest and thighs. Or forget the bath and simply hold some champagne in your mouth before enveloping his testicles. Either way, you'll leave him tingling.

The Tantra of India

Look upon a woman as a Goddess, whose special energy she is, and honor her in that state of Goddess.

—UTTARA TANTRA

THE ROOTS OF Tantra reach back thousands of years to a time when women were thought divine. Men worshipped their wives with burning kisses, elaborate compliments, and slow lovemaking that led the lucky ladies to a chain of orgasms. From this ecstatic peak, a woman could choose to bestow enlightenment — a state the man could achieve *only* through her generosity.

You The secret of the ancient Tantric women was focus. By centering their attention on the spot where his thrusts landed — or where his lips met their skin — they intensified the sensation. Soon, their pinpoint rapture was so intense it overflowed to every cell, making their bodies tremble and glow. Try it.

You Two Here's a lesser-known Tantric pose. Kneel astride and take him inside you. Then lean back, grasping his knees for support. This elongates your body and exposes your vulva to his worshipful gaze. If you move your hips in mesmerizing circles, his hands will be magnetized to your clitoris. Meanwhile, you're getting deep G-spot stimulation, and he's in stirring, creamy Nirvana.

No Matter How You Say It — Kiss Me!

WOULD YOU GET more smooches if you *demanded* them in German? Would they be sexier if translated into Italian? More exotic in Filipino? Find out by saying "Kiss me" in sixteen different languages.

Language	"Kiss me."
Dutch	Kus me.
Filipino (Tagalog)	Hagkan ako.
French	Embrassez-moi.
German	Küssen Sie mich.
Hawaiian	Ho'ni.
Hebrew	Tayn li neshika.
Italian	Bacilo.
Japanese	Watashi ni setsupun shinasai.
Latin	Basium mihi.
Polish	Calowac sie mi.
Russian	Pacuenynte mehr.
Serbian	Poljubac mene.
Spanish	Béseme.
Swedish	Kyssa mig.
Turkish	Öpmek beni.
Yiddish	Gib mir a kish.

Japanese Red

Perhaps the old monks were right when they tried to root love out; . . .
It is a blood-red flower, with the color of sin; but there is
always the scent of a god about it.

—OLIVE SCHREINER

**DAY
40**

IN JAPAN, RED is the color of beauty and happiness—and, behind the veil of public decorum, it's a code word for female genitalia. To titillate men, geishas wear ruby red lining under their kimonos and dramatic rouge made from the petals of crimson flowers. But even the Japanese housewife knows that a slash of scarlet lipstick will cause a man to lose his senses and think only of her bedroom.

You Like Japanese women, try wearing red undies to keep your reproductive organs healthy and stave off menstrual pain. Or use the geisha makeup tricks designed to suggest beauty, surprise, and eroticism—outline your eyes with deep crimson and black, or add delicate rose highlights under the outer curve of your eyebrows.

You Two Only because I was leaving Japan the next day, one of the workers at a famous Tokyo sex club was willing to reveal her secret for creating a besotted, repeat customer. Wearing red lipstick to intensify the visual effect, she gently pulls down on his testicles and laps the very base of his penis (upward licks only) until it shudders.

The Wise Women of Mangaia

A woman serves a man best when she has her joy above all other values.

—DR. VICTOR BARANCO

ON THE SOUTH Pacific island of Mangaia, boys begin their intensive sexual education around age thirteen. Female elders, still prized as sex partners, show the young men how to kiss, how to touch and lick a woman's vulva, and how to use their male equipment effectively. If the men don't learn to give a woman two or three orgasms a night, they lose their status in this sensual—and happy—society.

You A Mangaian woman tests the virility of her betrothed by requiring him to make her climax, using lips and hands only on her genitalia—without any direction from her. If he doesn't measure up, she discards him for another. If you experimented on *yourself*, using only your hands on your vulva and nowhere else, you could—unlike the silent island brides—tell your man *exactly* how to give you maximum thrills and chills.

You Two Restricted to the vulva and able to use only lips and hands, the hopeful Mangaian groom might achieve his goal by twirling his tongue over the beloved's clitoris in a figure-eight pattern. Ask your man to follow suit, perhaps switching to the alphabet for more variety. This way he shines every facet of your little gem—and feels so clever, so manly, and so turned on when he succeeds at the job.

A Day Off

The music of a culture says a lot about how the people think, feel, and make love. With no one else around, dance to a French torch song, an Indian raga, African drums, a Hawaiian hula. In which "language" do you feel freer, sexier, more beautiful?

DAY

42

Sense-ational Sex

Seeing

While the Fates grant it to us, let us fill our eyes with love-making.

—PROPERTIS

WHEN YOU SEE something beautiful, like a camellia or a lover's cheek, you automatically want to touch it. It's as if the photons that trigger sight enter your eyes and slip down your throat, often evoking tastes and smells. They flood your heart with longing and overflow out your fingers, wanting to complete the circuit by making physical contact. And as you touch, you feel you've exchanged something. You've seen and been seen in return.

DAY

43

You If you want your lover to caress spots he normally neglects, you have only to reveal them. Open your shirt. Flip over during sex. Pull back your hair. The vision of breast, behind, or nape will give him the irresistible urge to touch.

You Two For men, visual stimulants are stronger and last longer than almost any other brain activity. Send him a photo of you—almost naked. (Use your camera phone only if you're *sure* it's going directly to him. Either way, be sure he's truly The One.) Try a topless pose, but with your fingertips covering (or pinching!) your nipples. Or a rear view in a Brazilian thong. The sexy visuals will have him racing home—hands atremble and heart afire—with one outrageous thing on his mind. You.

Hearing

*His voice rumbled over the surface of her skin, like another caress ...
She could stuff her ears and still it would find its way into her blood
and make it rise.*

—ANAÏS NIN

DAY

44

SOUND IS A physical thing. When an object vibrates, it moves
air molecules that ripple out in waves to touch your ear and skin.
And because even solids transmit sound, the deep thrum of a bass
guitar or a lover's voice can travel through your skin to resonate
in your bones—where they turn into mild heat. No wonder music
and whispers can stir our emotions and make our bodies melt.

You Orchestrate your (and your lover's) emotions by using
musical sound cues. For instant optimism, try the last movement of Beethoven's Ninth Symphony. To relax, play Paul
Horn's *Inside the Taj Mahal.* Anything by Barry White can
warm you up for a quickie, while Rachmaninoff's *Rhapsody on
a Theme of Paganini* evokes lush romance. And for simple lust,
try Roxy Music's *Avalon.*

You Two Here's a *Kama Sutra* kiss he can hear as well as feel.
Sit in his lap, facing him, your legs around his back. Place your
open mouth over his and hum. Because bones transmit sound,
the vibrations will resonate in his skull and travel down to his
pubic bone—where his erection is trapped and "humming"
between your pelvis and his. Try this with him inserted, for
vibrations that go all the way to the soul. (By the way, according to Amy Wechsler, MD in *The Mind-Beauty Connection*, humming boosts nitric oxide, a body gas that reduces stress and
helps your skin produce new collagen.)

Smelling

My soul is bound
By the scents of her body,
Jasmine and musk
And rose of her body,
Amber and nard,
The scents of her body.

—*THE THOUSAND AND ONE NIGHTS*

DAY
45

WHEN YOU SEE a photo of your man or hear his laugh, you may smile with delight. But when you smell his shirt, you feel like you're actually in his arms. That's because you have more receptors for smell (about 10 million to 20 million) than for any sense except vision. And while sights and sounds get processed by the cortex, smells go *directly* to the brain center for emotion and memory—zapping you with strong feelings and vivid recollections.

You Scents not only trigger emotions but passions and perceptions too. To energize both of you, wear a citrus fragrance. Jasmine and musk light sexual fires, while vanilla evokes home and warm comforters. To help your guy remember things positively, dab on a floral scent. And according to the Smell & Taste Treatment & Research Foundation, a floral-spice perfume can reduce your perceived weight by seven percent!

You Two The next few times you make love, light a candle with a scent you'll use only for sex. Or mist the sheets with it. Then take the position you like best—say, woman-on-top. Soon, whenever he smells that aroma, he'll be primed to get in bed and put you in the driver's seat. Want more kisses on your breasts or neck? Spray the special fragrance there.

Music to His Ears

SOMETIMES WE THINK men just don't listen. But you can perk up his sense of hearing with the sweet sounds of approval. Caress him with your voice by saying:

1. You make me think dirty thoughts.
2. I love the way you taste. I could stay down here for hours.
3. You're so clever.
4. Your arms look bigger. Have you been working out?
5. I've never felt this good before.
6. I love the smell of your skin.
7. Impressive, babe. (Used after he's fixed the car or grilled a great steak.)
8. You're so exciting.
9. You make me feel so safe.
10. When can you do that to me again?

Tasting

Seeing is deceiving. It's eating that's believing.

—JAMES THURBER

IT'S NOT ENOUGH to simply look or touch. When you desire someone, you feel compelled to put lips to skin and taste him. Why? As babies, we put things in our mouths to learn about them. We still discover how salty, sweet, or tender a man might be with a taste test. But even more, tempting flavors make the brain cells that sense pleasure fire rapidly, and they carry yummy, gotta-have-it messages to the limbic brain—the seat of primal emotion.

You After a long day, make your sensual palate come alive with a cocktail of flavor opposites. Mix three parts raspberry liqueur, one part raspberry-flavored vodka, and three parts lime juice with a glass of club soda. The fizzy, sour, and sweet concoction will tickle your nose and your taste buds.

You Two In *203 Ways to Drive a Man Wild in Bed*, I recommended spreading honey on your nipples (as the Roman courtesans did) to invite licking. But tasty combinations are even better. Dollop chocolate on one nipple and Kahlua on the other (or ice cream on your neck and caramel sauce on your thigh). To get the whole treat, his tongue must travel from one location to the other—leaving a yummy "impression" on your skin and in his emotional memory.

Touching

For lovers, touch is a metamorphosis. All the parts of their bodies seem to change, and they become different and better.

—JOHN CHEEVER

MORE THRILLING THAN any other sensation, a lover's touch can change a moment into paradise. Not only does it bring sensitizing blood to the surface and release endorphins (the bliss chemical), but some indefinable essence seems to pass through his skin to yours—his heat, his electricity, his love. By touching, you enter a shared private world where you are still separate but no longer alone.

You According to the Touch Research Institute at the University of Miami School of Medicine, being touched slows heart rate and lowers blood pressure. If you aren't getting enough touch, pet a cat, sleep with a velvet comforter, scrub bubbles on your skin with a shower brush, get a massage or a mud wrap. Your sense of well-being will soar.

You Two To touch as much skin as possible, try doing the missionary with a pillow under your hips. Drape one leg over his shoulder but keep the other straight, pressing him into you. Put your hands on his face and neck. Entangled and caressing, your flesh—your very souls—seem to melt into one.

A Day Off

Follow Hugh Jackman's daily prescription for stress relief and happiness. Sit quietly for two minutes and get in touch with each of your five senses. Smell, feel, taste, look, and listen without judgment.

DAY

49

Heavenly Bodies

Moon

Every one is a moon, and has a dark side which he never shows to anybody.

— MARK TWAIN

DAY 50

BLAZING WITH REFLECTED sunlight, the full moon is 33,000 times brighter than Sirius, the brightest night star. But for the ancient Greeks, the moon's power lay in her *dark* phase—the part symbolizing our shadowy inner world. They understood that true power lay in combining the light of reason with the dark of intuition—a gift that only women, creatures of the cycling moon, possessed.

You Indigenous cultures plant crops and ideas during the new moon, knowing they will grow with the swelling of its light. To give your goals a growth spurt, write them down and place the paper under your pillow from new to full moon. Cut your hair during the waxing moon to make it grow faster; toenails during the slow-growing period of waning.

You Two In Renaissance astrology, Moon governed the eyes—those arbiters of personal light and dark. Cover his eyes with your palms before kissing him. Besides being an intimate gesture that warms and relaxes the eye muscles, it plunges him into the dusky world of imagination, where he can know your kiss in a deeper, more sensual way.

Comets

A learned woman is thought to be a comet, that bodes mischief whenever it appears.

— BATHSHUA MAKIN

IN THE MIDDLE Ages, people thought shooting stars augured the death of kings and brought the plague. But some scientists now believe comets may have planted the first seeds of life on Earth. Composed of ice, rock, and organic dust, the comets that stormed our planet during its formation may have delivered the water for our oceans and the spores that evolved into flora and fauna. Some mischief!

DAY

51

You A comet's impact both destroys and creates. Think about this. Your painting of a barn may have more "impact" if you first *destroy* your idea that it must be red and have four sides. This frees you to *create* a much more interesting structure with, say, eight sides, shaded in blues, purples, and yellows. Like a comet, you're not predictable.

You Two Blasted by solar winds, the trail of dust released by a comet always faces away from the sun. But here on Earth, we see both fiery core *and* sparkling tail—much more exciting. Try spreading your legs extra wide when assuming the doggy position so he views your shimmery "tail" *and* the molten "core" of your sex, waiting beneath. Your sensitivity goes up and his thrill quotient goes over the moon.

Orion

So when rosy-fingered Dawn made love to Orion,
you precious gods were all of you furious.

— HOMER, THE ODYSSEY

APPARENTLY MEN THAT are both hunky *and* loyal do exist, even if only in the sky. According to Greek mythology, the masterful hunter Orion fell deeply in love with Eos, goddess of the dawn. But he was killed by a giant scorpion (sent by jealous Artemis, goddess of the wilderness) before having a chance to marry Eos. Now, as a constellation, the faithful swain hunts the heavens for his eternal love—staying on the opposite horizon from Scorpio. No idiot was he.

You Egyptian myth associates the constellation of Orion with Osiris, god of the afterlife. Unfortunately, he got chopped into fourteen scattered pieces. But his wife Isis found every part except his penis, which she re-created with her breath—now the star-birthing nebula hanging from Osiris/Orion's belt. You too have the power to re-member a lover, to "invent" him with your thoughts or bring him to life with your mouth.

You Two I imagine Isis fashioning her husband's new equipment with a combination of breath, tongue, and hands. While stroking his penis slowly, you might, for instance, hold your mouth close by so he can feel your breath steaming the sensitized skin. And every time the bulging tip dances by, give it a quick lick. Sure to raise the "dead."

A Sense of Your Sun Sign

YOUR SUN SIGN can provide clues to the things that best please your senses. That of your lover can tell you where he's most sensitive to touch.

Sun Signs	Aries	Taurus	Gemini
Dates	3/21–4/19	4/20–5/21	5/22–6/20
Colors	Red	Turquoise	Yellow, white
Gem	Diamond, bloodstone	Sapphire, turquoise	Moss agate
Flower	Wild rose	Violet	Iris
Scent	Geranium, pine	Musk, rose	Jasmine
Body Part	Head, cheekbones	Throat, lips	Arms, hands
Sun Signs	Cancer	Leo	Virgo
Dates	6/21–7/22	7/23–8/22	8/23–9/22
Colors	Silver	Gold	Pastel blue
Gem	Moonstone, emerald	Amber	Carnelian, jade
Flower	Poppy	Sunflower	Lily
Scent	Hyacinth, myrrh	Red sandalwood	Lavender, citrus
Body Part	Stomach, breast	Heart, back	Abdomen
Sun Signs	Libra	Scorpio	Sagittarius
Dates	9/23–10/22	10/23–11/21	11/22–12/21
Colors	Green	Deep red	Purple
Gem	Opal, lapis	Aquamarine	Topaz
Flower	Violet, white rose	Heather	Carnation
Scent	Rose	Vanilla	Daffodil, nutmeg
Body Part	Ears, lower back	Genitals, nose	Hips, buttocks
Sun Signs	Capricorn	Aquarius	Pisces
Dates	12/22–1/19	1/20–2/18	2/19–3/20
Colors	Black	Electric blue	Purple
Gem	Onyx	Garnet	Amethyst
Flower	Nightshade	Snowdrop	Heliotrope
Scent	Frankincense	Violet, pine	Lilac
Body Part	Hair, knees	Legs, ankles	Feet

Sun

Don't separate me from the sun of your face.
Because I am totally wet with fear and hope,
Like this gazel.

— RUMI (TRANS. NEVIT O. ERGIN)

ALMOST EVERY ANCIENT culture worshipped the sun. The Egyptians, Greeks, and early Europeans saw him as male — penetrating, brash, and so mighty he contains 99 percent of the solar system's entire mass. But the Japanese, Hindus, and the Vikings saw the sun as a garment of light for the Great Goddess, who birthed all things from her round, shining belly. For them, she was the very essence of Woman — nourishing, radiant, and necessary for life.

You According to Aboriginal legend, Sun-woman wakes to light a fire in her eastern camp every morning. While preparing a torch to carry across the sky, she spills some of her makeup — a red ocher that stains the clouds crimson. If you want to feel "brilliant," wear something orangy red and imagine yourself, like Sun-woman, the true source of light for the day.

You Two In astrology, the sun rules both heart and back — implying some kinetic link between the two. Perhaps that's why a man often feels bonded to the woman who rakes her nails down his back during missionary sex. Don't be afraid to dig right in. The mix of pain and pleasure will leave an unforgettable brand of passion on his heart.

Clouds and Rain

A promise is a cloud; fulfillment is rain.

—ARABIAN PROVERB

CHINESE ARTISTS PAINT clouds—soft, ethereal, and moist—to symbolize female sexuality. For the male, they sketch rain, spilling big fat drops of penetrating wetness. In the meeting of the two, Chinese poets tell of the lyrical, damp beauty of lovemaking—as if two lovers float in a dreamy cloud world, pillow each other, and create something fresh from their humid mating.

DAY

55

You Though we often think of rain as sad or inconvenient, its *fragrance* is one of the most frequently cited "favorite smells." The aroma comes from an oil made by plants, released when rain hits the surrounding soil. It's impossible to synthesize, but perfumers copy it by blending citrus florals, woods, and musk to create linen sprays and colognes meant to refresh both body and soul.

You Two If you can arrange to have sex in the rain, do. You'll never forget the drizzly, stolen-moment romance of it. But the shower is good too. You can fulfill all his wet dreams by sliding down his body to wrap your lips around his favorite appendage. Warm wet mouth plus warm wet torrents equals *very* warm, wet heaven.

A Day Off

Tonight, gaze at the evening star.
Though we call it Venus, the ancient Babylonians
believed the gleaming planet was the goddess Ishtar
herself, shining magic and beauty onto those willing to receive it. As with the planet and the goddess,
often it's the soft glow, not the flashy bling, that
makes for real magic.

Skills You Never Knew You Had

Love Muscles, Part I

Her sex gripped and milked me, with an extraordinary strength and cleverness, such as I had never before imagined possible.

—FRANK HARRIS, *MY LIFE AND LOVES*

IN THE 1940S, the standard treatment for weak bladder control (common after childbirth or menopause) was surgery. Instead of cutting, Dr. Arnold Kegel taught his female patients to *strengthen* the muscle that hangs like a hammock from pubis to tailbone, and suddenly they were having more orgasms too. The ancient secret for milking both a vagina and a penis had popped out of the scientific closet. About time.

You Contracting your PC muscle (the one that stops urine from flowing) tones your vagina and makes it more sensitive. Working it out fifty times a day helps you lubricate faster and arouse easier too—especially helpful for menopausal women. And since the muscle contracts about once every 0.8 seconds at orgasm, the stronger it is, the more powerful your climaxes are.

You Two If you squeeze the muscles around your vaginal opening, then the actual PCs a little further up, and finally your anal and stomach muscles, you'll achieve the rolling motion that makes a guy feel like he's being milked. It takes practice but, once developed, this skill will knock his socks *way* off.

DAY 57

Opening

Love is always open arms. If you close your arms about love you will find that you are left holding only yourself.

—LEO F. BUSCAGLIA

WHEN YOU LOOK at a piece of art, you open yourself to what it has to give. You take in the artist's vision, mix it with your own, and come out richer and truer to yourself. So it is with sex. You open yourself to a lover—and through the gates of your body, you both enter a world where you can give of yourselves, be filled with another, and emerge from the experience bigger and better. As blooming and beautiful as you really are.

You In the missionary position, the wider you open your thighs, the more you stretch and sensitize the skin of your labia—and the more you expose your clitoris to his thrusts. The more you open your whole body, the better you can sense the mood of your lovemaking and arrange to get what you need next.

You Two When you open your legs, you issue an ancient and coveted invitation. So pick a time to catch his eye—at home watching TV, or even out to dinner. Hold his gaze, then very slowly open your thighs—as if to say, "Here I am. Come on over and nestle in my rich fields." If you understand that it's an act of immense power, he'll feel as though the gates of heaven have been flung wide just for him. And, in reality, they have.

Ejaculate? Moi?

Graze on my lips; and if those hills be dry,
Stray lower, where the pleasant fountains lie.

—WILLIAM SHAKESPEARE

BOTH ARISTOTLE AND the author of the *Kama Sutra* wrote about it. Ancient Taoists called it moon flower medicine. The clear or milky fluid that up to 54 percent of women emit at orgasm is *not* urine but an alkaline liquid secreted by the paraurethral glands. Many doctors believe *any* woman can ejaculate—assuming she wants to—if she's treated to prolonged clitoral and G-spot stimulation. Liquids aside, wouldn't the *massage* be lovely!

You To try it yourself: 1) empty your bladder; 2) stimulate your clitoris; 3) caress the upper wall of your vagina, from outer rim to G-spot (you may need a dildo to reach), focusing on sensitive spots; 4) continue both massages, taking a *long time* to build your arousal; 5) as you climax, push out and down. Whether you stay leak-free, ooze a teaspoonful, or squirt across the room, you'll find the journey is most of the fun.

You Two First explain: you're not urinating, you're producing a special fluid that shows you're really, *really* turned on. Then, let him watch (woman masturbating and oozing wetness—he's in heaven) or guide him in performing the long, delicious massage. If he's like most men, he'll be in awe of your "powers," turned *way* on, and proud you're so wet "for him."

DAY

59

Body Talk

ACCORDING TO BODY language experts Dr. Monica Moore and Allan and Barbara Pease, our stances and eye movements communicate silent but powerful messages. Why not use every weapon in your arsenal?

Signal	What It "says"
Eyebrow Flash (both eyes)	"I'm interested. I want more."
Power Glare (aimed at his forehead)	"You're boring. Please stop talking."
Power Look (meet eyes, narrow lids)	"I am your equal." OR "Don't mess with me."
Object Fondle (caress glass or pen)	"I want to touch you."
Lone Dance (move to the music)	"I want to dance with you." (Duh.)
Wrist Exposure (underside)	"I feel feminine around you."
Foot Dangle (cross-legged)	"Come closer."
Pointed Toe Dangle (directed at him)	"Come *a lot* closer."
Knuckles on Cocked Hips	"Check it out, baby!"
Leg Wrap (foot behind other calf)	"I'm shy right now. Be soft with me."
Crossed Arms	"Convince me, dude."
Belt Rest (thumbs tucked into belt)	"I've got something pretty interesting under here."

Love Muscles, Part II

I want you to do Kegels in the car—not while driving! And I want you to look over at the people in the car next to you . . . and wink.

—DR. RUTH WESTHEIMER

A LOT MORE fun than pushups, Kegel exercises can actually cause that swelling sensation you get after he's massaged your labia for about four hours. The clenching brings blood there. So you may want to liven up boring meetings, conversations with your mother-in-law, and endless waits in the bank line by having a private party at your internal gym. No one will guess that you're getting stronger and happier by simply hanging around.

You Most women don't know that squeezing is not the only amusing trick your PC muscles can perform. Pushing them out (or bearing down) puts pressure on your clitoris and moves your G-spot closer to your inner walls and vaginal opening. So both become more engorged and rub more firmly against his thrusting member.

You Two Pelvic contractions not only make *you* feel more, they also make *him* feel more. To perform the "Mare's Trick," clench and hold just as he's about to come. Or squeeze and release as fast as you can. This increases friction and compression on his about-to-burst organ and makes the fireworks last even longer.

Suckling

When she saw me she smiled in my face and took me to her embrace and clasped me to her breast; then she put her mouth to my mouth and sucked my tongue.

— TALES FROM THE ARABIAN NIGHTS
(TRANS. RICHARD F. BURTON)

**DAY
62**

AS AN INFANT, you learn that nourishment, intimacy, and bone-deep happiness can come from suckling your mother's breast or your own thumb. Your mouth, in fact, is your first erogenous zone. But as you mature, you forget to notice the visceral pleasure of sucking a lollipop or a sore finger—until one day you feed on a lover's lip, he gives you his flesh, and you dissolve into each other, aching to possess, to be taken, to submerge yourselves in this wet molten fire.

You The part of the brain that receives input from the mouth is much larger than that for any other part of the body. When you suck on something—a mango, a bonbon, a man—you can *absorb* it, become one with it, in a way your fingers and eyes can't. Try performing oral sex by feasting with your lips, slowly sucking and imbibing every morsel of skin. An entirely different experience, no?

You Two Suckling activates primal instincts in *both* of you. So instead of the usual peck on the cheek, welcome him home tonight by drawing his tongue into your mouth and sucking softly on the very tip. He'll immediately feel it in his groin, and somehow in his heart too—almost as if he *belongs* to you. Sucking anything else is almost overkill.

A Day Off

The courtesans of fifteenth-century Venice had very talented tongues. They practiced by rolling a grape in their mouths, biting off the end, and extracting the pulp without breaking the rest of the skin. Try it. Either you develop a spectacular new skill to use on your man, or you feast on grapes. What could be bad?

DAY

63

The First Love Goddesses

Aphrodite

The gold-filleted Hours . . . adorned her with golden necklaces over her soft neck and snow-white breasts. . . . Each one of [the gods] prayed that he might lead her home to be his wedded wife, so greatly were they amazed at the beauty of violet-crowned Cytherea.

—HOMERIC HYMN TO APHRODITE

**DAY
64**

A RECENT STUDY at the University of Toronto, finding that females were more aroused by pictures of naked women than those of naked men, led researchers to wonder if all women weren't a little bit bi. No disrespect to the scientists, but I think we're excited by our *own* beauty. Like Aphrodite (who often posed to display her shining hair and admire her own plump rump) and the Hours (who adorned her), we know a fine piece of erotic art when we see one. And it's us.

You Aphrodite's golden ornaments enhanced her glow and expressed the delight she felt about her body. Gold even feels warm and sexy-sleek to the touch. Wear a pair of gold hoop earrings, a gold waist chain with a bikini, or a gold pendant between your breasts to remind yourself—and everyone else—of your rare dazzle.

You Two Strike an erotic pose, as Aphrodite would have done, by *standing* during woman-on-top sex. He lies on the bed, butt at the edge, feet on the floor. You stand over him and move up and down at will, stimulating all kinds of new hot spots on *both* of you.

Inanna

The priestesses of Inanna . . . through their union with the men who came to the temple, bestowed on them an ecstatic experience that was, so to speak, the "life" of the goddess.

—ANNE BARING AND JULES CASHFORD,
THE MYTH OF THE GODDESS

FIVE THOUSAND YEARS ago in Mesopotamia, the most important event of every year was the Sacred Marriage—the sexual coupling of king and High Priestess that made the spring ground fertile. Representing Inanna, the Priestess bestowed the gift of sublime pleasure, as well as the wisdom and compassion that gave a monarch the right to rule. On that day, *every* woman participated, making love in the fields and becoming the goddess whose honeyed caress made her lover's fate so very sweet.

DAY

65

You The women of ancient Sumer felt that giving themselves to erotic ecstasy (the life force of the goddess) made them Virgin—meaning a woman who is one-in-herself, independent, free. We too can know that in making love, we don't surrender ourselves to another. Instead, we share a powerful passion that belongs completely to us.

You Two In a Sumerian hymn, Inanna promises to caress her bridegroom's loins. For a new angle on this ancient pleasure, stand behind and grasp his penis as if it were attached to your body. Stroke down only, alternating your hands over and over. He'll feel as though he's entering you again and again—at a slant he usually feels only when pleasuring himself.

Xochiquetzal

You alone bestow
intoxicating flowers,
precious flowers.
You are the singer.
Within the house of springtime,
You make the people happy.

— KING NEZAHUALCOYOTL (AS QUOTED FROM *THE HEART OF THE GODDESS*
BY HALLIE IGLEHART AUSTEN)

DAY

66

XOCHIQUETZAL, OR "PRECIOUS Flower," was the Mayan goddess of pleasure, song, and blossoms. Just as music and flowers relieve our everyday cares, so her sacred sexuality transports us to a world of spring-like enchantment. Every woman possesses the intoxicating gifts of Xochiquetzal in the precious flower of her vulva—with a nectar that makes her lovers dizzy with sweet ecstasy.

You Xochiquetzal loved to decorate her pubic hair with hummingbird feathers. On her festival day, women wore animal and feather masks and wove blossoms into their own hair. I don't know about a flower in the panties, but wearing a bloom behind the ear can make you look, feel, and smell like a goddess of humid and exotic pleasures.

You Two Most men *love* kissing a woman's vulva but feel intimidated by the mystery of how. 1) Spread yourself with whipped cream. He doesn't need instructions on lapping up cream pie. 2) Ask him to keep his tongue still but move his *head* from side to side. Much easier. Puts him into a ravenous trance. 3) Place one of his fingers inside you while he licks. Both of you will be trembling—no, quaking—with passion.

Goddesses in Bloom

JUST THE WAY Giorgio may be your perfume, certain plants seem to resonate with the beauty and style of different goddesses from around the world. Try planting a flower or herb sacred to the love goddess of your choice. As it grows, you'll be reminded of your blossoming sensuality.

Love Goddess	Origin	Flower/Herb
Aphrodite	Greece	Anemone, rose, freesia, thyme
Freya	Norway	Daisy, cowslip, mistletoe
Hathor	Egypt	Rose, myrtle, myrrh
Ishtar	Babylon	Lily, myrtle, juniper, cinnamon
Oshun	Africa	Jericho rose, cinnamon, parsley
Parvati	India	Lotus, jasmine
Xochiquetzal	Mexico	Marigold, cacao bean (chocolate!)

The Apsaras

*And possessing slim waists and fair large hips, they began to per-
form various evolutions . . . capable of stealing the hearts and reso-
lutions and minds of the spectators.*

—VYASA, FROM THE *MAHABHARATA*

THE APSARAS OF southeast Asia are celestial nymphs who
dance to entertain the gods. Their name means "moving in
water," and their motions are as fluid and hypnotic as the sea.
Sent to distract the sages from their meditations, the Apsaras
surprised everyone by providing a *different* path to enlightenment — the sacred sexuality of their swaying bodies.

You While dancing, the Apsaras usually rest one hand just
above the top of the pelvic bone — source of their powerful
erotic energy. Try it, and you'll find your hips rocking gently
and sensually, as if your hand is a pivot around which your
whole body gyrates automatically.

You Two To bring new hip-action to the plain old missionary,
slide your fanny off the edge of the bed, supporting your weight
with your feet on the floor. He kneels before you and enters.
Freed from the bed, your pelvis can mambo in *every* direction — putting his penis in touch with nooks and crannies inside
you that were never before explored.

Hathor

To Hathor belong the gifts of sexual attraction, radiance, fertility and love. Of all the pantheon, it is she who sparks the desire for relationship and life.

—ALISON ROBERTS, *HATHOR RISING*

HATHOR, THE EGYPTIAN goddess of music, joy, and female sexuality, had a face so lovely (even with her cow's ears) it decorated temples, combs, mirrors, and the tops of hundreds of columns. During her fourteen-day "feast of the beautiful embrace," women floated her striking image down the Nile (for a conjugal visit with her god-husband), raising their skirts to seduce men along the shore with their own brand of earthy beauty.

DAY 69

You Hathor's worshippers often fashioned naked images of themselves out of clay and prayers, to ask the goddess for a soulmate. They understood that to find true love, you must first love yourself (no matter your size, shape, and cellulite) and then be willing to bare your body and soul to another. Are you willing to be that open for love?

You Two Hathor often changed the minds of gods and men by displaying her pubic triangle. If you want impassioned oral sex, try brandishing your own female equipment. Sit in an armchair with one leg resting over each arm. It's beautiful, brazen, and inviting—and it gives him a perfect platform on which to worship you.

A Day Off

Imagine you are Aphrodite—golden-crowned, beautiful, erotic. As Aphrodite, what will you wear today? How do your hips move when you walk? What do you think when you look at a rose, a banana, a pillow? What do you say to your lover? How do you feel about your body?

DAY

70

Taking a Different Position

The Squat

Don't squat with your spurs on.

—COWBOY PROVERB

NOWADAYS, WE DON'T think of squatting as a particularly attractive or comfortable thing to do. But for the ancient goddesses, it was a position of sexuality and power. Isis squatted to dispense grains from her pelvis and to bring new life to her lover's penis. Kali crouched over Shiva to enlighten him with her womb. And, as a warrior and shaman, the Aztec goddess Tlazolteotl squatted to give birth — facing death to bring forth life and ecstasy.

DAY

71

You One reason goddesses squat is to get near the earth. Crouched close, you can feel its heat and fertility coming into you. It's a grounding and sensual thing to do. But when you squat, you also stretch the skin of your labia, making your clitoris and vaginal opening more sensitive and more available — a very sexy thing to do when close to your lover.

You Two In *302 Advanced Techniques for Driving a Man Wild in Bed*, I detailed nine variations on the squatting woman-on-top position. Here, I'm suggesting that *he* squat on the balls of his feet, and you straddle his hips and perch atop. Balanced on your feet, you are still free to bounce and jiggle as you please, but in this pose you can snuggle in to slide your chest against his. And your spread-out vulva means his thrusts go deep and rub against your more exposed parts.

The Backbend

*Bending back and opening the chest also unlocks the spirit within . . .
teaching you to move with ease and grace and to live with an open
heart and a passion for life and love.*

—J. CHAPMEN, *YOGA FOR INNER STRENGTH*

THE ANCIENT YOGIS were fans of moves that produce
strength on the outside *and* the inside. So they developed many
back-bending poses (from the slightly bent Cobra to the
Upward-Facing Dog to the full Backbend) because they
increase circulation to the chest and pelvis, making you robust
and vibrant. But the real goodies lie on a subtler level; these
postures stretch open your heart to love and your genitals to
bliss.

You Because it gets cerebral-spinal fluids pumping, a backward stretch can even clear up a foggy brain. Opening your
chest and belly, it helps you breathe more deeply and face the
world with confidence and power. Try a *very gentle* backward
stretch after a mind-numbing session at the computer or before
an important meeting or big night out.

You Two Lean against the back of an armchair, resting your
rump on the top. With your man standing in front of you, hold
his hands and bend backward, letting your hips seesaw up to
make the perfect open target for his erection. This stretch
brings extra energy and sensation to your vulva while providing quite the view for him—to say nothing of the outrageous
angles of penetration.

Note: Do not attempt back-bending poses if you have back trouble.

Colossus of the Bedroom

Why, man, he doth bestride the narrow world
Like a Colossus, and we petty men
Walk under his huge legs and peep about . . .

—WILLIAM SHAKESPEARE, *JULIUS CAESAR*

THE COLOSSUS OF Rhodes, a giant bronze statue of the god Helios, stood for fifty-six years at the mouth of Rhodes' main harbor—a third-century B.C. symbol of victory over those who had tried to besiege the city. Though his pose was probably similar to the Statue of Liberty's, legends picture him straddling the harbor, ships sailing between his legs. Why? Because the classic wide-legged stance is body language for "I'm bold. I'm invincible. See if you can take me on." Much more potent. Much more sexy.

You A man standing with legs fairly wide gives off a certain bravado, a sense of control. In contrast, a woman looks more powerful with legs only about twelve inches apart, head held high, arms and palms open—as if she's expanding into space. But in the bedroom, spread legs are both brazen and vulnerable, making your genitals more visible and physically more sensitive.

You Two If you stand naked on the sofa, legs spread wide, you give off *all three* signals—"I'm powerful. I'm attackable. Come and get me, big boy!" Plus, with him upright in front, you have just the right height and stability for randy standing-up sex. Hips can wriggle freely. Hands can roam all over the place. And wide-open genitals can rub together in ways they've never met before.

The Legs Have It

SOMETIMES ALL YOU need to spice things up is a new leg move. By rearranging your thighs, you can change the slant of your pelvis, the width of your vagina, and the availability of your clitoris and G-spot. And your man, who will think you've invented an entirely new position altogether, will be in reverent and aroused awe.

DAY

74

- *Legs together* — Squeeze your legs together during missionary (so they're inside his) to tighten the fit and move his penis more onto your clitoris.
- *Leg lift* — In scissors, lift your top thigh toward the ceiling and support it with your hand. You stretch and sensitize your labia and open more pleasure spots to his thrusting.
- *Bent leg* — During missionary, bring one knee close to your chest and lie the other flat down. It makes a tighter fit and angles him onto your G-spot, especially if he strokes toward your bent leg.
- *Leg up* — Sex on the desk, with you perched atop and him standing, gets even racier when you bring both feet up to sit flat on the desk, spreading your vagina wide and exposing just about everything to his pounding pelvis.
- *Power legs* — When on your back, set your feet flat on the bed so you can lift your butt and mambo in midair. Gives great range of motion, lets you guide him where you want him, and brings more sensation to your pelvis.

On Your Knees —
In a Good Way

*The first time I kissed Brad my knees went weak —
I literally lost my breath!*

—JENNIFER ANISTON

A KISS CAN make you weak, even bring you to your knees. But you probably don't stay there long. You might fall onto your back in a swoon or slide down his body to perform a different kind of kiss. If, instead, you both remained on your knees, you'd find you could squeeze your bodies close from shoulder to knee, and, because kneeling makes you tighten your thigh muscles, you'd feel a sweet, trembling pressure in your loins.

You When you change from doggie to missionary, you're often briefly on your knees. With a repertoire of kneeling poses, you cleverly transform those moments into rapture. For instance, you might stop to clasp his knees with your ankles, turn your head back for a kiss, and put his hands on your breasts or vulva. Try this facing a wall—the resistance allows him to thrust harder.

You Two When on your knees facing each other, lift one leg to set your foot on the bed behind him. This gives stability and an opening for him to enter. For even more balance, he can do the same with his opposite leg. Great for extracurricular kissing, fondling, sliding a hand down to caress his swinging testicles, or his reaching around to grab your rump. There's something quite ravenous about it.

Crouching Tiger, Hidden Sexpot

So low she was crouching now that she seemed flattened to the earth except for the upward bend of the glossy back as it gathered for the spring.

—EDGAR RICE BURROUGHS, *TARZAN OF THE APES*

WHY DOES A tiger crouch before she attacks? As any Olympic sprinter will tell you, crouching helps your legs first concentrate and then release their driving force. But more important, it taps into the elastic energy of your pelvis so that, instead of muscling your way out of a starting gate, you simply let your haunches uncoil like a spring. It's the hips that give you serious dash.

You Martial artists know that moving from your hips, in a slight crouch, keeps you in balance. Virtuoso lovers know that working your hips gives you more thrusting power but also flexes and tones the genital muscles. So if you practice lunges, crouching squats, and hip stretches, you'll not only sculpt your butt but also increase the feeling in your moan zones.

You Two Stand by the edge of the bed and lean forward, resting your elbows on the mattress. He comes in from behind. Simulate a runner's crouch by setting one knee on the bed and straightening the other leg out behind. While he thrusts, slowly switch leg positions and hold, then switch again, constantly changing hip angles and skin sensations for both of you—and making your vulva pulse with pleasure.

A Day Off

Take a new position on exercise. Do your whole routine backward. Look only to the left on your power-walking route. On the treadmill, run to jazz instead of rock. Just as with a rarely used sex position, you'll have new sensations, fresh emotions, and quirky ideas you can extend to the rest of your life.

Animal Magnetism

Queen of Beasts

It is better to be a lion for a day than a sheep your whole life.

—ELIZABETH KENNY

IF YOU WERE a Roman god who wanted to make his mark, you wrestled lions bare-handed—as Hercules did. But the Phrygian goddess Cybele actually harnessed the beasts' brawn by riding atop their backs, as if driving a chariot. Their raw sexuality became her strength, not because she withheld or gave it too freely, but because by sharing it proudly, she made others feel their *own* wild joy and fierce power.

You Sheathing her claws until ready to grasp her prey, a lioness saves her coiled strength for life's most important battles. No one knows her true might until the last moment. Then, pow! The strike is over and she's the one with all the goodies. Great timing. Sharp focus. Exquisite results.

You Two One simple move turns you into a lioness-on-top. Hold his wrists down firmly against the bed, like a lioness restraining a deer. Pinned by your legs and hands, he feels completely at the mercy of you and your flesh, not some steel handcuff. A bite to the jugular, as lions employ, is optional.

Your Significant Otter

At home in both of these elements [Earth and Water], Otter is the personification of femininity: long, sleek and graceful.

—JAMIE SAMS AND DAVID CARSON, *MEDICINE CARDS*

NATIVE AMERICANS OFTEN use otter skin to make medicine bags for powerful women. To them, the animal represents the best of everything female. Brimming with grace and sensual joy, the otter is also a caring mother and noble humanitarian. And with a sense of adventure that often leads to brilliant inventions, she reminds us that everything has potential if we view it from the right angle.

You In our search for every scrap of information, we may be tempted, like baleen whales, to skim only the surface. But otters dive deep. Retrieving rough shells that others discard, they rise to the surface, float comfortably on their backs, and dig in for the tasty morsel hidden inside. Yummier food. Truer understanding. Better jewels.

You Two Otter foreplay involves the male biting the female's nose and holding her underwater, followed by a playful chase through the kelp. Less violent and even more effective is the dry kiss to *your* lover's nose. Brushing your lips across the bridge transmits heady pheromones and activates nearly invisible vellum hairs that send shivers to all points south.

A Gift Horse

To ride a horse is to ride the sky.

—AUTHOR UNKNOWN

ATOP A HORSE, flying like the wind, we humans feel like gods. In fact, until the mid-nineteenth century, a naked woman astride a white horse became goddess-for-a-day in many European villages. Her exposed ride through town was essential for making crops and wombs fruitful. In England, she was called Godiva (meaning "goddess"), a Lady and her horse simply following a centuries-old tradition of primal power.

You Even pulling a plow, a horse maintains a noble bearing. And when set free, she soon recaptures her magnificent, wild spirit. In the new field of "horse as medicine," where being around these creatures serves as therapy, inner dignity is one of the animal's greatest teachings. Like the horse, stand proud, and you'll have the strength to confront anything that comes your way—and look gorgeous while doing it.

You Two While mating, a stallion nibbles and licks the mare almost continuously. This kind of sensory overload is especially effective just before orgasm. At that crucial moment, suck his earlobe. Hard. Or bite his lower lip and immediately lick it. Intensify your nips and licks as he moves through climax. You'll make his whole body shudder.

Love in the Wild

WE MAY THINK we invented the elaborate rituals of romance, but our animal brethren have been there, done that, and moved onto something far more flamboyant:

- Like knights in a medieval joust, male sage grouse compete for a crowd of admiring ladies. By inflating huge air sacs in their chests, they make popping sounds that resonate for three miles. The ladies choose winners and offer appropriate "favors."

- Alligators have a gift for foreplay. They touch snouts, bellow, rub backs, blow bubbles, and swim circles that sluice water over the other's skin—for hours.
- Snails prefer light S & M. First they circle each other. Then one hisses and fires a "love dart," piercing the other's body. The stab-ee circles some more and fires back. Now fiercely aroused, they come together and do the slimy deed.
- A Meller's duck has a long corkscrew penis. So the female evolved a vagina with spirals and side pockets where she stores sperm—later ejecting it if she's not satisfied.
- The snake comes equipped with *two* penises, in case one gets tired. He keeps the operative tool inside out and then inflates it like a long balloon right into his mate's dry and otherwise inaccessible opening.

The Charm of the Snake

There be three things which are too wonderful for me, yea,
four which I know not:
The way of an eagle in the air; the way of a serpent upon a rock;
the way of a ship in the midst of the sea; and the way of a man
with a maid.

—PROVERBS 30:18–19

DAY
82

THE MINOAN SNAKE Goddess from ancient Crete is perhaps the most famous of all the world's serpent deities. Bare-
breasted and holding a live snake in each hand, she offered the
creature's power of immortality (it continually rebirths itself
by shedding old skin) and its sinuous, female sexuality to all.
With snaky secrets at hand, she ruled a culture that was
woman-centered, egalitarian, and at peace for more than a
millennium.

You Australian Aborigines believe the writhings of Rainbow
Snake created the rivers. In India, the undulations of life-force
energy up the spine (*kundalini*) caused enlightenment. In any
culture, serpentine movements seem to waken the creative,
erotic energies of the body. When your libido is stalled, undulate your hips (keeping PCs relaxed) for two full minutes. Better than pink Viagra.

You Two Give the missionary snaky new life by propping
your feet on the headboard (your whole body faces that direction) and lifting your hips off the bed—so you can writhe and
swivel all *over,* all *around,* and *against every surface* of his shaft.
Perhaps *this* is why the Minoans were free from war for fifteen
hundred years.

Dove Love

*O my dove, that art in the clefts of the rock, in the secret places
of the stairs,*
*let me see thy countenance, let me hear thy voice; for sweet is thy
voice, and thy countenance is comely.*

— SONG OF SONGS 2:14

AS THE SACRED bird of Aphrodite, the dove originally represented the female soul and the delicate beauty of a woman's genitalia. The birds were often depicted on Aphrodite's coins, facing each other, wings spread, flanking the sacred stone of Delphi—looking for all the world like an aroused clitoris nestled between two feathery labia. No wonder the stone itself was thought to facilitate direct communication with the gods.

You A male dove struts, bows, and sings loudly to attract mates and claim territory. A female dove simply sits in her nest and coos. Soon, the male, drawn by her soothing call, flies in with a beak-load of nest-building twigs. In courtships of any kind, it's often the soft voice, so flirty and hypnotic, that wins all the sticks.

You Two Dove couples preen each other, often by stretching their beaks across the other's neck in an intimate nuzzle. Perhaps they have the same extra-sensitive spot we do—the tendon running from ear to shoulder. Pull your man's head to one side and kiss-kiss-bite up and down the exposed ridge. To him, it feels slightly dangerous, very tender, and all kinds of goose-bumply.

DAY
83

A Day Off

Try walking with the liquid grace of a panther. First lift your thigh, then your knee, letting the motion tumble into your calf and flow out through your foot as it lands on the ground. Because movement activates feelings and attitudes, walking like a big cat will bring out the slinkiness in you.

DAY

84

Delicious Danger

Open to the Public

My dear, I don't care what they do, so long as they don't do it in the streets and frighten the horses.

—ATTRIBUTED TO MRS. PATRICK CAMPBELL,
BRITISH ACTRESS, CIRCA 1910

MOVING A SEXUAL encounter into the hallway is refreshingly hot. But taking it out to Macy's dressing room is downright incendiary. You're in a fever of excitement—the risk of exposure causing your body to flood with adrenaline and testosterone. Your heart pounds. Your skin is on fire. And your brain goes ballistic with the thrill of breaking the rules.

DAY
85

You According to the book *The Day America Told the Truth*, written by James Patterson and Peter Kim, sex in public is one of six top male fantasies. Kinky and exhilarating for *both* of you, it's one of the easiest dreams to make come true, yet one that gains you tremendous sexual and emotional currency—as well as the power of a shocking secret.

You Two At a party—wearing a flirty cocktail dress and no panties—pull your man into the shadows of an open bedroom door. (If you're really daring, do try Macy's dressing room.) Simply raise your dress and let him do the rest. Or kneel, unzip his fly, and lick him right through his briefs. The covering adds sensation and extra furtiveness to your already dangerous tryst.

Biting

Every part of my body receives in turn his love-bites,
And he covers me with kisses of fire.

— *THE PERFUMED GARDEN*

DAY
86

IN THE WHITE-HOT moments of sex, your desire-swollen flesh aches for more than soft caresses. It craves intensity. Edge. Sting. The kind of firm nip that draws blood to the surface and makes your skin tingle and throb. Seals, who munch each other while mating, seem to understand this naturally. But we humans know something more — a good bite brings out the sexy animal in even the tamest lover.

You A love bite is a token of trust that binds two people more profoundly than words. When you nip your lover, you reveal a deep, ravenous need — and he makes himself vulnerable to it. The marks you leave behind will remind him of your hot, shared passion. According to the *Kama Sutra,* such bonds "will not be lessened even in one hundred years."

You Two 1) Nip the small, sensitive hollow below his hairline. Very unexpected. 2) Graze his thighs with your teeth during oral. 3) Bite lightly beside his windpipe and hold until you feel the artery throbbing just beneath. Very intimate and primal.

The Remington Challenge

We can't
Provide you
With a date
But we do supply
The best darn bait.
Burma Shave

—SERIES OF 1950S ROAD SIGNS

AROUND 3000 B.C., the pharaoh's wife set a new standard of beauty by removing her pubic hair with a paste of oil and honey. Roman women plucked their pubes with tweezers. And in fifteenth-century European castles, ladies clipped their privates in specially built shaving rooms. But in America, it was the teeny Brazilian thong and endorsements from stars like Gwyneth Paltrow that made shaved pubic hair seem daring, new, and sexy.

You Some women say shaving their pubes enhances oral sex because exposed skin is more sensitive, your clitoris gets more stimulation, and it encourages men to dive in more often. Hints: to avoid itching and irritation, trim first; use shaving cream with aloe (not soap!); stroke each area no more than twice (or use a beard trimmer); and apply baby oil afterward.

You Two Invite your man to bathe with you (the best way to soften hair). After toweling off, sit on the bed, legs lifted and open. With a glint in your eye, apply lotion to your vulva, and hand him a small scissors and razor. This intimate invitation says, "I trust you with my tenderest self. Let's take a risk." Scorching hot.

12 Places to Have a Dangerous Liaison

WHEN HAVING SEX in a semi-public place, always have a good excuse ready, like: a) you're trying to get pregnant and just found out you're ovulating; b) you're looking for a dropped contact lens; c) you have to apply sunscreen. Then grab your man and go for it:

DAY

88

1. Behind the shelves at a bookstore
2. In the haunted house at a carnival
3. Under a pier at the beach
4. On the roof of the Bellagio in Las Vegas
5. In the lobby during the first half of a live theater show
6. In a friend's closet
7. In the trees around the seventeenth hole of a golf course
8. In the backseat of a convertible with the top down
9. In the elevator of a skyscraper
10. In your parents' kitchen while they're asleep
11. In the stands at a football game, covered by a blanket
12. Behind a tree, just off the Bear Lake Trail at Rocky Mountain National Park

Risky Positions

Don't be afraid to go out on a limb. That's where the fruit is.

—H. JACKSON BROWNE

MEN GET INTO very deep ruts. They know what positions make them climax and, by god, they're gonna stick to 'em. But after eighty-three nights in missionary, you may develop a raging desire to swing from the chandelier. Okay, that's out. But you *can* inject just enough physical danger into a pose to renew your sense of fun, adventure, and untapped erotic possibilities.

DAY 89

You Though slightly precarious, the position described here will wake up spots inside you never knew existed. Because your vagina is "hanging" in a new position, inner walls shift, cavities open, and G-spots come out of hiding. And since risk and novelty stimulate the brain, you may find yourself becoming audaciously creative at the office too.

You Two Make like a wheelbarrow. Kneel down and brace yourself with forearms on the floor—your arms are like the front wheels of the cart. Bend your knees and rest your head in your hands. He stands behind and lifts your ankles up as if he's grabbed the handles and is ready to roll. You'll be wobbling and laughing but enjoying penetration deeper than the Mariana Trench.

Surrender

"What is Love?" they ask. "Tell them that love is
To abandon all desires, all wishes and the will
To do or not to do; to reject choices and selections."
The one who doesn't give this up
Is not worth mentioning.

—RUMI (TRANS. NEVIT O. ERGIN)

DAY
90

IN WAR, SURRENDER means losing. But in love, surrender means opening—letting yourself bloom with pleasure and intimacy that goes way beyond words. It's not losing yourself to another; it's giving yourself to your body, allowing your passions to guide you. It's the magic that happens when you stop dancing to the music and let the music tango *you*.

You Scary as it may feel, when you abandon yourself to sensation, you lose self-conscious doubts and acquire a bone-deep sensuality. Simply by going with the flow, you *know* how to kiss your lover into ecstasy. Orgasm becomes a rush of energy that circulates between you and your man, unifying and elevating your love.

You Two Few things are more enticing than offering yourself as a love slave. Secure in your own sex goddess-hood, kneel before him bare-breasted and, oh so submissively, tickle his legs with your nipples. Hand him several silky scarves and ask him to tie you to the bed until you've had three orgasms.

A Day Off

Do something slightly scary. Bake a berry torte from scratch. Go ice skating — without knee pads.

Doing new things creates new brain cells. And adrenaline gives you a rush you can carry into the bedroom.

DAY

91

Romancing the Bath

The Hedonistic Bath

Everything is a miracle. It is a miracle that one does not dissolve in one's bath like a lump of sugar.

—PABLO PICASSO

DAY 92

TO THE ROMANS, bathing was an all-day social event with performance theater and separate rooms for every bathing purpose. They put on bathing togas in the dressing room, acclimated in the tepid bath before soaking in the hot, cinnamon-scented bath (where they gorged on fruit and honey), sweated copiously in the desert-hot dry room, received a massage and skin-scraping in the rest area, and finished off in the *frigidarium*, an icy bath that invigorated them for group delights.

You For a private Dionysian bath, scent the water with sandalwood oil (or vanilla, which engorges the labia) and let it reach the perfect soaking temperature of 98 degrees Fahrenheit. Put on some John Coltrane, turn off all the lights, and sink in. Being in the dark will intensify every sensation — slippery soapsuds, exotic aromas, scrubby washcloth, smooth music.

You Two Scent bathwater with ylang-ylang and float rose petals on top. Then lead him blindfolded into the tub. Sit facing him and plop cut-up figs or peaches into his mouth. Drape your thighs over his, snuggle close, and soap him sensuously. Slide your hand underwater to tickle his balls. Then mount him, grab the sides of the tub for leverage, and rock your hips till you make his wet dreams come true.

The Towel

The towels were so thick there I could hardly close my suitcase.

—YOGI BERRA

BATH TOWELS WERE not always plush, but they often had ritual significance. In sixteenth-century Turkey, a sultan's daughter gave only one gift to her groom—a woven linen towel for the Turkish bath. And in Japan, the small hot towel before a meal or tea ceremony has always served to cleanse spirit as well as hands. Today, fluffy terry cloth does more than dry your body; it establishes the mood of the room where you prepare for the day.

You Your bathroom's beauty is only towel deep. Adorn yours with spa-quality, 900 GSM (grams per square meter of cotton) towels—much thicker than the usual 300–800 GSM. For over-the-top luxury, add a towel warmer. The plug-in kinds are easy to install, don't use much energy, and dry your delicates too.

You Two A cushy towel by the bedside can protect the sheets from sex stains or simply tidy you up afterward. But one of the most sensual things it can do is drape over your man's rump during long, slow lovemaking. It keeps his body heat snuggled in (around you too) and makes him feel as pampered as a sultan.

The Shower

Everyone who's ever taken a shower has an idea. It's the person who gets out of the shower, dries off and does something about it who makes a difference.

— NOLAN BUSHNELL

IN THE BEGINNING, you stood under a waterfall. If you were rich enough, like Babylonian King Nebuchadnezzar, you had slaves pour water on you from above. In ancient Athens, you showered under a spout at one of the city's large fountains. But in 1767, when Englishman William Feetham patented a piped contraption with a hand pump, you could finally have the voluptuous pleasure of falling water in your own home.

You Why not make a daily task into a sybaritic delight? Pretty towels, a sheer, flowered shower curtain, scented foaming gels, and an exfoliating body brush can transform any shower experience. For the ultimate, a detachable, massaging showerhead will set your scalp, nipples, and several other things aquiver to start your day off right.

You Two Step into the shower behind him, get soapy, and press your naked body against his. Reach around to give him a slippery genital massage. Then turn him around by his "handle" and let him watch suds slide down to pile on your nipples like whipped cream. Rub your sudsy breasts against his chest. Then rinse. Finally, brace yourself against the tiles to offer him rear entry while water cascades all over both of you.

Bath Accoutrements

FOR A TRULY sybaritic or restorative bathing experience, you
need supplies:

- Flowers to feminize the room and generate heat—white
  lilies for purity, red roses for romance, freesia or gardenias
  for aroma, orchids to connote ecstasy
- Cushy towels and bath sheets—ideally, heated by a towel
  warmer
- Candles—pillars in various sizes, candles-in-a-can, floating
  tea lights
- Scented oils and bubble bath—stress-relieving aromas are
  orange, nutmeg, lavender, chamomile, lemongrass; romantic aromas are sandalwood, ylang-ylang, rose, jasmine,
  ginger; uplifting are thyme, lemon balm, bergamot, lime
- Bath salts, muds, and seaweed soaks—salts detoxify; mud
  removes excess oil and dead cells; seaweed rehydrates
- Bath fizzes to tingle, smell good, and supply skin-nourish-
  ing minerals
- Loofahs and bath brushes to scrub and soften skin
- Drinks—ice-cold spring water, hot green tea, wine, cham-
  pagne, raspberry and vodka frappés
- CD player for Kenny G, Rachmaninoff, Miles Davis,
  Andrea Bocelli, Chopin, Anita Baker, or Gregorian chant
- Bath pillow
- Rubber ducky

The Healing Bath

*I used to lie between cool, clean sheets at night after
I'd had a bath . . . and talk to God.*

—FRANCES FARMER

IN JAPAN, BATHING is a ritual—an easy way to attune with water and deep thoughts. Its purpose is not really to remove dirt but to cleanse mind and spirit. Whether steeping in a stone pool fed by hot springs or a neck-deep private tub, one first washes *outside* the bath, then steps in with a pot of jasmine tea to soak up the soft, harmonious qualities of water, contemplate life, and become one with Nature.

You To cure what ails you, put on the soothing sounds of Kitaro or Bach and drop some lavender oil into your bath water. Then sink into it inch-by-inch, allowing the warmth to seep down to your bones. To detoxify, add a spa seaweed or bath salt mixture. Cover your eyes, lay your head on a bath pillow, and allow your mind to drift.

You Two Prepare bathwater with oils of cedarwood (relieves anxiety) and geranium (romantic and restorative). Sit behind him in the tub, legs wrapped around his torso. Feed him raspberries and brandy. With a cup, pour water over his chest and shoulders—it's blissfully soothing. Drag a soapy sea sponge over his back and chest, then down to the underside of his shaft. Repeat endlessly. Afterward, treat him to slow, Zen-like sexual healing.

The Loofah

Let us roll all our strength and all
Our sweetness up into one ball,
And tear our pleasures with rough strife
Through the iron gates of life.

—ANDREW MARVELL

DEEP IN THE tropical jungle grows a most versatile vine. Its gourd-like fruit, the loofah, can be cooked and eaten like squash, or crushed to produce an insect-repelling odor. But beauty queens like Nefertiti and Cleopatra treasured the fruit most when it matured and became tough, making a superb exfoliating sponge that gave their skin a luminescent glow.

You Give yourself a spa treatment that removes dead skin, improves circulation, and makes you tingle. After a hot bath, wet a loofah to soften it, apply scented soap, and brush your skin in long slow strokes, beginning at the ankles and moving upward. Rinse and pat dry. Then nuke body lotion for ten seconds and smooth it all over.

You Two Lay some towels on the bathroom floor or tub bottom, and invite him there for a slippery, tingling massage. Drizzle warm oil on his back and butt cheeks. Then stroke and circle with a dampened loofah. At some point, turn him over, lay a warm towel over his eyes, and continue massaging. The contrast of slippery oil and rough sponge, plus not knowing where you're headed, will shiver his timber but good.

A Day Off

Retreat to the sanctuary of a bath.

Read, dream, tweeze, fantasize, apply a mask, sing, meditate, or simply luxuriate in warmth, slipperiness, and comfort. No thinking allowed.

DAY

98

Simple but Deadly

A Hint of Mint

As for the garden of mint, the very smell of it alone recovers and refreshes our spirits, as the taste stirs up our appetite.

—PLINY THE ELDER

ACCORDING TO GREEK mythology, the beautiful nymph Minthe was turned into a plant by her lover's angry wife. Unable to undo the spell, her paramour endowed the lowly herb with a scent so enticing and capricious it would beguile the world forever. Cooling as well as soothing, mint does create the kind of complex sensations that are hard to forget.

DAY

99

You Mint tea can help relieve headaches and tension. But crème de menthe icing on something chocolate will cure the blues. Combine 4 cups powdered sugar, ½ cup soft butter, ¼ cup milk, and ¼ cup crème de menthe liqueur to frost a pan of your favorite brownies. Easy and wickedly good. Minthe would be proud.

You Two Hold a sip of crème de menthe in your mouth and let some ooze out over his penis before closing your lips over it. Exhale warm breath to heat the minty liqueur, then inhale as you slide your lips upward to give him the cold shivers. Or pour crème de menthe on his belly, collect it on your tongue, and trace it over his body. Then fan him with feathers to create hot/cold tingles everywhere.

"V" as in Vagina

She — the woman shows in turning up her robe
An object — the vulva — developed full and round,
In semblance like a cup turned upside down. . . .
You'll find it flaming hot as any furnace.

— THE PERFUMED GARDEN

LONG BEFORE WINSTON Churchill raised his hand in the victory sign, the "V" signified everything female. For ancient peoples, it resembled the spread of a woman's legs, but more important, it reminded them of a vessel — the sacred container of life and ecstasy that is her body. Thanks to *The Vagina Monologues*, the V has returned to its roots, as today's women proudly proclaim their anatomy by flashing the two-fingered sign for V-Day.

You If you place the open V of your first two fingers over your vaginal lips, you can frame the exact area where you want oral attention. Guys love the visual and the big go-ahead. Plus, you can squeeze, press, and massage to increase your pleasure — while still allowing him full access. It's a win-win situation.

You Two During doggie-style, set the V of your fingers atop your clitoris and on either side of his shaft. Knead and compress your outer lips around him, matching his rhythm. If you slide the point of the V along his stem *between* thrusts, he gets two kinds of intense stimulation every single second.

Good to the Last Squeeze

But whilst her busy hand would guide that part
Which should convey my soul up to her heart,
In liquid raptures I dissolve all o'er,
Melt into sperm, and spend at every pore.

—JOHN WILMOT, EARL OF ROCHESTER

DID YOU KNOW that a man's orgasm occurs in *three* distinct spurts? First comes a small drop of lubricating juice from the Cowper's glands—that lovely, slippery pre-cum. Then the prostate squeezes semen into the tube leading out of the penis, causing the feeling of "Oh boy, it's coming." Finally, the testicles squirt out semen to the beat of 0.8 second—those rhythmic contractions he may beg, borrow, and even steal for.

You Use this information to your advantage. Stage 1: While he's rapturous but still has functioning brain cells, ask him for diamonds. Stage 2: If you want to keep him hard longer, use the squeeze technique NOW. (Grip his penis firmly for about three seconds, just below the glans.) Stage 3: Whatever happens during these climactic moments imprints on his subconscious—so smooch him now and he'll associate your kiss with mind-blowing ecstasy.

You Two The last part of his three-stage ejaculation is by far the most potent. But you can give him a fourth stage—a smaller, aftershock orgasm. Keep him inside and, shortly after he's spent, gently pulse your fingers around his testicles. Orgasm causes a spike in prolactin which, according to research at the University of Calgary, triggers new cells in the brain's smell center. Result? Your unique scent imprints in his memory and makes him more attracted to you.

At the Movies

WHAT COULD BE simpler than popping in a porn DVD? It's erotic imagery that goes straight from brain to groin. And, after all, women are visual too. A study at McGill University found that, when shown porn clips, men *and women* showed signs of arousal (measured by genital temperature changes) in about thirty seconds—even though many of the women said they didn't like porn.

DAY
102

True, there are a lot of sleazy blue movies, but women are changing the market, and today many sex films have woman-friendly story lines and are tastefully photographed. They can give you frisky new ideas and flip *your* hot switch as well as his. Try these. The ones with stars are especially recommended.

*Beauty

Blonde Ambition

Brandy and Alexander

*Christine's Secret (Candida Royalle)

Platinum Paradise

Real People, Real Life, Real Sex (series)

A Taste of Ambrosia (Candida Royalle)

Ecstasy Girls

Jenna Jameson Is the Masseuse

*The Opening of Misty Beethoven

Outlaw Ladies

*The Devil in Miss Jones Part II

Dreams of Desire

Exposed

Suzie Superstar

(Try *www.blowfish.com* for easy renting. It has stringent privacy policies and helpful reviews.)

Naughty Pillow Talk

Style is knowing who you are, what you want to say, and not giving a damn.

—GORE VIDAL

ACCORDING TO A survey in *Sex: A Man's Guide*, written by Stefan Bechtel and Laurence Roy Stains, the only thing guys love more than filmy lingerie is hearing four-letter words in bed. It gives them confidence (if you're that aroused, he's doing something *really* right), inspires creativity (if you like this, maybe he can try—*that!*), and makes them pant with excitement (anything taboo is scorching hot). And somehow it makes them last *much* longer!

DAY
103

You Have you ever noticed that when you say "I'm tired," you feel more exhausted? In the same way, when you whisper "I love the feel of your _____ in/on my _____," you feel naughtier and more turned on. Talking dirty gets you in the mood. And if you do it with your own style, the words won't sound silly or raunchy. The best part is that you're getting across your deepest wishes.

You Two Start slow. Your face hidden as you brush your mouth over his hips, murmur, "Running my tongue along your thigh like this gets me so excited I want to suck your c**k." A guy *loves* racy talk about how much his body arouses you. When you get bolder, look him in the eye and say, "Please let me f**k you right now." He'll probably ravish you on the spot.

The Moistness of You

What would the world be, once bereft of wet and wildness?

—GERARD MANLEY HOPKINS

DAY

104

IN THE RICH moisture of nature—or of woman—lies a promise. Life will be renewed; seeds will grow; thirsts will be quenched. By granting him entry to your secret, moist places, a man can bathe in the primordial waters of life. In return, he penetrates and protects you with his male vigor. In this exchange lies a silent oath—to give yourselves to the deep, wet, and binding pleasures of ecstasy.

You In the animal kingdom, males contribute part of the moist slickness needed for sex. Kinsey reported that boars and rams, for example, "may dribble or run continuous streams of such secretions as soon as they approach a female in which they are sexually interested." But in humans, women own the juices of love. Is that why men are so wild for our wetness?

You Two In the middle of a French kiss, take one of his fingers and insert it deep in your vagina. He'll feel as though he's "drowning" in your two types of moistness—and as though he's mysteriously bound to you.

A Day Off

Imbibe the smell of something clean — hair, fresh laundry, the air after a storm.

Simple, but . . .

Hawaiian Honeymoon

Getting Lei'd

How can one help shivering with delight when one's hot fingers close around the stem of a live flower, cool from the shade and stiff with newborn vigor!

—COLETTE

DAY

106

FRAGRANT, VELVETY, AND sensual, a flower lei imparts vibrant femininity to any woman who wears one, and a sense of kindheartedness to any man. But the custom of making these garlands, dating back hundreds of years, actually comes from the aloha-like desire to weave different ideas together—friendship and beauty, nature and human handiwork, even the views of two contending chiefs into an aromatic wreath of peace.

You Often, a lei's magic lies in its *combinations*. White ginger blossoms, without the essence of mango and fragrance of neroli, would make a far less potent perfume. But the separate elements woven together—like smarts *and* sexiness—create something new and stunning enough to turn any stranger into a lover.

You Two When pleasuring his erection, *blend together* your lips and hands. Lick your fingers to lubricate, then wrap a hand around his base—fingers snuggled up tight against your mouth. The slippery combo will feel like one seamless, hot vagina, taking in every greedy inch of him.

Volcano

Lei of Mauna Loa, beautiful to behold.
The mountain honored by the winds
is known by a peaceful motion.
Calm becomes the whirlwind.
. . . I am alive for your love.

—HAWAIIAN HULA CHANT,
AS QUOTED FROM *HAWAIIAN GODDESSES* BY LINDA CHING

TO LIVE ON the slopes of Mauna Loa, home of Hawaii's active volcano, is to walk the razor's edge. At any moment, rivers of molten lava can destroy homes, memories, and lives. But in that same moment, new land of stark, massive beauty is born. One day, hot and impetuous. The next, serene as a forest of ferns. In this way, Pele, the unpredictable volcano goddess, keeps the fires of passion alive.

You Creativity is like a volcano. Lightning fast. Wild. Destroying old ways of thinking as it brings new ideas to life. Try sparking imagination or passion by writing, painting, or dancing out the thoughts you usually suppress—the really outrageous, crazy, lusty ones. In the private island of your mind and body, you'll set off the fireworks of creation.

You Two Pleasure yourself for his eyes only, but with this volcanic addition. Bring yourself to the boiling point, then ease off to a trembling, panting plateau. Fire then steam, over and over. These flowing cycles, so different from his single-pointed eruptions, will amaze him and feed his hunger for more.

Lehua's Look of Love

As she stood and lifted those blue eyes, those soft dark loving eyes shyly to mine, it seemed to me as if the doors and windows of heaven were suddenly opened.

—THE REVEREND FRANCIS KILVERT

DAY
108

WHEN PELE THE volcano goddess found that her man of choice loved another, she turned him into a tree—the Ohi'a. In a repentant mood, she later reunited the lovers by transforming her rival into a Lehua flower and placing her on the tree. Now, with hundreds of soft, quill-like petals—red, tipped in gold—Lehua forever raises her slender arms and shining eyes to the branching embrace of her constant lover.

You When you rest your eyes on something—a blossom, a painting, a lover—for a full minute, you open a communication of secrets. You might learn why the bloom is more beautiful when it's "over the hill," how the artist created a brushstroke that moves your soul, or where your man's skin is translucent—and so, exquisitely sensitive.

You Two Next time you're giving him oral, stop mid-slurp to lift your eyes and stare straight into his. Then resume licking. It's sassy, suspenseful, and tigerish. But, more important, the eye contact brings his mind and soul—heated up about 100 degrees—into an act he usually feels only in his body.

Bringing the Islands to Bed

SOMETIMES IT'S EASIER to be wild in bed when you're on vacation. Make your bedroom into an island getaway, and anytime you want, you can have motel sex in your own tropics:

- Hang a mosquito net around the bed. It creates a filmy cocoon that conjures up lazy afternoons and tropical breezes.
- Paint one wall plumeria pink or ocean turquoise.
- Install a double hammock in the corner and add some tropical print pillows. Good for all kinds of swinging positions.
- Set out several Hawaiian potpourris. My personal faves are white ginger, tuberose, and pikaki (frangipani). One whiff transports you to a lush garden of love.
- Replace your usual bedroom chair with a rattan love seat or king chair to give the feel of the islands—and to help you sit atop him regally and comfortably.
- Add flowers. Real, of course. Lots of them. Exotic birds of paradise, elegant orchids, brilliant proteas, and aromatic ginger and tuberose.
- Fill the room with island music—the Brothers Cazimero's *Hawaiian Paradise*, Elvis's *Blue Hawaii*, Don Ho's *A Night in Hawaii*, or anything from *www.mele.com*.

Happy aloha dreaming—and sexy scheming!

Lomi Lomi

When you do dance, I wish you
A wave o' the sea, that you might ever do
Nothing but that.

—WILLIAM SHAKESPEARE

EVER HAD SOMEONE hula all over your body? That's Lomi Lomi massage. Instead of kneading a bicep, then a calf, the masseuse might glide her forearms in one fluid movement all the way from your shoulder to your foot, moving energy through the body in waves. Continuous and flowing, one stroke melts into another, merging mind with heart, and body with soul.

You For fast, deep relaxation, try the Lomi Lomi trick of massaging two opposite parts of your body at once—for example, one hand rubs your left forearm while the other kneads your right thigh. Because the brain can't focus on two areas at once, you drift into a state of mindless, oceanic bliss.

You Two Lubricate your hands with lots of oil, then Lomi Lomi his erection. Swirl one hand from head to base—but before it reaches bottom, start smoothing and twisting with the other. Hand over hand, again and again. It's perpetual, mind-altering, tongue-lolling rapture.

Fountains of Life

I only wish to be the fountain of love from which you drink, every drop promising eternal passion.

—ANONYMOUS

THE *WAI* IN *Ha-wai-i* means "life-giving waters." To the Polynesians, this meant any fluids other than sea water—rain, coconut milk, semen, a woman's lubrication. Holding them sacred, the Hawaiians believed these liquids not only sustained life in our bodies, but were also the source of wisdom, love, and spiritual well-being.

You A simple bowl of water with flowers floating in it promotes beauty and tranquility in your office or bedroom. But you can make it into a vibrant wellspring by adding an inexpensive pump (found in most garden stores) and covering the pump with smooth rocks. Instant, soothing tropical waterfall.

You Two When you are *between* positions, take him into your mouth for a few seconds. Very unexpected and sexy. He feels as if he's drowning in you, deluged by your lovely moistness. Meanwhile, you are literally drinking from the fountains of life.

A Day Off

Wear a sarong around the house. You feel like you're at the beach. And as you walk, the loose folds create a soft breeze against your hips and thighs.

DAY
112

Kicky and Kinky

Ohhhhm, Hot Doggie!

Blessed are the flexible, for they shall not be bent out of shape.

—AUTHOR UNKNOWN

WHILE BENT OVER in Downward-Facing Dog, your tush waving high in the air like an invitation, have you ever thought how similar yoga poses are to sex positions? It's no accident. The *Kama Sutra*, like yoga, was originally developed as a physical path to enlightenment, and many of its postures are derived from asanas that improve the agility of hips and thighs, open your heart, or release sexual power.

DAY

113

You Make your next Downward Dog a sensual experience. Feel each finger caressing the floor, each thigh muscle lifting into your PCs, each skin cell being sensitized with fresh blood. Among other things, this pose strengthens flabby arms, relieves menstrual discomfort, and helps prevent osteoporosis.

You Two Receive health as well as sexual benefits with the Full-Tilt Downward Dog. From the inverted-V yoga pose (hands and feet on the floor, butt in the air), flex your knees to position your hips at the right height for his entry. For the Half-Tilt Downward Dog, lower knees to the floor and rest your head on folded arms. Either way, he's going in *very deeply* against your natural vaginal curve—more friction for him, more sensation for you. This position also tilts your cervix lower, so instead of feeling slammed, your deepest sex spot will feel "kissed."

The Newlywed Game

"She's my girl . . . She's my blue sky. After sixteen years, I still bite her shoulders. She makes me feel like Hannibal crossing the Alps."

—JOHN CHEEVER, *THE COUNTRY HUSBAND*

IF YOU COULD re-create the heart-fluttering, champagne dizziness of brand-new love, would you? Would you sacrifice for it the comfort, the trust, the bone-deep contentment of a long, if less romantic, relationship? After years of togetherness, toe-curling passion doesn't just happen. It's a state of mind that, like the finest perfume, needs to be refreshed every single day.

You According to the book *How to Improve Your Marriage Without Talking About It*, written by Dr. Patricia Love and Dr. Steven Stosny, women can make relationships more passionate by talking less (conversation about feelings increases muscular blood flow and makes guys fidget) and touching more. While men, says the *Journal of Marriage and Family*, could fire things up by learning to share power with their wives. Hear, hear!

You Two Jump-start your romantic motors by registering as newlyweds (even if you aren't) at a nearby hotel. Many include services and amenities such as in-room massage for couples; aromatherapy candles; champagne on arrival, or bedside martini service; a Barry White CD; breakfast in bed for two; and even male and female edible underwear. Whenever you feel the urge to chat, even to say, "Isn't this romantic?" kiss him instead.

Lather Up

What soap is for the body, tears are for the soul.

—JEWISH PROVERB

ACCORDING TO LEGEND, soap was discovered by accident when rain washed together with spilled animal fat and wood ashes, and some ancient Roman noticed the bubbles. The fortuitous chemical reaction had created a brand new molecule that suspends oil and traps light—magically transforming those homely ingredients into something iridescent, playful, and purifying.

You To find the perfect soap for you, smell it, feel it, and read the label. Olive oil holds moisture on the skin, while palm and coconut oils are drying but make big bubbles. Apricot kernel oil is great for sensitive skin, cocoa butter makes creamy lather, and milk and aloe vera aid chapping and eczema. Herbs and flowers nourish the spirit and smell nice.

You Two One of the most expensive treats in Thai bordellos is the soap massage. He lies on a plastic air mattress in the tub and watches while she soaps her body erotically. Then she lathers him up by sliding her slippery, hot hands over his chest, thighs, and genitals. At last, she climbs on top and slithers between his legs, around and even under his foamy body. The beautiful part is that it's just as much fun for you as for him!

Scoff at These Laws

ONE PERSON'S GOOD time is another's way-too-much-fun-to-be-legal taboo. But still—what were some of these legislators thinking? It's actually against the law in:

- Harrisburg, Pennsylvania—To have sex with a truck driver in a toll booth.
- Newcastle, Wyoming—To have sex while standing inside a store's walk-in meat freezer.
- Oxford, Ohio—For a woman to take off her clothes while standing in front of a man's picture.
- Connorsville, Wisconsin—For a man to shoot off a gun when his female partner has an orgasm.
- Kentucky—For a woman to appear in a bathing suit on any highway unless escorted by at least two officers or unless armed with a club.
- Florida—To have sexual relations with a porcupine.
- Nevada—For members of the state legislature to conduct official business wearing a penis costume while the legislature is in session.
- Alexandria, Minnesota—For a man to make love to his wife with the smell of garlic, onions, or sardines on his breath. Law mandates that if his wife requests, he must brush his teeth.
- Cleveland, Ohio—For a woman to wear patent-leather shoes. Apparently, a man might see the reflection of something he shouldn't.

Thank goodness there's *something* that's legally permitted. In Hong Kong, a betrayed wife may kill her adulterous husband, but only with her bare hands. The husband's lover may be slayed in any manner desired.

The Brush Off

She kissed the hairbrush
By mistake
She thought it was
Her husband Jake.
Burma Shave

—SERIES OF 1950S ROAD SIGNS

DAY

117

YOU DON'T WANT a man's cheek, or a hairbrush, to be too rough. But the right amount of bristle can make a guy feel excitingly rugged and a hairbrush seem almost decadent. Those little stings of pleasure grazing your lips or tingling your scalp have a soothing but savage appeal—as if you're being fondled by an affectionate panther. And you're the one who's purring.

You Most hairdressers say a brush combining boar bristles (which distribute your natural oils and smooth the hair shaft) and nylon (which detangles better) does more for shine and manageability than any shampoo or conditioner. Or try a hairbrush massager. Vibrating 6,000 times a minute, it will invigorate your scalp and, um, any other area you want to "brush."

You Two When kissing him all over isn't quite enough, bring in a hairbrush. The wild but gentle swirl of hundreds of little "fingernails" across the side of his torso, armpit, back, or foot bottom will wake up sleepy nerve endings, add a little wild to your reputation, and make him feel like a thoroughbred being groomed for the sweepstakes.

Liquid Gold

A woman waits for me — she contains all, nothing is lacking,
Yet all were lacking, if sex were lacking, or if the moisture of the
right man were lacking.

— WALT WHITMAN

WHEN A MAN gets aroused, he produces a few glistening drops of clear liquid at the tip of his penis. Mostly water and protein, this slippery fluid helps to clear his tubes for the passage of sperm and to lubricate him for sex. Though it is *not* ejaculate, most guys consider it part of their Sacred Sperm — an elixir so unutterably divine that, to be strictly proper about it, one should actually kneel in its presence.

You In reality, this mucus-y fluid is similar to the more copious lubrication we women produce. The difference is the pH factor. Pre-cum is higher in alkaline, which helps neutralize the acidity of the vagina — increasing the odds of sperm living through the long journey to fertilization. And yes, Virginia, there are sperm (capable of impregnating you!) in those first few drops.

You Two One of the few times I've seen a lover literally shake with desire (I'm talking 6.0 on the Richter scale) was when I collected his pre-cum on my tongue and fed it to him with a French kiss. Over and over again. It didn't insult my taste buds at all, and for him, the earth actually moved. Clear over to Cleveland.

A Day Off

Paint your toenails with glittery stripes. It makes your toes look thinner and more delicate.

And you feel just a bit more outré.

DAY
119

Girly Things

Panties

The warm close substance that passes close to her flesh . . . between her thighs, has, all senseless leather, cloth, or silk, as the case may be, something of the nature of a man's hand in it.

—"ETONENSIS"

THAT'S THE THING about panties—they go where a man wishes his hand could be. As the original cancan dancers knew, if a guy can just lay his *eyes* on a lady's knickers, he's delirious. But, in truth, most men don't even have to touch or see the frothy things. Let the average male know you're wearing cheeky bikinis beneath your party dress, and the *idea* of them, the tension of how he's going to get you out of them later . . . well, it becomes almost unendurable.

You When asked what their favorite item of women's clothing is, most men say panties. Hands down. Take him to a lingerie store and model styles in silk and lace. He'll be thrilled he's getting a private peep show, and you'll end up with a new wardrobe of panty presents.

You Two Panties can multitask. Use them to "tie" him up— put one of his hands through a leg hole, twist the rest, and slip the other leg hole over the bedpost. Or wear skimpy panties and knee-high boots to distract him from watching an after-noon-ruining basketball game. Or set your undies in the fridge for an hour, then use them as a massage mitt on hot skin.

Fingernails

Men like long nails; in old movies couples were always scratching each other's backs.

— BRITT EKLAND

IN CHINA AROUND 3000 B.C., nails were grown long to show that a person was too high in rank to perform manual labor. Cleopatra painted her nails deep red because that was the color of the royal class — and to draw attention to her naughty fingers. But it wasn't until the 1970s that really long nails returned to fashion. Were we celebrating our liberation from scrubbing clothes on washboards or simply reveling in our freedom to be as sexy and dangerous as we want to be?

DAY
121

You Both hair and nails are made of a protein called keratin. So you can make fingernails grow faster and healthier by eating more protein and calcium, but also by rubbing cuticle cream into the nail beds frequently, cutting your nails more often, typing on a keyboard daily, or living in a warm climate.

You Two During a kiss, run your fingernails lightly along the inside of his arm — a tender spot. Tantricas use this technique to make the fine hairs of the whole body become erect. But you're also showing appreciation for his biceps — the size of which most men are terribly insecure about. And even though fingernails don't have feeling, the nerves around your cuticles send messages to the brain that it interprets as a delightful tingling on your own fingertips.

Fleshy Pillows

And then I fell gently
To sleep on her breast —
Deeply to sleep
From the heaven of her breast.

—EDGAR ALLAN POE

DAY
122

THE GODDESS OF Willendorf, a 20,000-year-old limestone figure with oversized hips and mammaries, was an object of worship to ancient man, her plump breasts representing the fertile bounty of Earth and Woman. Deep inside, men have never stopped seeing those pillows of flesh as a place to go for nourishment—solace in times of trouble, nurturing "milk," and the erotic spark that makes life worth living.

You Your breasts don't have to be 38DD's to serve as enchanting, primeval soul food. The fact that they protrude, have nipples, and are reasonably soft is all it takes to trigger a man's ancient cravings. Allow him to rest his head there occasionally, and he'll be happier than a Paleolithic clam.

You Two As you move into position for oral sex, slide your breasts down his belly and let them envelop his erection. Give him time to enjoy the view and the sensations, because when you press into him, your bosom will look twice as plump as usual and feel like heaven itself.

The Girliest Thing of All

YOU MAY LIKE to avoid thinking about your vagina—the very thing that makes you a girl—but it can be your most alluring and feminine asset. Let's explore.

It's versatile. Though the average vagina is about 3 inches long and 1.3 inches in diameter, it dilates during sex to fit perfectly around almost any size penis.

It's buff. Strong enough to push out a baby, your vaginal muscles remain fairly toned throughout your whole life. But, by doing regular Kegels, you can pump them up enough to squeeze your guy like a vise—and make your orgasms super-intense.

It makes its own perfume. Think you should smell like a gardenia? Actually, the aromatic juices of an aroused female are the most powerful aphrodisiac known to man. Try wearing some behind your ears. P.S. You smell sweeter during the first two weeks of your cycle (more estrogen); spicier for the last two (more progesterone).

It's self-cleaning. Because it regularly sheds parts of its lining (creating a creamy discharge), the vagina is one of the cleanest—and slickest—parts of your body.

It has the only human organ made purely for pleasure. With as many nerve endings as the head of a penis, the tip of your clitoris is only ⅙ inch long. But the tissue extends deep inside to spread orgasmic shudders through your entire pelvis.

It's unique. Your vagina may look as smooth as an apricot or as ruffled as a conch shell. It may be pink, brown, or splotchy maroon. It may have a thatch like a grass hut or just a few silky strands. It's a personal wonder of nature that lures a man to explore and worship.

DAY
123

Lotions and Oils

How much better is thy love than wine!
and the smell of thine ointments than all spices!

—SONG OF SONGS 4:10

DURING BIBLICAL TIMES, one of life's few luxuries was skin ointment. As precious as gold and glory, perfumed lotions anointed royalty, welcomed esteemed travelers (following a foot bath), and softened the complexions of those who could afford it. To be massaged with ointment, so hands could glide over the body like silk and heady perfumes be released into the air, was a rare treat—and ambrosial foreplay for the world's first hedonistic lovers.

You Even though lotions and oils are inexpensive now, we don't use them enough. Rubbing cream on your hands each time you wash keeps skin young and makes you feel pampered. Massaging a lover with oil sensitizes flesh and creates an intimate bond. Add scent and you create sense memories too. Make a note to include perfumed lotions in your *everyday* beauty and lovemaking arsenal.

You Two 1) Using a kitchen baster, squirt warm oil all over his body. 2) Holding his penis, pour oil over your hand and let it cascade onto his skin. Then knead his erection with it. 3) Rub warming lube on both of you just before penetration. It will make your privates radiate and tingle even more than usual.

Lace

It is difficult to see why lace should be so expensive; it's mostly holes.
—MARY WILSON LITTLE

LACE ACTUALLY BEGAN with holes. When Roman togas frayed, clever wives twisted the threads together to make intricate borders of open filigree. But lace didn't become high fashion until the upper-class women of fifteenth-century Venice, housebound and bored, started sewing *punto in aria*, literally "stitches in the air." When Venetian courtesans began dressing in it, every woman wanted to wear the frothy fabric that allowed men small but seductive glimpses of their skin.

You How do you wear lace without looking like you're fresh from the bedroom or your grandmother's funeral? Use it sparingly and team it with something spiky and modern. Wear a lace-trimmed tank under a tailored suit. Pair a ruffled lace top with skinny jeans or a pencil skirt and stiletto boots. Mix black lace and leather. Team it with tweed or tartan. It's ultra feminine but with a glamorous, sexy edge.

You Two Top his erection with your discarded lace nightgown or cami. Smooth it over head, shaft, and testicles. Lick him through the fabric; then take the whole package into your mouth. The lacy threads add silky-rough texture, while the holes allow unexpected moments of tongue-on-skin contact.

A Day Off

What would make you feel more feminine? Perhaps wearing flirty dresses instead of slacks.
Maybe learning about women's history or sharp-
ening your intuition. Maybe a soul-nourishing
gab session with girlfriends? Or wearing heels on
a date or into the bedroom? Dig deep to find your
answers. Then implement a girly plan.

Places in the Heart

Aching

His heart was full of tenderness and sorrow: the longing to return to her was more than he could resist.

— WILKIE COLLINS, *I SAY NO*

THE PORTUGUESE CALL it *saudade* — the beautiful ache that occurs when two lovers are apart from each other. That one word, untranslatable in English, combines several feelings — sadness, wishing for completeness, and yearning for the lover's return. It means that you're happy to feel such intense desire, and may even relish it; yet it's crushing your heart.

DAY

127

You Because it's painful, we often try to push our aching for love aside. But the Portuguese, who dedicated a music genre to it, know this feeling is sweet. It's one of the few ways, besides sex, that we can experience love viscerally. Listen to the mournful songs of Ramana Vieira or revel in pining for someone, and you'll locate the deepest places in your body and soul.

You Two Sometimes it's what you do *after* he's come that matters. If you keep undulating your hips and squeezing your PCs, or if you hold him in your mouth for a few minutes, you extend the blissful ache of orgasm into intense longing. He'll feel like he can't get enough of you.

Dreaming

Dreams are illustrations . . . from the book your soul is writing about you.

—MARSHA NORMAN

A DREAM IS a place for your heart to explore things you don't understand or that you can't allow yourself to do in real life. Maybe that's why 40 percent of women say they've had an orgasm while dreaming about sex, but not while doing it. If you heed them, your nighttime reveries can help you find ways to love more freely and live more boldly.

You Scientists have found that, in dreams, the brain transforms thoughts by associating them with memories and images in creative new ways. So when you have a burning question, program your dreams to answer you. Think about the issue as you fall asleep, then pay particular attention to the dreams that come toward morning, when your subconscious dives the deepest.

You Two While he's still awake but thinks you're asleep, pretend to have an erotic dream, full of the kisses and caresses you wish for. Use vivid sound effects and undulations. Then wake up and describe the dream he starred in that made you so very hot. He'll do his best to make your heart's desires—now his too—come true.

Wanting

The act of longing for something will always be more intense than the requiting of it.

—GAIL GODWIN

WHAT WE WANT comes from our heart, but *how* we want it is controlled by our brain. According to the *Journal of Neuroscience*, we have separate brain circuits for wanting and liking. When the two work in sync, we feel wild desire. Wonderful. But . . . we have fewer circuits for pleasure than for desire. So sometimes when we get what we crave, we're left feeling empty. The secret is not to overdose on our desires but to leave a little in reserve—to fuel our need for wanting.

You Evolution designed us to binge on high-calorie foods that get stored as fat, so we could survive the long winters. But this overloads our brain circuits for liking, and does not make us happy—or thin. So when you crave peanut butter cookies, eat just one bite slowly. You satisfy your wanting without destroying your liking—or your figure.

You Two Have him take you to dinner at a restaurant with long tablecloths. Then either let him touch your pantiless crotch—just a little—or fondle him through his trousers. This will make him want, desperately, but will postpone the "getting it and liking it" phase for hours. The perfect brain circuitry combination.

Mood-making

THOUGH IT OFTEN feels like emotions are out of our control, sometimes we can open the door to places in the heart through our senses. Smells send nerve messages directly to the limbic brain (seat of emotions), and taste is closely connected to memory. So dial up the kind of lovemaking you want by using different scents and tastes. Sprinkle an essential oil or perfume on bed linens, drop it into the bath or the water you use to wash lingerie, or dab it behind your knees. Then picnic in bed on the flavors that conjure up sense memories.

Mood for Lovemaking	Scents	Tastes
Erotic, exotic	Musk, sandalwood	Oysters, olives, asparagus
Zesty, giddy	Lemon, grapefruit, geranium	Oranges, apples, champagne
Slow and relaxing	Orange blossom, lavender	Warm honey on fresh biscuits
Earthy, primal	Cedarwood, patchouli	Red wine, blue cheese, beets
Bold and saucy	Jasmine, vanilla	Cinnamon, vanilla ice cream; chili peppers, salsa
Romantic, sensual	Rose, gardenia, vetivert	Strawberries, chocolate, caramel, whipped cream
Spiritual bonding	Frankincense, myrrh	Artichoke hearts, fish

Cuddling

Millions and millions of years would still not give me half enough time to describe that tiny instant of all eternity when you put your arms around me and I put my arms around you.

—JACQUES PRÉVERT

CUDDLING IS AN intimate language. Without words, a snuggle can say, "I love you. I want to smell you. I want to crawl inside you." But because the skin all over a guy's body is almost ten times less sensitive than a woman's, men are not natural cuddlers. Try citing a recent survey conducted by the Berman Center for Women's Health, which found that couples who cuddle not only have a closer bond but also hotter sex, and — because snuggling releases oxytocin — they even have less stress. Science always gets 'em.

DAY
131

You Touch brings a woman back to herself. It makes her aware of her body and her sensuality. Even if there's no one else to do it, you can cuddle yourself every day. Massage your neck and glide your hands up and down your arms, giving yourself a hug. You'll feel sexier, more desirable, and better loved.

You Two Get into spoon position with him behind you. Then raise your top leg so he can slide his thigh between both of yours and prop his foot on the bed for leverage. He partly kneels on the other leg. You're still nestled together but now you have deep penetration and hard thrusting too. A great way to show him that cuddling can be a very hot activity.

Remembering

When you remember me, it means that you have carried something of who I am with you, that I have left some mark of who I am on who you are.

—FREDERICK BUECHNER

LIKE PLASTIC SURGERY, memory is a reconstructive process. We take pieces of things we've sensed—smells, sounds, emotions—fill in some gaps, and weave them into a "story." When we do, we refire many of the original nerve paths and *almost* re-create a lover's kiss or the smell of his hair. Except that—unlike plastic surgery—the re-creation, full of the tastes and longings we've dubbed in, is often *better* than the original.

You While women are good at recalling words and pictures, men are better at remembering spatial tasks, like finding their way out of the woods. Help him remember to touch you more gently by giving him landmarks—perhaps likening your breasts to mountains topped with delicate flowers or powdery snow.

You Two When you're on top, rest the heel of your hand above your pubic bone. Then pulse your fingers rapidly on the base of his erection and against your clitoris. This snappy sensation intensifies both your climaxes. And when later you thrum your fingers on his arm, he'll *remember*—and crave again—a thrill, a throbbing, and an orgasm even more earth-shattering than the original.

A Day Off

Write down all the little things that make you ache with love or longing — the call of a whippoorwill, the smell of his pillowcase, a searing pink sunrise, the crook of his little finger.

Be grateful for them.

Come into My Boudoir

Between the Sheets

Lifting an edge of the sheet he pulled it away, exposing the entire body, altogether naked . . .

—AMBROSE BIERCE, *CAN SUCH THINGS BE?*

DAY

134

AFTER ROUGHING IT in a sleeping bag, or in a confirmed bachelor's ratty-ass bed, you come to appreciate the luxury of fresh, soft sheets. We think Egyptians invented the first bed linens out of, well, linen—hand-spun to become buttery and lustrous with use. During the Renaissance, women softened itchy straw mattresses with silk or velvet covers. But even percale can set the stage for sumptuous loving and turn into a slinky sex toy.

You Transform everyday bedding into something sybaritic. Occasionally have your linens professionally cleaned and pressed, even starched if you like. Spray them with linen water in a subtle fresh scent like verbena, cucumber, or melon. Or spring for the newest thing in sheets—modal jersey. It's softer than your favorite T-shirt and comes in a myriad of blazing hot colors.

You Two Begin with a grand gesture. Fling the sheets aside as if clearing the altar for some primitive sex rite. Have him lie down. Pull the sheet seductively between your thighs, then drape it over him and wriggle atop his body with the sheet between you. The fabric traps body heat and creates soft, kinky friction.

Mirror, Mirror on the Wall

And if I looked at myself in the mirror, I found myself flushed and more beautiful at such moments. I felt like kissing my own reflected image.

—GEORGE SAND, *LÉLIA*

A LARGE, STRATEGICALLY placed mirror is *not* for noticing how your tummy sags or how the underside of your arms flap; it's for admiring the sheen of your skin when you make love, and for multiplying moonbeams and candlelight. Since mirrors reflect only 80 percent of the incident light, they also create the sense that something infinitely mysterious lies waiting just beyond the looking glass.

DAY
135

You Part of the reason doggie-style sex feels less romantic is the lack of intimate eye contact. But with a mirror beside the bed, you can turn your head to catch his eyes in the looking glass. You also get a spectacular view of him thrusting against your beautiful bum.

You Two Have him sit on the edge of the bed, facing a large mirror. Then straddle him from behind, pressing your breasts into his back and your pubis into the crack of his behind. Slide your hands around front. Looking in the mirror, imagine *you* are the one with the huge erection as you stroke it to orgasm. He'll never forget seeing his own equipment operate from a completely different angle.

Candles

When was the last time you spent a quiet moment just doing nothing—just sitting and looking at the sea, or watching the wind blowing the tree limbs, or waves rippling on a pond, a flickering candle or children playing in the park?

—RALPH MARSTON

THE FIRST CANDLES, cone-shaped and with a wick of reeds, illuminated the tombs of ancient Egypt, their light linking humans with the divine. In sixth-century China, tapers with evenly spaced notches marked the passage of time. Today, candles are a tool for romance, with the power to lend drama to any room and turn ordinary sex into a sublime and incandescent ritual.

You Arrange a collection of scented pillars atop a table or in your summer fireplace. The luxuriant fragrance will soothe you. Then really look at the flames—fiery and fluid, soft and dangerous, unpredictable yet eternal. How could you create those passionate, enticing qualities in yourself?

You Two For a sexy evening, Justin Timberlake prescribes a room filled with a bazillion candles, musky incense, a bowl of strawberries and cream, and the sultry sounds of Al Green. "Being surrounded by candles and incense," says Justin, "amplifies everything." There's a bonus: besides transforming the night and the room, candlelight hides figure flaws and makes your body glow with mystery.

The Well-Dressed Bed

YOUR BED SHOULD create its own world—one where cares melt away and only the two of you exist. Consider dressing it like one of these:

Bacchanalian Bed
- 400+ thread count cotton (or satin) sheets
- Piles of feather pillows
- A goose-down comforter
- A quilted feather bed
- Several faux fur and velvet throws
- Lavender or jasmine sachets
- Silk or velvet canopy drapes
- Two full-length body pillows
- Bouquet of red hibiscus on bedstand
- A sheepskin rug on each side
- Chocolates on each pillow

Zen Bed
- Linen or starched white sheets
- Two king-size natural foam pillows
- A chenille or soft wool blanket
- A pillow-top mattress
- One cable-knit cashmere throw
- Sprinkles of rain-scented perfume
- Mosquito netting
- Two body pillows stacked at foot
- One white calla lily on each side
- Bali natural fiber or bamboo mats
- A mint on each pillow

Incense

Perfume and incense bring joy to the heart; as does earnest counsel from a friend.

—PROVERBS 27:9

THE ANCIENT EGYPTIANS believed incense was the sweat of the gods and could protect you from disease and the dark spirits of the night. Hippocrates, the Greek healer, used it to treat coughs, wounds, and depression. Oriental priests, more interested in magic, conveyed their prayers to heaven on its rising smoke.

You Scents go directly from the nose to the lymphatic system, which distributes hormones and affects emotions. Burn jasmine to inspire confidence, lavender to calm nerves (men love it too), rosewood to conjure up summer, geranium for afternoon tea, sandalwood for exotic evenings, and ylang-ylang for romance.

You Two According to the Smell & Taste Treatment & Research Foundation in Chicago, lighting *floral* incense increases penile blood flow. You can stimulate libido by wafting scented smoke up the front of both your bodies, from genitals to nose. And for fun, lead your blindfolded lover (incense under his nose) on an erotic trail from front door, to table of tasty treats, to champagne bath, to fur rug, to . . .

The Altar of Love

Love beds are altars. People are temples encountering temples, the holy of holies receiving the holy of holies.

—MATTHEW FOX, *THE COMING OF THE COSMIC CHRIST*

MOST COUPLES IN ancient Rome created a bedside shrine to the deity that presided over their marriage. Offering fresh flowers, scented water, and special shells or poems to it each day kept them focused on the magic at the heart of their union. By worshipping at the homemade altar, the lovers hoped to attract the gods and goddess of passion, thereby ensuring many years of marital bliss.

DAY
139

You It's good feng shui to have a love altar in your bedroom (see You Two), especially in the right, rear corner—that of love and marriage. The fresh flow of energy will attract new romance into your life or strengthen the love you already have. And every time you light a candle on it, or simply pass nearby, you'll feel just a little sexier.

You Two Cover part of your dresser or nightstand with a red cloth and adorn the area with a candle, flowers, a photo of you and your man, jasmine incense, a favorite sex toy, an erotic statue, a shell from your honeymoon beach—whatever means passion to *you*. Add a small bowl that contains "playing" cards ("Lick my toes," "I'll be your slave," etc.), and your guy will visit the shrine every day too.

A Day Off

In the middle of the day, get into your luxurious
bed with a good novel and some hot chocolate.
And maybe your cat.

Give yourself permission to nap.

DAY
140

The Tease

Anticipation

Anticipation — It's a ticklish thing really, quivering, exciting, waiting.

— DAL PERRY

REMEMBER THE MOMENT in *Unfaithful* when Diane Lane literally shivers in anticipation of her illicit tryst? Sometimes the best part of sex is waiting for it. In fact, science has found that anticipation releases dopamine, triggering the brain to generate the pleasurable sensations of the event itself. No wonder we savor every fantasy, every butterfly in the tummy, every sleepless night on the long road to an absent lover's kiss.

DAY

141

You To the anticipator belong the thrills of suspense. But to the anticipatee — the one he's waiting *for* — belong the delights of power. How long will you make him "suffer"? Will you make him *earn* his reward with a gift or boon? Is a flash of naked breast all he gets? Or a deep, wet kiss? Or is it a night of slow loving — the way *you* like it?

You Two Make him crave you like a (healthy) drug. Don't have sex for several days (maybe even a fortnight!), but *do* rub up against him fully clothed, kiss his neck, parade around in sexy underwear, caress his thigh while watching TV. On the last night, when sexual tension is thick as syrup, lay him down on a fur rug, climb on top, and make all his long-awaited dreams come true.

Gauze

A woman sits and weaves with fingers deft
Her story of the flower-lit stream,
Threading the jasper gauze in dream,
Till like faint smoke it dies.

—L. CRANMER-BYNG, *A LUTE OF JADE*

DAY
142

KNOWN AS "THE woven wind," silk gauze was the sexiest fabric in ancient Rome. If allowed, a man might undrape the many layers of a woman's street garments to reach his final prize, the famous *Coa vestis*—a brilliantly dyed, sheer gauze tunic worn next to her skin that *almost* revealed her bare beauty. Embellishing her charms yet still veiling a mystery, it was the ultimate erotic tease.

You Diaphanous fabrics surround you with a rarefied aura. If you wear an innocent gauze shift to, say, apply your makeup or vacuum the living room, you can be enticingly "naked" while still hiding your imperfections. They even make gauze bikinis now which, after a dip in the pool, are much sexier and more elegant than the usual wet T-shirt.

You Two 1) Dressed in gauze, dip your finger into his glass of champagne and swirl it around your thinly covered nipple. Now you really stand out. 2) Tent your bed with gauze to create a secluded island of love. 3) Drape his erection with gauze and lick. The fabric adds layers of silky, fine-grained sensation.

His Own Petard

There are two things I like stiff—and one of them's Jell-O.

—DAME NELLIE MELBA

A MAN BECOMES erect when ten times the usual amount of blood pours into the two tubes that run the length of his penis. The bloated vessels strain outward, pressing thousands of nerve endings hard against his skin. Hypersensitive and ready to burst, he's driven to burrow inside a tight, wet cove as quickly as possible. Delaying his journey, then, makes for delicious slow torture.

You Use him like a pleasure wand to tease your own private parts. Dip him inside just enough to lube him up, then part the delicate lips of your vulva with long, slow strokes. Vibrate him in circles. Hold his shaft firmly and tap the very tip against your clitoris. Nothing yummier.

You Two Tantalize the most sensitive skin on his body *without* letting him inside you. Roll him between your hands like pastry dough—a favorite self-pleasure move for many men. Rub his wand on your thighs, breasts, pubic hair; perhaps give it a little slap. Position his shaft high up between your legs and wiggle against it. Wait till he begs before you allow him to enter.

Sneaky Seductions

HE'LL KNOW YOU'RE making him hot, but he won't really understand why, if you:

1. *Lift your arm.* A subliminal reminder of saucy pin-up girls with hands posed behind their heads. Displays your breasts beautifully.
2. *Smile coyly.* Especially when combined with a downward gaze, it makes him think *you're* thinking something very naughty.
3. *Lick your lips.* Glistening, wet, ripe, they're a subtle invitation to juicy oral sex.
4. *Whisper.* Forces him to listen—and to look at your lips.
5. *Hike your skirt a teensy bit.* Looks like an invitation. Makes him think you're Sharon Stone.
6. *Lock eyes.* Tells him you know what you want—him—and aren't afraid to go after it. Deadly when combined with #3.
7. *Brush his arm lightly.* Raises the fine hairs and says you long to caress him. Everywhere.
8. *Toss your hair.* Tells him you're sassy and you know it. Makes him imagine those fine strands whipping around his privates.
9. *Tickle him with your toes.* Signals that you will use any part of your body on any part of his.
10. *Eat with gusto.* Says you have lusty appetites and will undoubtedly love feasting on him.

Words

Your words are my food, your breath my wine.

—SARAH BERNHARDT

ACTIONS MAY SPEAK louder, but words paint bigger, tastier pictures. Even just one word ("Tonight") or two ("Bring leather") can set off an explosion of scents, memories, colors, and electrifying ideas. In fact, PET scans show that simply *looking at* words stimulates the visual memory cortex. Quite strongly. But *thinking about* words animates even more parts of the brain, including imagination and emotion.

You Use the power of words to create a mood of your choice. Throughout the day, think or say "tropical breeze" for relaxation, "tigress" for power, "mink" to feel beautiful. And when your erotic fires need stoking, make a mantra of "soft lazy hands," "Matthew McConaughey," or "hot rolling surf."

You Two A few teasing words can rivet his attention all day. Wedge a note under his windshield wiper: "Thinking of your hands all over me." Later, e-mail him: "You're naked and doing naughty things to me." Text a cryptic "Still thinking . . ." On his cell, say, "I took my panties off already." He may even come home early.

Items of Serious Quality

Your breasts are snow, I breathe them like sea foam.
I taste them like white salt.

— THE THOUSAND AND ONE NIGHTS
(TRANS. JOHN BROUGH)

DAY

146

IN 2500 B.C., the warrior women of Crete advertised their ferocious femininity—and cleverly distracted the enemy—by wearing tight bodices that bared their breasts. Except for a brief flirtation with nipple-exposing empire dresses in eighteenth-century France, we've kept our breasts demurely covered ever since. No wonder a University of Missouri study found that kissing a pair of snowy, naked breasts was the second most popular male fantasy.

You Get a feel for the powerful sensuality of your breasts by occasionally going without a bra. The sensation of silk, or a cotton T-shirt warm from the dryer, against bare skin makes you aware of every nerve ending, every graceful sway, and every gorgeous contour of these items men find so riveting.

You Two The act of removing your bra can be a compelling tease. First, catch his eye. Then arch your back slowly, undo the clasp, and wriggle a bit as the material falls away. Or leave the bra on during sex, but remove your breasts from the cups so they pouf up and spill over. Naked breast sightings (translate: "rhapsodic glimpses of succulent melons topped with juicy cherries") release massive amounts of testosterone into a man's bloodstream.

A Day Off

Maintain eye contact with a lover, a coworker, or a friend for a full five seconds.

Daring to offer a small taste of who you are opens your heart to deeper love and passion — while fascinating the heck out of the one you've locked eyes with.

DAY
147

Flowers

Magnolia

Robed in lustrous ivory-white linen were those figures of undress marble, the wealth of their glorious bodies pressing out into bosoms magnificent as magnolias.

—RICHARD LE GALLIENNE, *THE QUEST OF THE GOLDEN GIRL*

DAY

148

THE MAGNOLIA MAY have been one of the first living beings to adorn itself with lustrous, plush-to-the-touch "accessories." Dating back 95 million years, even before bees appeared, the plant needed something sturdy yet irresistible to attract the only pollinators available—beetles. Its solution? Bosomy flowers that smell like heaven and labia-red seeds that dangle from the fruit by delicate, come-hither strands.

You If you ever needed a justification for showing cleavage, wearing bright red lipstick, or spritzing on a succulent perfume, the magnolia is it. Sure, we know we glow from within. But sometimes a girl just *needs* to go over the top with sexy, all-female adornments. When you do, remember the magnolia and feel great about it—it's *natural!*

You Two To get your "beetle's" undivided attention, magnolia-up. Don a lacy, ivory-toned bustier that plumps up your breasts. But don't leave it at that. In the same way that a magnolia dangles its seeds, let a garter or fastening ribbon waggle about seductively. And, if you feel really outrageous, use that labia-red trick too—rouge your vaginal lips. It's a killer.

Daffodil

I wander'd lonely as a cloud
That floats on high o'er vales and hills,
When all at once I saw a crowd,
A host, of golden daffodils;
Beside the lake, beneath the trees,
Fluttering and dancing in the breeze.

—WILLIAM WORDSWORTH

THE DAFFODIL'S GENUS name, *narcissus*, comes from the Greek youth who was endowed with great beauty by the gods—with one catch. He must never view his own reflection. But when he came upon a forest pond, he blew it. Instead of using the shimmery surface to admire the beauty of the nymph who loved him, he fell in love with his *own* reflection and simply faded away. The daffodil, which displays its beauty to delight *others*, sprang up in his place.

You Deep in the Ukraine lies the Valley of Narcissi. Millions of years ago, it was a huge lake but now is home to the largest habitat of narrow-leafed daffodils in the world. For a golden dose of what the Oriental sages called "bread for the soul," visit this utopian valley at the Ukraine website, *www.wumag.kiev.ua*.

You Two Sometimes, a reflection can be your friend. Make love on a comfy chair in front of a full-length mirror. Concentrate on things you never see—the arch of your undulating back, the muscles flexing in his butt, the interesting angles provided by the chair. Watching your bodies in the act of passion makes sex kinkier, hotter, and more surprising—but also deeper and even more intimate.

Lilac

I am thinking of the lilac-trees,
That shook their purple plumes,
And when the sash was open,
Shed fragrance through the room.

—ANNA S. STEPHENS, *THE OLD APPLE-TREE*

DAY
150

THE PLANT THAT gives off a sweet, female scent turns out to have a masculine history. In the Turkish court of Suleiman the Magnificent, pithy lilac stems were hollowed out to make pipe stems. (Apparently, the Turks cared nothing for the flower's heady fragrance!) So when the plant first came to the West, it was given the botanical name *syringa*—the Greek word for "pipe."

You Like a woman, a lilac is both beautiful and tough—able to thrive even when left completely on its own. Maybe that's why the flower's aroma is considered a mood lifter. Brighten your spirits by placing fragrant lilacs (don't skimp, get a whole heap of branches) in your bedroom, kitchen, and office.

You Two Play his penis like a pipe. Place your fingers as if holding a panpipe, lining them up along the underside ridge, thumbs on the other side. Enclose the head with your mouth and suck gently while your fingertips flutter and press on the ultrasensitive skin.

The Language of Flowers

BASED ON GREEK myth (Aphrodite covered her nakedness with myrtle branches), Chinese folklore (the lotus represented divine female fertility), and Persian poetry (flower names helped lovers remember rhymes), Victorian women created a secret language of flowers to convey feelings that strict propriety forbade them to reveal. You too can attract your heart's desire by keeping blooms nearby or sending a bouquet to your lover.

Ambrosia — Your love is reciprocated

Azalea — Take care of yourself for me; Chinese symbol of womanhood

Bird of Paradise — Magnificence

Carnation — (*pink*) I'll never forget you; (*red*) My heart aches for you; (*solid color*) Yes!

Daffodil — Respect

Gardenia — Secret love

Gladiolus — Love at first sight

Hyacinth — (*purple*) I'm sorry; (*red or pink*) Play or sport

Jasmine — Attracts wealth; exotic sensuality

Lemon verbena — Attracts opposite sex

Marigold — Comforts the heart

Peach blossom — I am your captive

Peony — Aphrodisiac

Quince — Temptation

Rose — (*red*) Love; (*white*) Secrecy; (*pink*) Please believe me; (*yellow*) Friendship; (*red and white*) Togetherness

Spiderflower — Elope with me

Tuberose — Dangerous pleasure

Tulip — Perfect lover; fame

Viscaria — Will you dance with me?

White violet — Let's take a chance on happiness

Lily

Erect and alone, under an ancient flood of light,
Lily! And of you all the most artless.

—STÉPHANE MALLARMÉ (TRANS. THE AUTHOR)

SOME SAY EVE birthed the lily—the flower springing from her tears when she learned she was pregnant. The Romans believed the blossom was made from Juno's breastmilk. Others opine that the pure white bloom is the Madonna herself. Whether associated with chastity and hope or fertility and sex, the lily is always ripely, gloriously female.

You Though flagrantly beautiful, the lily's main sexual weapon—the one it uses to attract pollinators into its womb—is its scent. There's something languorous, loamy, and decadent about it, like sex on a veranda surrounded by steamy jungle. When you want to feel dazzlingly wicked, splash on Donna Karan Gold perfume, made with white Casablanca lily.

You Two Make your hand look like a lily's blossom—palm cupped, fingers slightly spread and coming out like surrounding prongs. Add the stamen "tickler" in the middle by tying a thin strip of terry cloth around your palm. Now set this cap atop your lover's penis and, slowly and repeatedly, caress it up and off, pinching and drawing out the tip at the very end. A novel sensation that will really make his erection bloom.

Orchid

Vivid orchids and wonderful colored lichens smoldered upon the swarthy tree-trunks ... the effect was as a dream of fairyland.

—SIR ARTHUR CONAN DOYLE, *THE LOST WORLD*

CITING THE ROUND, paired bulb of one orchid variety, a student of Plato named the flower *orchis* — Greek for "testicle." Medieval herbalists used the plant in aphrodisiac and love potions, believing the young, firm tubers would help conceive a male child, while the more mature, soft ones might conceive a female. Later, orchids became one of the main ingredients in ice cream. No wonder we crave it so much.

DAY

153

You Many orchids have no scent. But the ones that do, give off the alluring fragrance of vanilla. The Smell & Taste Treatment & Research Foundation has found that the scent most arousing to men is vanilla — an aroma that conjures up both the elegant sexiness of the orchid and the homey treats of the kitchen. Cook with it. Dab it behind your ears. Await ravishment.

You Two His orchid-like bulbs are jam-packed with nerve endings that make them a garden of sensual delights. Get on top, facing away, and cup his testicles. Then gently pull them to the tempo of your thrusts. May cause mindless blithering.

A Day Off

*For patients with problems of the mind and heart,
the physicians of ancient Egypt prescribed walking
among flowers.*

Wander in a garden and be uplifted.

DAY
154

Unexpected Treasures

Underarms

She slowly tiptoed over to him, and gently tickled his armpit.
Benye bit his lips, the pleasure ran through his entire body, every
nook and cranny. He wouldn't turn around, but he gradually
stopped groaning.

—MOYSHE KULBAK,
THE MESSIAH OF THE HOUSE OF EPHRAIM

YOU'VE ALREADY CONQUERED the obvious hot spots. Time to branch out and discover one of your man's most well-hidden erogenous zones. Because it shares in the nerve network that radiates out from the nipple, the much-neglected underarm is a treasure trove of erotic sensation—tender and ticklish, yet animalistic and all male.

You A man's underarm brings out the savage in a woman. Here you can lay claim to his coiled power, his private scent, his helpless trembles. And because smell and emotions overlap in the brain, sniffing your man can even make you feel better. According to researchers at Duke and Rutgers universities, his unique "odor print" becomes a personal aphrodisiac that actually boosts your immune system.

You Two Slide your fingertips along the curving ridge where arm meets chest and feather your nails down the center of his arm cavity. Tease the tips of his hair with your breath. Or, when feeling frisky, pin his arms above his head and use your tongue to flick delicately sideways and to dip in and out of the deep, warm hollow.

DAY
155

Twists and Turns

*His touching was like a dance in which the two bodies turned
and deformed themselves into new shapes, new arrangements,
new designs.*

—ANAÏS NIN, *THE DELTA OF VENUS*

TRYING OUT A new leg wrap in the scissors position or
attempting the Tantric Shoulder Stand can be playfully randy.
But sometimes it's what happens *between* positions that kindles
the real fire. When sex is like a rumba—bodies glued together,
legs entangled, hips grinding—you wring the delight out of
every touch and make switching sides not just fun but scorching hot.

You When changing positions, take it slow. Focus on the
points where skin brushes against skin. Don't just raise and
lower, but skim your leg across his belly. Rock your pelvis and
squeeze as you swivel around. Notice the difference in suction
when you release and reinsert. A well-executed turn can stimulate your G-spot, pick up the rhythm and intensity—and even
burn a few calories.

You Two Next time you're on top, spend some quality time
in the face-to-face position. Then, keeping him inside, *slowly*
pivot around to face his feet. Besides affording him a titillating
view, the corkscrew action swizzles together parts of you that
never met before—and creates the sensation of churning warm
milk into hot butter.

Pearls

The shimmer of pearl belongs of right to her whose soul reflects the colour and quiet radiance of a thousand dreams.

—L. CRANMER-BYNG, *A LUTE OF JADE*

WITH THE MILKY luster of a breast and the firm roundness of a clitoris, pearls possess an allure far beyond their beauty. To symbolize *purity,* brides in ancient India presented an undrilled pearl for their groom to pierce. During the belle époque, courtesans flaunted their *sensual* prowess by piling on the rows of pearls given them by besotted lovers. And in the 1920s, Coco Chanel revolutionized fashion by dressing bare backs with the *elegance* of long pearl ropes.

You Natural pearls have undertones ranging from pink to yellow to bluish-black. Match them to your skin tone to make your complexion luminescent. For a different kind of glow, wear a pearl thong like Samantha did in *Sex and the City.* The pebbly jewels, which hang in a U-shape from a lacy waistband, hug your pelvis and stimulate important erogenous zones as you walk.

You Two Oil your palms and rub a string of pearls between them. Because they retain your body heat, the gems will feel deliciously warm and shivery when you roll them over your man's lower belly and thighs and wrap them around his ultra-sensitive shaft.

The Mighty Clitoris

DID YOU KNOW the clitoris is the only organ whose sole purpose is pleasure? Made from the same embryonic tissue that forms a penis, it contains the same sensitive nerve endings packed into a much smaller space. Actually, it may look tiny but it extends about two centimeters inside your body, giving you even deeper options for excitement. To maximize pleasure:

- Use your PCs to bear down or push out. Since those muscles are connected to the interior section of your clitoris, they massage the clitoris and make it bloom open and close up tight in alternating rhythms.
- Stand for oral sex, bringing more blood and sensitivity to your clitoris and all its internal tissues, sensitizing them. He kneels before you, puts his hands between your thighs, cradles your derrière, and rocks your pelvis forward—exposing you even more.
- Get on top and grind in circles, applying pressure to both outer bud and deep clitoral tissues.
- During missionary, pull on the skin between vulva and anus. Because the perineum and the clitoris are internally joined, this move retracts the clitoral hood and exposes more skin to his thrusts.
- Hormonal fluctuations change the quality and *location* of clitoral sensations (deep or shallow tingles). So experiment with new manual techniques at different times of the month. Then *show* him how to please you that day.
- Sit in a chair with your legs draped over each chair arm, which pulls wide the skin around the outside of your clitoris and the muscles inside. Then, whether he applies his tongue or his penis, you are open for business.

Icy Hot

You are ice and fire,
The touch of you burns my hands like snow.

— AMY LOWELL

IN THE HEAT of love, icy cold can be electrifying. While warmth brings blood to the surface of your skin, cold startles it away, causing your pores to open and close like little vaginas in the throes of orgasm. Also, heat slows your pulse. Cold speeds it up. Oscillating between two extremes, your body is literally shocked with pleasure—skin atingle, heart racing, and nerve endings on high alert for fiery shivers.

DAY
159

You 1) While sitting in a hot tub, glide an ice cube over your lips, toes, and nipples. 2) Alternate from hot to cold water when using the showerhead for self-pleasuring. 3) Use a cucumber, icy cold from the refrigerator, as a personal sex toy. 4) For purely subliminal zing, dab on some Fire N Ice lipstick and *feel* like a hot Ice Queen.

You Two In the middle of a torrid blow job, pause to sip some ice water and reapply your frosty lips to his delightfully shocked organ. Alternate by drinking hot tea. Even more unexpected—chill your panties in the freezer; then smooth them over his entire body. His erection may shrink a bit, but it will be very happy.

On the Up-and-Up

I once had a rose named after me and I was very flattered. But I was not pleased to read the description in the catalogue: "No good in a bed, but fine up against a wall."

—ELEANOR ROOSEVELT

NO WOMAN WANTS to be thought of as a wall ornament. But there is something spicy and intensely urgent about having sex pinned up against a door, tree, or shower partition. It's a lot like slow dancing, yet you feel deliciously ensnared. Ravished even. Gravity brings blood and heat to the floor of your pelvis. And because his legs support him, your man can use his hands and hips more freely—the better to please you with, my dear.

You To make standing work for *you*, hook one of your legs around his thigh to position his thrusts onto your G-spot. Or stand on a phone book so your hips, now level with his, can rock and roll. If *he's* against the wall, lean back to make his pelvic bone press against your clitoris with each stroke. Or turn your back to him and lean forward, creating ocean-deep penetration.

You Two Turn the tables and throw him up against something really interesting—like, say, the refrigerator. The combination of being upright, getting a change of scenery, and feeling the heat and vibrations of the fridge will shoot tingly sensations up and down his whole body.

A Day Off

Practice seeing ordinary things through passionate eyes. Could that flight of stairs be a place to make love at new angles? Might your old coat hide the secret that you're wearing nothing beneath it? Perhaps that grapefruit would taste better dribbled across his chest than simply peeled and eaten.

DAY
161

We'll Always Have Paris

The Seine

Beneath the Pont Mirabeau flows the Seine
And our love . . .
While under the bridge of our arms
Passes the eternal gaze of the languorous waves.

—GUILLAUME APOLLINAIRE (TRANS. THE AUTHOR)

DAY
162

THE VERDANT GREEN, sometimes sunset-colored waters of the Seine are not only beautiful, they also contain the ancient soul of a people. From her Roman river-goddess namesake, Sequana to her roles as carrier of grain and muse of Cezanne and Monet; from her glory as Joan of Arc's final home to her famed banks where lovers stroll and poets rhapsodize, the Seine is a voluptuous river that flows through every romantic's spirit.

You To the French, the most beautiful woman is one with a rich history and ripe smells—like the Seine. What if volunteering for a political campaign, rafting a river, or flinging yourself into an impossible affair is a better beauty routine than a weekly comb-out? What if your natural aromas are more alluring than Shalimar? Fifty million Frenchmen can't be wrong.

You Two The crevice where inner thigh meets groin is like a sexy river—musky, damp, slightly mysterious. It's a border between public space and private territory. Lick slowly along this crease, occasionally straying over to the VIP area (right next to his penis) where skin is thin and sexual sensations run deep. It's an elegant tease that will unlock in him an eddy of desire.

Iron Lady

Do people think that because we are engineers, beauty plays no part in what we build, that if we aim for the solid and lasting, that we don't at the same time do our utmost to achieve elegance?

—GUSTAVE EIFFEL

IN 1887, A long list of prominent writers, artists, and architects wrote a letter to the newspaper *Le Temps*, protesting the construction of the Eiffel Tower. They called it a "monstrous . . . hateful column of bolted iron." Yet by the 1920s, the 1,000-foot-tall monument had become an icon of the avant-garde — praised by artists like Chagall, Gounod, and Maupassant. The graceful Iron Lady reminds us all that just because a body is different, large, or "solid" doesn't mean it's not achingly beautiful.

You The Iron Lady wears three different shades of bronze paint — darkest at the bottom, lightest at the top — to complement the hues of the Parisian sky. We can all take a hint from this stylish French "woman": a monochromatic, graduated color scheme makes large look statuesque and turns "big bones" into graceful architecture.

You Two Turn his erection into a full-blown Eiffel Tower with this trick. During oral, press your thumb at the base of the tube running along the underside — hard enough to keep semen from running through it. Keep sucking energetically all the while. Your pressure delays ejaculation but allows him to swell and to have orgasmic muscle contractions, more intensely than he ever thought possible.

Rodin's Kiss

One has the impression of seeing the delight of this kiss all over these bodies; it is like a sun which rises and its light is everywhere.

—RAINER MARIA RILKE, ABOUT RODIN'S *THE KISS*

ONE OF THE most famous sculptures in the world, *The Kiss* portrays two real-life lovers at the very instant they become aware of their feelings. Through Rodin's genius, you can actually *see* their passion—in the grip of their toes, in the space of a breath between their lips, and in the man's hand. Resting on her hip, his hand no longer belongs completely to him but instead becomes the incandescent, shivery property of his beloved's thigh.

You Rodin believed that passion changed a person's physical features, making any woman in love beautiful. If you can't believe a great artist who studied the human body in every mood, who can you believe? All you have to do to look stunning or sexy is feel passionate about something.

You Two Like Rodin's *The Kiss*, a really ardent smooch should involve more than the lips. It should make you feel dizzy, as if you've lost your boundaries. Expand a kiss by drawing your tongue down the tendons of his neck, fluttering it over the edge of his ear, and gliding the tip firmly down to his nipples. Nibble up to his lips and repeat. If you let your passion flow through your mouth, you'll both feel it in *every* part of your bodies.

Paris in Cincinnati

CAN'T FLY OFF to the City of Love for the weekend? Re-create the romance of Paris in your own "backyard":

- Invite your sweetie, not to the Eiffel Tower, but to the highest rooftop in town. Wrap one blanket around both of you and snuggle to the view.
- Make love to the sultry, soul-searing ballads of Edith Piaf.
- If your town has a bridge, walk to the middle of it at sunset. No bridge? Borrow a friend's deck, climb a lonely hill, or find a pond. Just do it at sunset.
- Rent *Casablanca*.
- Take a crusty baguette, a slab of Camembert, a bottle of Bordeaux, and a blanket to the nearest park. Feed each other. Toast each other. Read Baudelaire.
- Have escargots delivered to your door by Markys.com.
- Put on a beret, a tank top, a tight skirt slit up the side, and heels. Maybe even seamed stockings. Sashay into the room and ask, *"Voulez-vous coucher avec moi ce soir?"*
- Woody Allen said, "As long as you haven't been kissed during any of those rainy Parisian afternoons, you haven't been kissed at all." Kiss in the rain. Huddled in a store vestibule, if possible.

The Mystique of the Hermès Scarf

Much of what bears the still-discreet Hermès label changed from the object of an old person's nostalgia to the subject of young peoples' dreams.

—ANONYMOUS BUYER, ABOUT THE SCARF'S INTRODUCTION IN 1937

DAY
166

GRACE KELLY USED one as a sling for her broken arm. Madonna wore hers as a halter in the movie *Swept Away*. Sharon Stone bound her sex victim with Hermès in *Basic Instinct*. Made from the silk of 250 mulberry moth cocoons, crafted by one of fifty designers, and stitched by hand, the Hermès silk scarf is the kind of accessory that can surround any woman—or tie-him-to-the-bed occasion—with an irresistible aura of chic.

You Fortunately, you don't need to spend a week's salary on Hermès to get that certain *je ne sais quoi*. Fold a large silk square diagonally, then lap over the pointed end till you have an oblong. With the ends hanging down from around your neck, twist them once around each other *loosely*. Then once again. Now tie the remaining ends behind your neck. This French twist gives any T-shirt or suit jacket the perfect *ooh la la*.

You Two Before you kiss him, place the corner of a silk scarf in your mouth. With your tongue, glide the material over his lips and just inside his mouth. Suck it back into your mouth and then smooth it back into his. The silk makes your kiss feel even wetter and silkier than it does with the usual French kiss.

Musée d'Orsay

People who cannot invent and reinvent themselves must be content with borrowed postures, secondhand ideas, fitting in instead of standing out.

—WARREN G. BENNIS

LIKE A FASCINATING woman, the Musée d'Orsay (Orsay Museum) has reinvented herself several times. She was born as a railroad station, then became a mailing center, then a set for several films, and finally a temple for the works of Monet, Cézanne, and Rodin. Designed as a "cathedral of the modern age," the museum has great bone structure, but it's her many and varied "lives" and the gorgeous nuggets inside that make her beauty transcendent.

You The cavernous spaces of this former train station give its artwork room to become more than just paintings on a wall. Somehow they expand to become *insights*. It's like that with ideas. Give them space—a walk in fresh air, a brain-clearing yoga routine, a breath of Mozart—and they flower into inspiration.

You Two If you make a guy feel like a work of art, he becomes a bigger, better man. When he's undressing, grab a camera and say, "What a great behind [or chest, or bicep, etc.]!" Snap, snap. "You could be on the cover of *Playgirl*." Compliment him on function and feeling too: "I love the way your butt tenses when you're inside me. I feel the power of it under my hands." His behind, and a few other things, will be all atingle.

A Day Off

Today, eat and drink French — Perrier, café au lait, French Champagne, Brie, croissants, baguettes with chicken and herb sausage, and so on.

It's a sensual and Continental vacation from the ordinary.

DAY
168

Attitude

Nude Attitude

Women say they feel more comfortable undressing in front of men than they do undressing in front of other women. They say that women are too judgmental, where, of course, men are just grateful.

—ROBERT DE NIRO

WHEN WOMEN LEAVE Carson Kressley's TV show, *How to Look Good Naked*, they feel—and look—stunning, despite their bared cellulite, wattles, and under-bra skin rolls. They've learned their hips measure inches less than they thought and that others see only their gorgeous skin or smoky eyes. Like them, you don't need a perfect body to flaunt your own naked, sexy vamp. *That's* what leaves every man not only grateful but panting.

DAY

169

You Start every morning by smoothing on a luscious body lotion. It honors your naked skin. And under your business suit or yoga pants, you'll know the soft you, the voluptuous you, the all-female, zesty you is smoldering.

You Two Nudity has the power to warp men's minds. On a lazy weekend day, parade around the house naked. Find reasons to lean over in front of your guy or absent-mindedly caress your fanny. Tell him he can't touch you (which will make him literally ache) or let him use you as he will (which'll make him feel Las Vegas lucky). Surprise him that evening by lifting his shirt to rub your bare, oiled torso against his back.

A Slut in Your Own Home

The movie business divides women into ice queens and sluts, and there have been times I wanted to be a slut more than anything.

—SIGOURNEY WEAVER

EVER WANTED TO be Samantha Jones for a day? Now we have scientific backup! Anthropologists say that, among primates, the most promiscuous females are the most fertile. And citing more than twenty tribes who equip their kids for success by collecting genes—one father/contributor for smarts, one for strength, one for looks, and so on—the scientists conclude that a woman's loose behavior brings communities closer together and actually improves the gene pool.

You You don't have to be bad to be naughty. Try being just a little "looser"—with your walk, your hair, or the tie of your shirt. Or, why not be a slut in your dreams? Psychologists say that women who fantasize about multiple partners and wanton behavior are happier, healthier, and even more successful.

You Two A slut's attitude is, "Give me oral sex. Now." And guys just can't wait to have at her. Take a commanding position by kneeling over your man's head, facing his feet. Then roll your vulva over his chin, lips, and nose. Nice and slow. Nice and loose. As if wallowing in your pleasure and his lust. You sexy slut!

Edge

The artist never entirely knows. We guess. We may be wrong, but we take leap after leap in the dark.

—AGNES DE MILLE

YOU DRIVE ALONG the rim of the Grand Canyon, marveling at its hugeness, and you think, *This is what awe is.* But then you step right up to the edge, and the vast space physically pulls you. Heart pounding, skin prickling, you brace yourself to keep from falling—even diving—into the unknown. But you don't back away. You stay right on the edge of danger and awe because now you think, *This is what exhilaration is! This is living!*

You Put your toe just over the line of safe, familiar boundaries and feel the thrill. Be slightly subversive in a studded bracelet and three-inch snakeskin heels. Eat fried squid. Wear a perfume that makes you feel dangerous. In a bar, sing karaoke or play the saxophone. Daring is contagious and very, very sexy.

You Two Cross over one of the last sexual frontiers—down *there*, back there. Oh for crying out loud, his anus. It's got a ton of nerve endings and is much cleaner than you fear. Just before he comes, moisten a finger and massage the outer rim. Pull his butt cheeks apart a little to intensify the feeling. If you dare, put your fingertip just inside and pulse. He'll have an excruciatingly intense orgasm.

Luxurious Entitlement

An inordinate passion for pleasure is the secret of remaining young.

—OSCAR WILDE

PLEASURE AND LUXURY are not just for fun; they are vital food for the soul. As a woman who turns ordinary life into ambrosia just by being in the room, you *deserve* to indulge at every opportunity:

- Flowers on the coffee table—yes. Bouquets in the kitchen, bathroom, hallway, and even your car—*now* we're talking! Inhale them. Caress your cheek with them. Wear them in your hair. You are delighting the world.
- E-mails are fast, but a note on scented stationery is much more sensual and intimate. Like a queen, have yours engraved with elegant gold initials.
- A cashmere or faux fur wrap will make you feel—and behave—so much more like a film noir sex goddess than a cotton sweater ever will. For the sake of your about-to-be-bewitched lover, indulge.
- Dried herbs are so ordinary. With fresh-cut basil and chives, your cooking takes on the aroma and punch befitting a world-class gourmand.
- Why get a facial when you can have a volcanic-clay wrap that melts away tension, detoxifies, moisturizes, and va-va-voom-ifies?
- Enough with the boxed wine. At the end of a thoroughly ghastly day, every femme fatale deserves champagne, a chocolate martini, or a raspberry, ice cream, and vodka smoothie in a chilled glass. It's important for setting the mood.

Necessary Passions

Life without love and passion is a life not worth having lived.

—RUMI

DOCTORS KNOW THAT the inability to feel pleasure and passion is a hallmark of serious mental illness. Passion helps provide the will to live, releasing serotonin and endorphins — brain chemicals that fill us with contentment and zest. If it weren't for passion, we wouldn't mate or strive or give the best of ourselves. So when you're caught mooning over last night's hot date instead of working, say you're simply improving your performance and preserving the species.

You Treat yourself to something that makes you tingle, every day, even if it's just homemade whipped cream, a long novel, foot reflexology, a hundred new tunes on your iPod, a painting class with nude models — or a bodies-locked-together, tongue-all-over-the-place kiss on the elevator. Passion keeps you young, beautiful, and purring.

You Two Nothing says lust like an up-against-the-wall quickie. Turn that lust into scorching passion. 1) Start early. Beforehand, fantasize about his tongue on your . . . wherever. 2) Just before he enters, wrench away, make eye contact, and then slam into him. 3) Pull his pelvis close so he fills you and presses your clitoris. 4) Prop your leg on a stool, for that midair excitement without falling over. 5) Ensure afterglow — put his hand to your cheek, kiss him quick, then leave feeling fabulously ravished.

Power

It's babe power, which means you don't have to look, walk, or act like a man to be his equal.

—DIANE BRILL

WE MAY NOT be able to bench-press 200 pounds, but women wield a force much deeper and longer-lasting than brute strength. Instead of "power over," we specialize in "power with"—*connecting* to each other, to nature, and to our sensuality as well as our brains. That way we learn more and actually *multiply* our assets and beauty. How clever are we?

DAY
174

You Business analysts now agree that feminine leadership styles—in which relationship, intuition, celebration, and vulnerability are high priorities—often decrease turnover and improve the bottom line through innovation. So, why bother to beat a man at his own games when it's smarter and more high-powered to manage the office like the woman you are?

You Two Men are not gifted at making connections. Sometimes you have to do it *for* him. If you want more G-spot stimulation, flip over to doggie position and reach between your legs to grab his erection. Rub it between your moist vaginal lips, then suddenly push it in—reaching the desired location—and moan. Using your female brain and body to make you *both* happy is true babe power.

A Day Off

To access your true gifts, you need time to commune with your soul. Make today your personal attitude-adjustment "hour."

Slow down. Contemplate. Imagine. Make a place for your inner life to grow.

DAY

175

Dressing for Sex-cess

High Heels

We do it [wear heels] for the image in the mirror, the reflection of ourselves as hot and in charge, an extraordinarily satisfying goal that we can live with more happily than with a man; who needs him?

—NANCY FRIDAY

DAY

176

LESS THAN FIVE feet tall, Catherine de Medici did not want to seem inferior to the lofty Duke of Orleans. So she designed a new-fangled shoe with high heels for their 1533 wedding. In 2005, Condoleezza Rice sent a message with shoes too. Arriving in Germany to meet with the chancellor, she wore knee-high, spike-heeled boots—her footwear proclaiming, "I'm sexy, powerful, and ready to kick some butt."

You High heels may prevent you from running, but they put a come-hither wobble in your walk, raise your rear by 25 percent, and create a level of authority that's sexy as hell. Their sneakiest secret, though, lies in the leather, which holds in sweat containing fatty acids also found in the vagina—thereby giving off an aroma completely irresistible to men.

You Two Strut into the bedroom in nothing but five-inch stilettos and a cheeky smile. Keep the shoes on during foreplay, gliding them over his calves, thighs, and erection. During sex, wrap your heels around to scratch his back. A few nights later, wear them out to dinner. He and his penis will remember *exactly* where those puppies have been.

Jeans

Blue jeans are the most beautiful things since the gondola.

—DIANA VREELAND

WHEN THE SAILORS of eighteenth-century Genoa needed trousers tough enough to withstand laundering by being dragged behind the boat, some clever fellow invented the forerunners to modern-day blue jeans (named for the *blu* dye of *Genoa*). But in 1980, jeans acquired major sizzle when Calvin Klein photographed fifteen-year-old Brooke Shields in skintight dungarees, purring, "Nothing comes between me and my Calvins."

You No other pants accentuate a woman's derrière and crotch quite the way jeans do. Yet, they still look innocently casual. To get a fit that makes you feel happier-, livelier-, and sexier-than-thou, the experts at *Oprah* offer these guidelines: boot-cut legs offset wide hips; a back yoke makes your rear look curvier; and a dark blue wash is slimming.

You Two Wear a lacy thong or nothing underneath your dungarees. Then, in a teasing voice, ask him to help you remove the jeans. Perhaps the zipper is "stuck." The gesture is simple, intimate, and racier than a red Ferrari. But to spike his temperature even higher, let the jeans fall around your ankles and then lean over a chair.

The Corset

As she spoke she loosed from her bosom the curiously embroidered girdle into which all her charms had been wrought — love, desire, and that sweet flattery which steals the judgement even of the most prudent.

— HOMER, *THE ILIAD*

DAY

178

IN 1700 B.C. Crete, both men and women wore tight corsets that made their bodies mirror the silhouettes of their double-headed battle axes. Evolving from that fierce role, corsets became a form of female "modesty" in the 1800s. And yet, a Victorian bride's hour-long unlacing was intensely erotic — the groom freeing her feminine assets by swishing each lace, slowly and provocatively, across her highly sensitized back. Once wicked, always wicked.

You As Kate Winslet, Halle Berry, and Catherine Zeta Jones have discovered, a sanely constructed, modern corset plumps up your décolletage, nips in a spreading waist (Catherine wore hers after a pregnancy), and makes you feel gently "hugged." Covered yet voluptuously displayed, you are Female with a capital F.

You Two You walk in wearing nothing but a corset, curves popping out in all the right places. You stand in front of his chair and lean forward, resting your hands on his shoulders. Or you lean back against the dining table, revealing a laced-up back and a naked rump poufing out atop the table. You ask him to lead you around by the ends of your laces. Your work is done.

Costumes Make the Woman

PUT ON A costume and—voilà!—you're someone else. Free to be raunchier, bossier, and more outrageous than the real you would ever dare. Forget the nurse, the schoolgirl, and the French maid and try these hot alter egos.

Role	Clothes and Props
Roller derby diva	Blades, hot pants, tight tee with "Amanda Smack-around" scrawled on it
Survivor castaway	Muddy bikini, buff, moth-eaten hat, fake snake
Xena, Warrior Princess	Torn tank, leopard shorts, wide belt, whip
Pizza delivery girl	Red-and-white striped shirt, pizza box, doorbell
Sopranos hit woman	Tight black dress, purple tie, stilettos of both kinds
Judge Judy	Drapey robe over Peter Pan collar, gavel, pursed lips
Little Red Riding Hood	Full-skirted dress, red cape with hood, basket, shy smile
Catwoman	Leotard, (for best results, cut the crotch out of the leotard), ears and tail (found in costume or sex toy store)
Biker bitch	Black leather everything, combat boots, chains, tattoo
Bunch of grapes	Purple leotard, green hat, pinned-on purple balloons (never have so many men wanted to feel my balloon bazooms)
Race car driver	Grease-monkey overalls (several sizes too small, covered with endorsement logos—copy these off the web), helmet

Seamed Stockings

You shouldn't wear them when out with someone you're not prepared to sleep with, since their presence is tantamount to saying "Hi there, big fellow, please rip my clothes off at your earliest opportunity." If you really want your escort paralytic with lust, stop frequently to adjust the seams.

—CYNTHIA HEIMEL

DAY

180

ON MAY 15, 1940, nylons were launched in the United States. No longer made of silk, the classy stockings—with seams that encouraged men's eyes to travel up the back of a leg—were finally available to working women. They bought four million pairs in the first four days. A few years later, Betty Grable raised money for war bonds by selling the sexy hosiery she wore in pin-up photos for a whopping $40,000.

You For a touch of haute glamour and sexy edge, team a pair of seamed stockings with your business suit. With the new seamed pantyhose, or Lycra stockings with stay-up silicone bands, you can even be comfortable. But for evening, stick with the real thing—perhaps seamed with pearls—and a man-magnetizing garter belt.

You Two According to David Zinczenko, editor of *Men's Health*, 43 percent of men think partially clothed sex is hotter than naked sex. So keep those stockings on! At some point, though, slip one off and tie it loosely around the bottom of his penis and testicles. If you tug the stocking while he thrusts, the build-up and release of pressure will cause volcanic tremors to ripple through his erection.

The Skirt

I knew I would like her when I saw how her backside moved under her red satin skirt.

—JAMES HADLEY CHASE

EVER SINCE THEY got out of loin cloths, men have been trying to wear skirts—animal skins, togas, kilts. But they always look so darn odd. That's because a skirt moves like a *woman*. It sways. It floats. It flirts. It swoops around your hips and ripples off into space, taking your curves out to forever. A skirt is all woman. And, when you wear one, so are you.

You By simply lifting her dress, a woman of the ancient world could end wars, cure the deranged, and make the gods smile. The simple gesture stopped people in their tracks and seemed to say, "Here's *real* power, buddy. Don't make me show you the whole thing or you might die with pleasure." You have that same power in *your* skirt.

You Two Wear a skirt with nothing underneath and—guaranteed—you drive him up the wall. During dinner out, give the guy a chance to think about what's only a hand-lift away. Then, in a secluded corner of the parking lot or on a park bench, unzip him, lift up your skirt, and mount—letting the fabric cloak your "private" activities.

A Day Off

Get professionally fitted for a bra—a necessary luxury that will change the way your breasts look and feel. Or buy real silk panties for every day of the week.

Wear them!

DAY

182

Mystery

An Invisible Treat

The visible is not the only truth, nor is it the whole truth; the invisible must be penetrated with the aid of the visible.

—MARC CHAGALL

MEN ARE SUCH visual creatures they often have trouble sensing the invisible—smells, feelings, tones of voice. But if you blindfold a man, he is forced to "look" deeper. Now he must find his way by identifying your scent, reading your skin like Braille, and listening for the meaning in your silences. In this mysterious world, he begins to use a new tool—his erotic imagination.

DAY

183

You When a guy is blindfolded, he can't see the cottage cheese around your thighs or the weird expression on your face mid-orgasm. In his mind, you are Jessica Alba. Furthermore, you're kind of *forced* to place his hands exactly where you want them. Don't be embarrassed to take full advantage.

You Two Blindfold him with your bra. Lick his inner thigh, then bite his shoulder. Kiss his thigh again, then suck his toe. Keep his senses on high alert by moving unpredictably around his body. Or waft an exotic perfume under his nose, then kiss the tip of his penis. Do it again—and again—but make him wonder when. Wear this scent next time you meet for drinks and see how fast he takes you home to bed.

Moon Madness

Such a slender moon, going up and up,
Waxing so fast from night to night,
And swelling like an orange flower-bud, bright,
Fated, methought, to round as to a golden cup,
And hold to my two lips life's best of wine.

— JEAN INGELOW

DAY 184

THOUGH SMALLER THAN any other planet in the solar system, the moon exerts a powerful influence on the Earth. She pulls on the tides, makes fish bite, and brings out the mischief in all of us. For ancient peoples, the moon's cycles seemed the answer to many of life's mysteries—showing us that life is change, that events move in cycles, and that things may not always be what they seem.

You Following an old custom, many Neapolitan women call on the moon to increase breast size. They stand naked in moonlight and chant nine times, "*Santa Luna, Santa Stella, fammi crescere questa mammella*"—meaning "Holy Moon, holy star, make this breast grow for me." Plants grow with the moon's waxing; maybe breasts do too. According to *Many Moons*, written by Diana Brueton, tests found that the breast-enhancement chant worked in 90 percent of the cases!

You Two Next full moon, cuddle up outside with your fella, some binoculars, and a thermos of hot toddies. As you gaze skyward, tell him that according to Tacana Indian lore, the moon can add vital inches to a man's equipment. "Prove" it by pressing on the protruding veins at its base (fingers on top and underside). This increases length about 10 percent. Feeling ten times the man, he'll be ten times the lover.

Texture

The minute you start reveling in the textures of life and the world of the senses, you find yourself thinking about love.

—DIANE ACKERMAN, *A NATURAL HISTORY OF LOVE*

RICH WITH NERVE endings—about 1,300 per square inch—our skin is constantly receiving messages about texture. We've even developed separate receptors for heat, cold, pressure, and pain. But, oddly, none for pleasure. Apparently, we create that only from *within*, when we satisfy our body's voracious hunger for the many textures of life.

You Wake up your skin—and your ability to fashion pleasure—with texture. Step out of bed onto a furry rug. In the shower, rough up your skin with a body brush. Then smooth and cool it with minty lotion. Slip into silky underthings and a crisp shirt. Eat crunchy toast spread with gritty apple butter. Bathe your face in the cool morning breeze. You've already begun inventing a day of delight.

You Two Massage his back and rump—places he can't see—with varied textures. Stroke him with a paddle brush, a pashmina scarf, a leather glove. Roll a baseball over his skin. Smear him with warm honey. Graze his flesh with a basting brush. Spread quick-evaporating rubbing alcohol on his back, then blow on it. The not knowing and the constantly changing sensations will make his whole body come alive.

Mystery School

WANT TO EXUDE an aura of mystery?

1. Spray on perfume that's a *mixture* of Oriental scents like ginger, jasmine, and sandalwood. The blend makes exotic, indefinable colors that float in midair.
2. Wear a half-smile, like you know a secret. The Mona Lisa has intrigued men for ages.
3. Go to bed in a Victorian nightgown. The following night, wear a red teddy. Next night, sleep in the buff. What fascinating creature will show up on night four?
4. Before entering a room, think about your most adventurous vacation. You will sparkle with a sense of the unknown.
5. Wear lip liner just a little darker than your lipstick. Sexy, defined lips make you seem provocative, mysterious, even a little dangerous.

Hunting for Pleasure

Pursuit and seduction are the essence of sexuality. It's part of the sizzle.

—CAMILLE PAGLIA

THE ALLURE OF the treasure hunt is as old as history. Odysseus searched for adventure. The knights of the Middle Ages quested after the Holy Grail. And modern-day treasure hunters still seek pirate ships filled with doubloons. Deep in our souls we long for mysteries to unveil, clues to solve, and adventures on which to embark. The prize intrigues us, but it's the search that truly quickens our blood.

You Hunt for pleasure treasures at the bookstore. In the art section, find the sexiest nude photo. Locate the island of your dreams among the travel books. Search the poetry section for a romantic sonnet. Soak up *all* the images of beautiful bodies, lush green fields, and evocative rhymes you find along the way.

You Two Let a trail of fishnet stockings lead your man to a bottle of wine and a note: "I can't wait to lick this off you." Feathers lead him to the next intriguing message: "Bring along an unusual sex toy." Lacy panties (still fragrant with you) urge him on to a gift: "Let me caress you in these silky boxers." By way of flower petals, satin gloves, and jars of Honey Dust body powder, he finally hunts down the treasure—you, on a fur rug, clad only in very high heels.

Love Ritual

Lovemaking is a ritual that invites the goddess of sex to be present . . . so that what goes on between people is inspired and infused with this spirit.

—THOMAS MOORE, *THE SOUL OF SEX*

OF ALL LIFE'S mysteries, sex is perhaps the greatest. When we make love, we are deep inside our bodies, and yet we experience our souls. At orgasm, we feel the earth move and the heavens open. Through sex, in fact, we perform a ritual that produces the same patterns in our autonomic nervous system as those of mystical trance. Is it because something enters us that turns us into gods?

You The following You Two ritual intensifies the feeling of sacred eroticism. It draws all his energy to his genitals, while making him more deeply aware of his whole body. Because of your mirror neurons (see Day 298), your body will follow suit, and your connection will be even more intimate. So put on something priestess-like and start making magic.

You Two Light candles all around the bed. Oil your thumb, gently rub it on his forehead, and trail down to his lips. Slide down his throat, breastbone, nipples, navel, penis, and testicles. Retrace the same path with incense, just above his skin. Then kiss down the pathway with your lips, repeating with oiled nipples. Now oil his thumb and guide him down your pathway, ending with his thumb inside you. Rub each other's genitals slowly. Then climb atop his penis and draw your hands down the same line, fondling both your genitals at bottom. Begin slow thrusting as you repeat, going deeper into mouth and nipples each time. Continue into eternity.

A Day Off

David Duchovny said, "Sex is great until you die, but it's never as great as it was when you were a kid, when it was a mystery." Think about a time when sex was still a juicy secret. What exotic pleasures did you imagine? Hold them in your heart when next you kiss your lover.

DAY
189

Paws

Hands

Love is blind; that is why he always proceeds by the sense of touch.

—FRENCH PROVERB

WITH TWENTY-NINE BONES and thirty-four eloquent muscles, each of your hands can speak a language that goes way beyond words. A hand on the forearm says "I'm here for you," in a way he *feels*. In a crowded room, a brush from your fingertips instantly calls him into the heat of your own private world. And, in a moment of passion, your fierce grip cries out to his skin, bones, and hair follicles that you want him *now*!

You Your hand has 17,000 tactile receptors. Think about this when you lay it on your lover's thigh. You'll receive tons of messages about how hot he is, where to touch him, and when to press harder. And each of these bulletins comes to you with a zing of exquisite pleasure. Ask him to kiss your palm slowly and you'll see what I mean.

You Two You've seen the *Survivors* participants try to make fire by spinning sticks between their hands. Try the same thing on your guy. Oil your palms, then rub them together quickly to build up tingly heat. Place a hand on either side of his organ and swizzle away. The twisting motion creates extra friction and makes inner sparks fly.

Feet

Wherever one sees the feet of woman, one should give worship in one's soul even as to one's guru.

—TANTRIC SCRIPTURES

IN BABYLONIAN AND Roman temples, people walked barefoot to absorb the sacred and fertile powers of Mother Earth. Footprints left behind were sacred, and the foot itself was a tactile instrument for communing with a deity or a lover. Oddly, we still "worship" footprints today, immortalizing those of celebrities in the sidewalk of Grauman's Chinese Theatre.

You Your feet cushion up to 1 million pounds of pressure during an hour of exercise and, during a lifetime, walk far enough to travel around the planet four times. Pamper them with a lemongrass foot bath. Fill a pot with warm water, add a few drops of this tangy oil (soothes sore muscles), and soak your feet for ten blissful minutes.

You Two In ancient times, priestesses washed a man's feet to symbolize his transition from ordinary citizen to king. Make your man feel royal by massaging his feet with cooling peppermint oil. Circle your fist firmly all over the sole. Wrap both hands around one foot (palms on the top of the foot), and press your fingers into the sole while gliding the heels of your hands sideways. Massage around the ankle (where several sexual reflexology points are located). Finish by sliding your thumb *between* the tendons running from ankle to toes.

Ankles

Oh, if a man could but fasten his eyes to her feet, as they steal in and out, and play at bo-peep under her petticoats!

—WILLIAM CONGREVE

EARLY CHRISTIAN ARTISTS defied the church's codes by painting robes to cover the body but leaving sexy feet and ankles bare. By Victorian times, the sight was considered so dangerously tempting that many houses had separate men's and women's staircases so that a man walking behind couldn't catch a glimpse of a lady's shapely and provocative ankle.

You When you can't take your shoes off, an ankle massage is a quick and easy way to relieve stress and brighten your outlook. Circle your fingers around both sides of one ankle, while stretching and flexing the joint. Some women can ease their menstrual cramps by pushing on the acupressure point just above the ankle on the inside of the leg.

You Two Lie on your back, raise your knees to your chest, and cross your ankles. When he enters you, press your feet into his chest to stimulate his heart. Your cross-ankle position squeezes his penis tighter inside, like one long PC contraction, and maneuvers him onto your G-spot. And the lower you slide your feet, the more blood and energy you force into his erection.

Love at Hand

PRACTICED BY ROMAN fortunetellers and Indian mystics, palmistry is the ancient art of evaluating a person's character by studying his or her hand. Here are a few things to look for in a lover's paw:

Shape of Hand
- Air (square palm, long fingers): restless, changeable, looks for a meeting of the minds
- Earth (square palm, short fingers): practical, energetic, earthy, straightforward lovers
- Fire (long palm, short fingers): passionate, confident, wants to take the lead in love
- Water (long palms, long fingers): sensitive, creative, emotional, focuses on caring

Heart line (starts under little finger, flows toward other side of palm)
- Straight and short: very sexual
- Placed high: passionate, possibly jealous
- Long and curvy: expresses emotions easily
- Goes straight across: controlled emotions
- Wavy: lots of lovers, doesn't get serious
- Ends at index finger: affectionate, content
- Ends at middle finger: selfish, materialistic
- Ends between middle and index fingers: gives heart away too easily

Space between middle and ring fingers
- Touching: miserly
- Narrow: frugal
- Wide: generous

Fingers

If there is reincarnation, I'd like to come back as Warren Beatty's fingertips.

— WOODY ALLEN

DID YOU KNOW your fingers don't have muscles? These nimble digits are moved, like puppets on a string, by tendons connected to muscles in the forearm. But each fingertip contains over 3,000 touch receptors — making your fingers as sensitive to a droplet of mist, a feathery touch, or a quickening pulse as a pair of freshly kissed lips.

You Because many of the acupuncture meridians end in the fingers, you can transmit relaxation and healing to your entire body by massaging them. Wrap your right index finger around your left thumb, securing the hold with your right thumb. Twist and pull as you slide your fingers off the held thumb. Repeat with all fingers of each hand.

You Two While giving oral sex, slip one finger into your mouth and tickle his penis with finger, lips, and tongue at the same time. Your finger adds deep, focused, and completely unexpected sensations. When it's nice and wet, slide the finger out to massage his perineum (the very sensitive area between his anus and testicles). His pleasure is literally at your fingertips.

Toes

Come, and trip it as ye go,
On the light fantastic toe.

—JOHN MILTON

TOE MANIA GOT really crazy in the 1400s, when people began modifying their Duck Bill shoes. The broad footwear was slashed on top, where the toes are, and lined with fur—to give the appearance of pubic hair. As you walked, your toes peeked through the slits, like little penises poking in and out of "vaginal" openings. Not surprisingly, this footwear was a favorite of Henry VIII—he of the six very unlucky wives.

DAY

195

You Not just fun luxuries, regular pedicures increase circulation and flexibility in overworked feet and prevent toenail disorders. Feel less profligate now? Beauty hint from Manolo Blahnik: "The secret of toe cleavage, a very important part of the sexuality of the shoe" is that "you must only show the first two cracks."

You Two With a high concentration of nerve endings, a guy's toes are even more sensitive than his penis! Take each of his toes into your mouth, one at a time, and suck with a vacuuming motion. Graze them with your teeth. Lick between the toes until he's squirming and fully erect. Then, thrust his penis tip in and out between the crotch of *your* nicely oiled toes.

A Day Off

Go barefoot all day.

With your tootsies, sop up the feel of damp earth, tickly grass, slick floors, and furry rugs. And, oh yes, enjoy the silence.

DAY

196

Perfect Figures

The Female Trinity

The Moon Goddess has three aspects: As She waxes, She is the Maiden; full, She is the Mother; as She wanes, She is the Crone.

—STARHAWK, *THE SPIRAL DANCE*

FOR THE ANCIENT Greek, Indian, and Aboriginal cultures, the downward-pointing triangle symbolized woman. Besides looking like the magical place between her legs, its three-sidedness seemed to represent a female's mysterious nature. She waxes, wanes, and becomes full, like the moon; and she is one person, yet with three distinct personas—the enchanting, erotic Maiden; the fertile and powerful Mother; and the wise, insightful Crone.

DAY 197

You Whatever your size, shape, or age, you too are a deeply mysterious woman. An ancient exercise for learning to wield your power, centered in the pubic triangle, is to pleasure yourself to near orgasm—*three* times—before finally climaxing. With regular practice, your body learns to stay on the orgasmic plateau longer, and you acquire awe-inspiring sexual stamina.

You Two According to ancient love texts, a triangular network of nerves links a man's penis (point #1) with his feet (points #2 and #3). Stimulating all three at the same time—like, say, cradling his feet while licking his shaft—activates this connection, sending orgasmic jolts through his legs and pelvis. An easy way to amp up the electricity of oral sex.

Figure Eight

Now in more subtle wreaths I will entwine
My sinewy thighs, my arms and legs with thine.

—THOMAS CAREW

IN ANCIENT INDIA, the sideways figure eight meant sexual union. With its intertwined, matching circles, the infinity sign gave a sense of two equals becoming one. The pagans of old Britain adapted the sign in their handfasting ritual. Legal in Scotland until 1939, this type of marriage consisted of joining a couple's right hands (like a handshake) and then the left hands—arms crossed in the ancient symbol of completeness.

You The power of symbols goes deeper than logic. Convey the idea of marriage—or simply a meeting of minds—by inscribing hypnotic figure eights on your man's skin. On his back during a massage, over his lips as you kiss, around his navel during oral love.

You Two When you're on top, skooch down so your legs straddle his thighs instead of his hips. Then grind your pubis against his in a figure-eight swivel. As you turn and churn, your pelvis sends shocks of pleasure to *every* part of his penis and creates heavenly friction on your clitoris.

Number Nine

Sex is one of the nine reasons for reincarnation. The other eight are unimportant.

—HENRY MILLER

NINE IS THE number of completion. But in the ancient world, it also signified rebirth and sex. Scandinavians of yore held nine-day fertility feasts every nine years, and the Celts celebrated the orgiastic rites of spring with nine groups of nine partners. Perhaps they understood that, as nine rounds out a cycle of numbers, sex *completes* us while also *birthing* us into something new.

You Sex usually occurs on date number three. But how about romance? If you hold off love talk until the *ninth* date, you can help the exploratory phase end and a new bonding begin. Or, want to change a habit? Repeat the new behavior for nine days—something unwanted will die in order to birth a healthier new you.

You Two You may have read about the Spiral of Nines, an ancient Oriental thrusting sequence, in my book *302 Advanced Techniques for Driving a Man Wild in Bed.* Here's a hot variation. When you're on top, move your hips in nine quick, shallow strokes, then one slow, deep thrust. Then eight shallow, two deep, and so on until you reach nine deep, slow ones. Repeat. Shallow stroking teases the sensitive tips of both your genitals and his, while alternate full thrusting reaches to the deepest core—both building to a delightful climactic frenzy.

10 Ways to Get in Sync

A MAN COMES to a boil quickly (pioneering sex researchers William Masters and Virginia Johnson found the average guy ejaculates within 2½ to 3½ minutes). But you simmer slowly and stay hot for hours. To help you cook in tandem:

DAY

200

1. Warm up early. During the day, read erotica, fantasize, ogle his cute butt.
2. Get on top. This way *you* control the love-making tempo.
3. Use *lots* of lube. It decreases the friction he feels, so it takes longer to crest.
4. Teach *him* to do the Spiral of Nines (see previous day). Counting distracts him.
5. Hold an ice cube, then palm his testicles. It delays orgasm.
6. Switch positions frequently. No more than thirty thrusts in each.
7. Invite him to give you oral. Before sex, it heats you up. During sex, it slows him down.
8. Widen your legs. Less friction for him. More clitoral contact for you.
9. Squeeze him. Put your thumb on his frenulum (the small web of skin that connects, or used to connect, his foreskin to the head of his penis), fingers on the coronal ridge. Hold for three seconds.
10. Squeeze yourself. Rapidly contracting your PC muscles speeds up your arousal.

The Incomparable 69

Oral sex is so pleasurable for both participants that the distinction between who is receiving and who is giving melts away.

—JACK LEE ROSENBERG, PHD, AND
BEVERLY KITAEN-MORSE, PHD, *THE INTIMATE COUPLE*

IMAGINE YOUR LOVER'S tongue deeply embedded in your sex, your mouth saturated with the feel of his. Some say it's the ultimate sensation. But, more than opening floodgates of pleasure, the mutual genital kiss may also heal you. Oriental sages believed that blending oral and genital fluids produced a therapeutic elixir—and that the heads-and-tails pose, so similar to the yin/yang symbol, turned emotional discord into sweet harmony.

DAY 201

You Receiving intoxicating sensations can distract you from focusing on him. Perish the thought. Fortunately, the solution is to concentrate on the titillations in your own pelvis. You'll fall into a rapture that actually *flows* from vulva to lips, pouring ecstasy through your mouth and onto his quivering organ.

You Two Have him sit on the floor, butt on a pillow, legs straight out in front. He tilts back about 45 degrees, propped up with his hands. You stand behind and lean over his head, supporting yourself with your hands beside his thighs. Do the usual 69 thing; but because you're both elevated instead of lying flat, nerve sensations move freely, causing even more shivers and tingles than usual.

Multiples

Like a fierce wind roaring high up in the bare branches of trees, a wave of passion came over me, aimless but surging.

—JOANNA FIELD

SOME ANTHROPOLOGISTS SAY female orgasm evolved to promote pair bonding—that is, a woman kept the mate with enough patience and imagination to scale her erotic heights. Even just once. But, according to Masters and Johnson, most women can orgasm five or six times before they are fully satisfied. While men may thrill to this challenge, we women are *still* more exhilarated by quality than quantity. And yet . . .

You If you want multiple orgasms: 1) Try doggie-style. You can massage your clitoris while he stimulates your G-spot. 2) Pant as you approach—and go through—your peak. This helps you tolerate intense sensations that may otherwise stop you after the first orgasm. 3) Post-peak, caress *anything but* the clitoris—labia, belly, rear. Stimulation continues, but oversensitivity does not.

You Two You can give *him* additional contractions—if not real multiples—by massaging his prostate. 1) During oral, insert a lubed finger about two inches inside his anus. Pump your finger on the walnut-like lump toward the front of his body. 2) During intercourse, press rhythmically on his perineum just as he nears orgasm. Waves of pleasure will surge through him.

A Day Off

Beauty—both inner and outer—can be a matter of numbers.

Today, drink three bottles of water—to hydrate your skin. Get eight hours of sleep—to energize your body. Read one poem—to refresh your soul.

DAY
203

Primal Play

The Cutting Edge

*The freedom of authentic masculinity is an amazing thing to see. . . .
Finally they can lead with firmness, then submit with humility.
They can challenge with a cutting edge, then encourage with
enthusiasm.*

—BILL HYBELS

**DAY
204**

MEN HAVE A love-hate relationship with their razors. Shaving makes them feel fierce and cutting-edge. And yet, they sense a primal fear, perhaps stemming from Neolithic days when the Seven Mothers were in charge. Annually, these ladies selected a "sacrificial king." The lucky man was slain with a sickle-like razor, or simply castrated, so that his spirit, and that of the whole community, would be reborn. Yikes!

You By giving a man shaving equipment, especially the kind with old-fashioned brushes and creams, you present him with power. It says you see him as all man—someone who needs incredibly sharp and dangerous tools to keep his potent masculinity civilized. Now he's free to roar like a lion, then submit like a lamb.

You Two Excitement will skyrocket when you announce you're going to shave him down below, the better to kiss him. As recommended on Day 87 (shaving *you*), bathe him first to soften hair follicles, trim with scissors, then apply foamy cream with aloe. For his tougher skin, shave first *with* the grain, then *against*, then *with* again to close pores. Now spread warm olive oil on the *entire* area. Voluptuously. Marvel at how much BIGGER he looks (which he will). Meanwhile, he'll be feeling sensations he's never *ever* felt before. And hoping he gets to feel some more.

Seeds of Life

All beings are born from an offering of sperm hurled into the fire of desire.

—ALAIN DANIÉLOU, *THE PHALLUS*

WHILE A WOMAN'S womb and breasts—in fact, her whole body—are vessels of the life force, a man's only link with creation is his "sacred seed." Through this small bit of fluid, a man feels connected to all those who have come before him and to the precious children he will leave behind. No wonder these few drops, the only evidence of his creative power, are so precious to him.

You It might be messy, but in a healthy man, ejaculate is pretty innocent stuff. Made of fluids that contain fructose, protein, citric acid, alkalines, and of course sperm, it adds up to only five calories a teaspoonful. Women of some indigenous cultures actually smooth it on like moisturizer to improve their complexions.

You Two When you're on top, bring him close to orgasm, then slide off. Let him stew in his own desire while you keep him warm with your hand. Then finish him with your mouth. By eagerly accepting his sexual fluids—pre-cum mixed with your lubrication, and vital sperm—you make him feel treasured as a man.

The Jungle Bite

She should take hold of her lover by the hair, and bend his head down, and kiss his lower lip, and then, being intoxicated with love, she should shut her eyes and bite him.

—KAMA SUTRA

A WOMAN WHO makes love with abandon is not civilized. She claws, scratches, and bites like a wild animal. Horses, for instance, nip each other continuously while mating. A male lion buries his teeth in his lover's neck, as if wanting to penetrate her not only with his penis but also with his roar. And do you know why the female praying mantis tries to bite off her mate's head? Because it spurs him on to better sex.

You A well-placed bite can act like passionate acupressure, stimulating your most primal instincts. It's a reflection of untamed lust—but it also incites it. So when you want to summon up the kind of jungle fever that makes sex hot, hot, *hot*, ask him to bite you on the nape of your neck.

You Two At the peak of your orgasm, dig your teeth into his shoulder. It lets him know he's driven you over the edge. He'll be proud. And wildly turned on. And, if you "bite" with your whole body, tensing and clasping with every muscle, it will intensify your delicious contractions.

The Primal You

IF YOU'RE NOT in touch with your wild, earthy instincts, you're cutting off the part of you that has an enormous capacity for pleasure. Besides, there's nothing sexier than an elegant woman with a hint of jungle underneath. Here's how to connect to the Primal You.

1. Burn musk or cedarwood incense.
2. Dance to the percussive music of Babatunde Olatunji.
3. Play with your man's biceps. And underarm.
4. Taste your own juices. Wear the scent behind your ears.
5. Belly laugh.
6. Cut open a fig—fresh, not dried. Look at it for a full minute. Smoosh into it with your finger, nose, and tongue. Eat it slowly, letting the juices drip down your chin.
7. Swim in the nude. Sleep in the nude.
8. Practice samba rolls. Roll your hips forward, then your rib cage. Then roll back, all in one fluid motion.
9. Drink a South African Cabernet. Or strong ginger tea.
10. Wear crotchless panties or a thong under your pencil skirt.
11. Walk barefoot in the grass.
12. Trim and perfume your pubes. Tickle your man's thigh with them.

Secret Weapon in the Back Room

Don't worry, it only seems kinky the first time.

—UNKNOWN

WOULDN'T YOU LOVE it if there were a place on his body that was rich in sexual nerve endings, made him come on command, and encouraged him to be more sensual? There is. The anus. From ancient times, this sensitive opening has been honored for its sexual fire and secret thrills. And since it's a passageway, not a storage bin (all the nasty stuff is stowed at least six inches deeper), it's actually quite clean and even inviting.

You Because it lies at the tip of a nerve saddle that runs from penis, through testicles and perineum, to backside, the anal opening is a major control point. When you touch him there, he'll very likely: 1) rock his hips, which loosens his pelvis and sensitizes his torso; 2) climax very soon, depending on your pressure; 3) over time, gain new ejaculatory control. In this way, you take the helm of his erotic ship.

You Two To soothe and cleanse him, massage his genitals and rear with a warm, wet washcloth or your fingers. Then spread his cheeks and gently lick his anal opening. As accompaniment, knead his cheeks or rub his penis. Just take it slow, or he may climax intensely but too soon for your own pleasure.

Ravishment

. . . Take me to you, imprison me, for I
Except you enthrall me, never shall be free,
Nor ever chaste, except you ravish me.

—JOHN DONNE

ACCORDING TO CATHY Winks and Anne Semans in *The Good Vibrations Guide to Sex*, one of the most common male fantasies is being "taken" by a dominating woman—especially for men who're usually in charge at work, like CEOs or sports coaches. When you are sexually aggressive, your guy can take a break from having to be in control and, instead, get lost in sensations and feelings. Plus, your keen desire to get at him makes him feel totally irresistible.

You When you decide to ravage your man, something happens inside you that carries over to the rest of your life. You walk taller, with or without spike heels. You're no longer shy about telling others what you need—in the bedroom and the boardroom. You *both* know that he's not the only one in your relationship with real power.

You Two After a few minutes of vigorous sex, whip out some Velcro hand ties and bind his wrists together over his head. He'll see he can easily escape if he wants, but since he's aroused, he'll be thinking, "*Yes*. Just give me more." Thrust atop him forcefully, nipping at his throat and chest—as if "taking" him against his will. Relish the power.

A Day Off

Bertrand Russell said, "Of all the forms of caution, caution in love is perhaps the most fatal to true happiness." Write down all the things you've never dared in bed because you thought they were too raw, risky, or rude. By acknowledging your primal desires, you're well on the way to the joy of expressing them.

WEEK 31

A Bigger Toy Chest

The Vibrator

There are a number of mechanical devices which increase sexual arousal, particularly in women. Chief among these is the Mercedes-Benz 380SL convertible.

—P. J. O'ROURKE

BACK IN THE late 1800s, before God created the Mercedes, doctors treated female disorders by hand. Through massaging a woman's privates, they aimed to bring on "hysterical paroxysm"—better known as orgasm. Always looking to save labor, enterprising physicians came up with the vibrator and marketed it as the scientific cure for headaches, asthma, fading beauty, and even tuberculosis.

DAY 211

You Swedish sex researchers say the perfect vibrator speed is sixty cycles per second—much faster than the average finger. But when you prefer a softer, smoother ride: 1) wear panties; 2) lay your finger across the right spot and vibrate your fingertip; 3) use the cup attachment to focus vibrations *around*, not *on*, sensitive areas; 4) smother the toy with a thin pillow and ride the cushion.

You Two Introduce him to your battery-operated friend through your body—literally. When you're on top or doing it doggie-style, press a vibrator against your mound and he'll feel tremors right through your pelvis with every thrust. Or—*really* hot—lay the toy against your cheek when giving him oral. Then ask him to return the favor!

Scrunchy

I don't wake up with perfect hair. It takes a certain creativity to get it right.

—RICHIE SAMBORA

DAY
212

LEAVE IT TO a woman to turn a personal disaster into a retail bonanza. Needing a job after a bad divorce, Rommy Revson was hesitant to go on interviews with hair that had recently been bleached into a haystack. Since even a barrette broke off the fragile strands, she designed fabric-covered bands called "Scuncis" to hold them back —and a billion-dollar industry was born.

You Indulging your senses can be as simple as lifting your hair. Pull your tresses back with a scrunchy and put on some long, dangly earrings. Focus on the delicate sweep of jewelry, and stray wisps of hair, against the sensitive skin of your neck. Offer this exposed flesh to the feathery and searing kisses of your lover.

You Two To compress fluids and make him more sensitive, wrap a scrunchy around the base of his shaft. Then lick him. Increase intensity by stacking up six scrunchies and stripping them off with your lips, one by one. The removal of each tingly piece releases a little more pressure and turns his orgasm into a veritable eruption.

Feathers

The day is done, and the darkness
Falls from the wings of Night,
As a feather is wafted downward
From an eagle in his flight.

—HENRY WADSWORTH LONGFELLOW

BECAUSE THEY FLY close to heaven, feathers hold magic. In ancient Egypt, they were the ticket to eternal life. If your soul weighed less than a feather, proving you free of impurities, you were in. Native American shamans use feathers to borrow an eagle's power, direct the smoke of healing herbs, or make their words fly true. A feather falling into *your* life reminds you to tickle your fancy and fly free of familiar boundaries.

You In natural magic, different feathers help to focus various kinds of power. Carrying a robin's feather can attract new things and induce fertility. Swans mate for life, so their feathers bring love, grace, and beauty. Nightingale feathers are good for communication, and those of the eagle promote equal balance between male and female.

You Two Uncover new erogenous zones by "feathering" your man. Dust an ostrich or peacock feather in body powder and trail it over his throat, underarm, fold between thigh and pelvis, butt crease, behind his knees, and between toes. Or dip a sturdy falcon feather in sandalwood oil for a similar, wetter journey. Tie him up first to increase the intensity, and keep it up till he shudders with wanting.

"Honey, Meet My Vibrator!"

YOU DON'T WANT your man to feel threatened, replaced, or be-"littled" by a machine. Better that he *welcome* your vibrator into mutual sex play, right? Here's how to make the introductions:

- Tell him sex researchers found that many couples enjoy their best lovemaking when they engage in mutual self-pleasuring or use toys during intercourse.
- Use a Swedish-style scalp massager—a small box that straps onto the back of your hand. Soothe his shoulders and back with your vibrating fingers, move on to butt and thighs, then belly and nipples. Make him *ask* for attention elsewhere.
- Invite him to massage *you* with a vibrating egg or Venus Butterfly pad. He'll get a kick out of your reactions and won't feel threatened by something LARGE.
- In the middle of a torrid blow job, gently vibrate his perineum, testicles, or anus.
- In the missionary position, lodge a small vibrating egg between your pelvis and his.
- Let him watch when you pleasure yourself. Then hand him the tool.
- Cover the vibrator with a sock—or your panties—to soften the sensation on his shaft.
- Show him the attachment designed to cover the head of his penis and ask if he wants to try it out.
- Unless he's *very* secure, keep the vibrator that's shaped like a dildo under lock and key.

An Old T-Shirt

My Love in her attire doth show her wit,
It doth so well become her:
For every season she hath dressings fit,
For Winter, Spring, and Summer.

—SEVENTEENTH-CENTURY MADRIGAL

ITCHY AND HOT inside their wool uniforms, American soldiers in WWI envied the European troops their light cotton undershirts. By WWII, T-shirts had become standard Army issue. But when Marlon Brando and James Dean shocked us all by wearing their "underwear" on national TV, the plain white T-shirt suddenly became the sexiest thing a guy could wear.

You Ninety-one percent of Americans own a "favorite" T-shirt, but do you take yours for granted? A tight little tee feels soft as a kiss on bare skin and, when worn without a bra, it can rivet the attention of almost any man. Plus, old cut-up tees become great eyeglass wipes, packing material, potpourri containers, and dog security blankets.

You Two Wear a torn T-shirt, put his finger through one of the holes, and tell him you won't mind if he rips it off. That'll get his blood flowing. Conversely, when he's lying around in a shabby tee you'd rather see in the rag bag, lick his nipple right through the fabric, and soon you'll both be tearing each other's clothes off.

DAY
215

Grapes

Let us get up early to the vineyards; let us see if the vine flourish,
whether the tender grape appear, and the pomegranates bud forth:
there will I give thee my loves.

—SONG OF SONGS 7:12

DAY
216

AS LONG AS 8,000 years ago, women near the Black Sea were
cultivating one of the first crops—grapes. Winemaking soon
followed. But one legend says the ancient women found a sec-
ondary use for the small fruit. By showing a man how to roll
grapes in his mouth without breaking the skin, they taught him
the delicacy required to lick a nipple. Even back then, we were
brilliant.

You Grapes are good for the heart (they reduce bad cholesterol), the breast (they lower the risk of cancer), the womb
(they lessen heavy periods), and the skin (they protect against
free radicals that age you). Pop a few into green salads or
freeze them and add to yogurt. Or insert one or two when self-
pleasuring—they rumble around and create lovely friction.

You Two With one hand, press the tip of his erection softly
against his belly. With the other, roll a couple of chilled grapes
up and down the shaft. When you start using both hands to
pleasure him, keep the grapes in your palms, even squishing
them slightly. The cool, smooth textures create sensations no
fingers or lips can match.

A Day Off

Grab a girlfriend, have a glass of wine, and make an expedition to your local sex-toy store.
Touch everything.

DAY
217

Twentieth-Century Sex Goddesses

Mae West

Let's forget about the six feet and talk about the seven inches.

— MAE WEST

A WOMAN AHEAD of her time, Mae West loved to wind up her throaty, breast-heaving contralto and deliver bawdy double entendres on film. When incarcerated for public obscenity in 1927, she insisted on wearing silk panties instead of prison issue — and the warden took her to dinner every night. In her fabulous fifties, Mae starred in a Vegas extravaganza, singing and vamping with a passel of tall, virile bodybuilders.

You Mae West was not classically beautiful, and yet she toted up a long list of famous and powerful lovers. What did she have? She believed in herself as a sexual powerhouse and acted accordingly — showing us that if you hang it out there with boldness and style, everybody else will believe in you too!

You Two Mae knew she'd make a guy hard all over again when she cooed, "Thanks, I enjoyed every inch of it." For a similar effect, try this. Throw his legs over your shoulders, raising and presenting his penis to you like a juicy drumstick. Then smoosh your face and tongue over his entire genital area. Really get lost in him. He'll feel adored, deliciously dominated, and revived.

Brigitte Bardot

I really am a cat transferred into a woman . . . I purr. I scratch.
And sometimes I bite.

—BRIGITTE BARDOT

IN THE 1956 film *And God Created Woman*, Bardot performed a barefoot table dance that scorched the brains of every man who saw it. It was part cat stretching, part child playing, and part woman having sex. You could see it all in her body. She wanted her "prey." She pouted that she might not get it. She was prepared to take it. As innocent, seductive, and savage as a cheetah in the wild.

You When you *think* like a cat, you *move* like a cat. Graceful, sinewy, dangerous. Your mesmerizing actions are natural—not a come-on, but very come-hither. Try stalking your man—like a lioness. You'll feel a new power, a burning intensity that stirs your blood. And, believe me, so will he.

You Two Before sex, a light scratch on the cheek or testicles will sensitize his skin. During sex, when the pain threshold moves closer to pleasure, maul him like a tiger—his shoulders, chest, sides, and bottom will thrill to the deepened sensation. After sex, feather your nails across his inner thigh to arouse him for a second go. And if you leave scratch marks, he'll tingle with remembering.

Sophia Loren

Sex appeal is fifty percent what you've got and fifty percent what people think you've got.

—SOPHIA LOREN

AT AGE FOURTEEN, Sofia Scicolone entered a beauty contest, wearing a gown made of curtains. Because she stood proud, the then "ugly duckling" won second place. After her first screen test, Sophia was asked to alter the nose and hips that were "too big" to be beautiful. But she knew better. Years later, her exotic face and extravagant body made sixty-five-year-old Sophia Loren "one of the world's most stunning and age resistant women."

You In the film *Two Women*, director Vittorio de Sica played down Sophia's glamour to focus on the originality and fire he'd seen in her all along. She won an Oscar. Like Sophia, you're usually more memorable and alluring when you concentrate *not* on your beauty, but on your passion—the flame inside that makes you radiantly *you*.

You Two Sophia played up her earthy image and was often photographed splattered with mud. Men love a woman who's not afraid to get "dirty" or to touch the coarser parts of his body. So get earthy. When giving oral sex, massage his sensitive anus with a lubed finger and gradually sneak it just inside. The dual stimulation will surely cause his earth to quake.

Female Wisdom

SENSUAL WOMEN ARE often wise women—because exercising your passion stimulates your brain. Here's food for thought from some of the other sexy-smart women of the 1900s:

- "Plain women know more about men than beautiful women do." – Katharine Hepburn
- "There are things that happen in the dark between two people that make everything that happens in the light seem all right." – Erica Jong, from *A Collection of Sexy Quotes*
- "Plunging necklines attract more attention and cost less money." – Shelley Winters
- "God made men stronger but not necessarily more intelligent. He gave women intuition and femininity. And, used properly, that combination easily jumbles the brain of any man I've ever met." – Farrah Fawcett
- "If goodness is its own reward, shouldn't we get a little something for being naughty?" – Lauren Bacall
- "All a man really wants is complete worship and adoration. He knows he's perfect, but he likes to hear it from you." – Zsa Zsa Gabor
- "Being a sex symbol has to do with an attitude, not looks. Most men think it's looks, most women know otherwise." – Kathleen Turner

Marilyn Monroe

[Marilyn Monroe] listens, wants, cares. . . . Every pore of that lovely translucent skin is alive, open every moment —even though this world could make her vulnerable to being hurt.

— MONTGOMERY CLIFT

FEARING SHE LOOKED too "girl-next-doorish," Hollywood studio heads taught Marilyn to smile with her upper lip drawn down to hide her delicate gumline. Though she now looked ready to devour any male appendage (with that famous open-mouthed pout), their new bombshell still had an endearing innocence—as if her artificially lowered lip was straining to keep some naive exuberance, or wounded child, safely inside.

You Marilyn possessed a volcanic eroticism that could have been threatening. But her vulnerability made this overt sexuality seem charming. Both dangerous and in need of protection, she made an irresistible combination. Good to remember when you want to enthrall, not scare, someone with your power.

You Two After visiting President John F. Kennedy, Marilyn once said, "I think I made his back feel better." Here's her supposed method. Sit naked on your man's bare rump and brace your hands next to his shoulders. Slowly press and slide your pubis up his spine, pausing occasionally to rotate your clitoris on a knobby vertebra. This massage should be "healing" for *both* of you.

Josephine Baker

Beautiful? It's all a question of luck. I was born with good legs. As for the rest . . . beautiful, no. Amusing, yes.

—JOSEPHINE BAKER

CALLED THE "BLACK Venus," Josephine had a sleek, exotic beauty that came from her Apalachee Indian and black slave ancestors. Wearing only high heels and a skirt of sixteen bananas, she performed sensual, no-holds-barred dance routines on the stages of 1920s Paris that earned her diamonds, cars, and 1,500 marriage proposals. But her most valued treasure was a decoration for aiding the French Resistance in World War II.

You Often compared to a snake, a giraffe, and a hummingbird, Josephine flung out the most savage and erotic dance moves Europe had ever seen. But her crossed eyes, wide grin, and crazy antics with a pet cheetah tamed her act with humor. Take a lesson from the "Creole Goddess"—fun makes intense sexuality even *more* exciting.

You Two Josephine flaunted her female assets with wit and artistry, making her, according to Ernest Hemingway, "the most sensational woman anyone ever saw." Be bold with yours. Decorate your nipples with caramel sauce (they'll look creamy and inviting), body paint (artsy and fun), or nipple clamps (aching to be attacked). This outrageous eye candy invites touch, adoration, and uncontrollable craving.

A Day Off

Are you bold and brassy like Mae, tigerish like Brigitte, fiery like Sophia, vulnerable like Marilyn, or outrageous like Josephine? Which one feels the most like the woman you are, or would like to be? Think about how to deepen those qualities in yourself—so that you light up your own world.

Sex Education

Love Lit

A dirty book is rarely dusty.

—OLD PROVERB

IN EIGHTEENTH-CENTURY BRITAIN, naughty books were read aloud in alehouses and coffee shops. Funny and politically astute, many came with questions meant to set off hours of group speculation and long nights of intimate arousal. How much more sensual and titillating were these spicy vapors of thought—read by another's lips, heard by every cell in your body—than the hard, over-bright images of a TV or computer screen!

DAY
225

You In 1940, when Anaïs Nin began writing erotica for $1 a page, her words gave power and poetry to desires we barely knew we had. Now we could sense more deeply the "sting of pleasure" and the feel of our breasts "undulating like waves" under a man's hands. To bring new colors and sounds to your flesh—or warm up for a quickie—browse through her incomparable *Delta of Venus*.

You Two Read to him from *The Memoirs of Fanny Hill* or Susie Bright's *Herotica*, choosing a passage that describes one of your fantasies. Make eye contact at each naughty word. Tear off your shirt when the heroine's bodice gets ripped. Apply crème blush to "these lips that she rouged as if they were a mouth." (Anaïs Nin, *Delta of Venus*.) He gets hot. You get kinky. Sex gets epic.

Higher Math

Mathematics is the language with which God wrote the universe.

—GALILEO

THE SPIRAL OF a nautilus shell, the design of a sunflower's petals, the notes of an octave, the contours of the human face — all are based on the Fibonacci sequence: 1, 1, 2, 3, 5, 8, 13, etc. (each number being the sum of the previous two). Only nature knows why these ratios are magic. But the curving, off-center symmetry they create is among the most beautiful and sensual the world has to offer.

You Divide a Fibonacci number (starting with 5), by its lower neighbor, and you get roughly 1.6, the basis for the graceful proportions of the Parthenon. Use this Golden Mean ratio to create your *own* beauty. Place a figurine ⅔ of the way across a credenza; cut some flowers at ⅔ the height of others; use lip liner (or a smile) to make lips ⅔ as wide as the outside corners of your eyes. (Google "Fibonacci face" for other beautifying diagrams.)

You Two For a Fibonacci hand job, start with two very slow strokes (up and down counts as one), then three slightly faster, five even speedier, eight pretty darn quick, and thirteen rapid-fire pistons before slowing down in reverse order. Repeat this perfectly modulated sequence five times to build plateaus of tension that will put him on the ceiling.

Sensual Geography

There is an eternal landscape, a geography of the soul; we search for its outlines all our lives.

—JOSEPHINE HART

EVER BEEN TO a forest so serene you could hear your heart beat? Or crossed a desert so empty you ached with loneliness? Like many indigenous people, you understood in those moments that the landscape is an extension of your own body. The more in tune you are with nature's caves and mountains, the more intimate you become with your own dark spaces and higher thoughts.

You Apply the adjectives that would define a valley—secluded, sloping, lush—to the hollow above your pubic bone. Describe your womb as you would a cave—deep, moist, secret, breathtaking. When you see your breasts and rump as gracefully rolling hills, your body takes on a new and sculptural sensuality.

You Two Claim new erotic territory by exploring his geography. Lick where his skin is thin as spring ice—wrists, inner elbows, back of knees—to break through to a lake of sensation. Massage his mountainous calf muscles, and you stimulate the veins of gold running straight to his penis. Tickle *behind* his testicles—a secret ravine of nerve endings.

Heart and Brain Science

WE OFTEN THINK of our hearts as warm and fuzzy and our brains as cool and rational—one diving headfirst into love while the other works up a profit/loss ratio for pleasure. But according to neurologist Louann Brizendine, psychologist Daniel Goleman, and heart researchers Gary Schwartz and Linda Russek, the two organs work together intimately:

- About 60 percent of heart cells are neural cells, having direct connections to the brain's reasoning, learning, and emotional memory centers.
- When you talk with someone, your orbitofrontal cortexes actually link up and stimulate emotions in each other.
- Three of the four default settings in the supposedly all-business brain are constantly processing information about relationships.
- A girlfriend-to-girlfriend chat activates the brain's pleasure centers, releasing floods of dopamine and oxytocin—a rush second only to orgasm.
- When checking out a potential mate, the brain ticks off biological "yeses" and "nos" to subconscious questions such as "Will he produce viable offspring?" If he makes the grade, the brain releases a jolt of dizzying love-and-lust hormones.

Applied Physics

In physics, you don't have to go around making trouble for your-self—nature does it for you.

—FRANK WILCZEK

PHYSICS MAY BOGGLE the mind, but it can also show you how to sensitize your skin. Blood pushing against tissues because of gravity or pressure (fluid dynamics) brings nerves closer to the surface. So, sensitize breasts by leaning forward to pool blood behind your nipples. Trap engorging genital fluids with a penis ring or by pinching your clitoris. And make your whole body tingle by clenching and releasing every muscle like a giant human pump.

You Does he move too fast? You can slow his thrusting rhythm by making love atop several comforters or pillows. The slower oscillating resonance of something soft and cushy makes it difficult for him to bounce fast. If it's speed you crave, install a very firm mattress. Or throw him to the not-at-all-oscillating floor.

You Two Here's fluid dynamics at its best. Stand facing the bed but lean forward to rest your forearms on the mattress. He stands behind, lifts one of your feet to his hip, and enters you. In this position, sensitizing blood collects in your breasts, labia, G-spot area, and in his penis. All major erogenous zones are now ready for takeoff.

Art Appreciation

A work of art enters life very much like another human being — complicated, loaded with overtones and meaning, mysterious, enticing, obsessive, and beautiful.

—BUDD HOPKINS

LIKE ALL GREAT art, Van Gogh's *Starry Night* and Ansel Adams's *Moonrise over Hernandez, NM*, were born of passion. Their simple, intense images reveal the mystery, the incandescence, the complex overtones of night — but also of one's deepest self. The more you dare to bare yourself — to such a piece of art or to a lover — the closer you come to the passion in your own soul.

You Paint the canvas of your skin with a *temporary* tattoo. A Swarovski crystal spray framing your navel, a mehndi pattern circling your buff biceps, a crescent moon accentuating the curve of your rump — elegantly hidden where only you and your lover can see them — make you feel like a million-dollar Rubens.

You Two Take photos of yourself — naked, or in a corset, or kissing a cucumber — when you are *feeling desire* for him. (Passion is what turns snapshots or scribbles into art.) Then plant them in his shaving kit, next to the beer, under the remote. As he searches for each one, these small masterpieces of naked emotion will excite him in all the usual places — but also inside.

A Day Off

Visit an earth sciences store or explore the lush landscapes on www.nationalgeographic.com.

Learn. Be dazzled. Find passion.

Good Enough to Eat

Apple

There's a sigh for yes, and a sigh for no,
And a sigh for "I can't bear it!" —
O what can be done, shall we stay or run?
O cut the sweet apple and share it!

—JOHN KEATS

DAY
232

AT GYPSY WEDDINGS, bride and groom sliced an apple crosswise and each ate half. When you cut the fruit this way, the core looks like a pentacle — the five-pointed star, made with one continuous line, that's a sign for magic. The new couple often repeated the apple ritual before and after sex, sharing something juicy, while also affirming the continuity and wonder of their love.

You Often given to a conquering hero by a goddess, the apple represented long life and health to the ancient Greeks. But it also signified the succulent fruit of her sexuality — an incomparable gift that every woman can bestow, enriching the vitality of her own and her lover's body. By the way, according to a study at Pennsylvania State University, eating an apple before a meal can help you consume about 190 fewer calories than if you take in the equivalent calories in the form of apple juice.

You Two With your tongue, make an unbroken line that unites five erogenous zones, something like the apple's magic pentacle. Begin at the tip of his erection (Zone #1) and slurp down the ridge of the shaft (Zone #2), between his two testicles (Zone #3), across the perineum (Zone #4), up to his anus (Zone #5), and back. It seems to unite all five points *inside* him like an infinite ring of fire.

Fig

. . . It stands for the female part; the fig-fruit . . .
The flowering all inward and womb-fibrilled;
And but one orifice.

—D. H. LAWRENCE

IF THERE'S ANYTHING that resembles a vagina—moist,
red-ripe, and inward-blooming—it's the inside of a fig. That's
why, for thousands of years, the fig tree has been a symbol of
female sexuality—and male enlightenment, with even the great
Buddha sitting under a fig, or *boddhi*, tree to attain perfect illu-
mination. For how else does a man reach divine heights but
through the ecstasy of loving a woman?

DAY
233

You Besides looking like a woman, figs are also very healthy
for us to eat. Each one contains about 26 mg of calcium (great
for our fragile bones) and .6 mg of iron (a good restorative
during our periods). And, according to the ancient Romans,
they make you look younger and have fewer wrinkles.

You Two Figs make succulent finger food for feasting in bed.
But slice one open and the games have just begun. Slide the
mushy insides up and down his shaft and twirl it atop the head,
like you're juicing a lemon. Then eat it. It looks and feels like
a little vagina rubbing all over him—and when you eat it, he'll
think he's watching two women make love.

Bread

If thou tastest a crust of bread, thou tastest all the stars and all the heavens.

—ROBERT BROWNING

IN ANCIENT TIMES, bread was the one essential food. Because it came from the Great Mother, whose own body supplied the grains that nourished life, bread was magic. When baked into the shape of a honeycomb, it supposedly increased the production of honey bees. But a loaf looking like a breast or penis served as a sex charm—aromatic, fleshy stuff that was eaten with great relish by the newfound lovers.

You In the Middle Ages, a British man would travel with several loaves of bread to sustain him. So his clever wife, hoping to keep the vagabond's mind on her—not on whatever female fluff he found along the way—made an impression of her vulva on the loaf before baking. Having tried this homey trick, I can confirm that it works.

You Two Plushy and pliable, your man's behind is like fresh bread dough. Have him lie on his tummy, while you straddle his thighs and knead the lower part of his butt with the heels of your hands. Not only is this a major erogenous zone, but your motions push his penis against the bed in ways that will make his loaf rise.

How to Eat for Pleasure

TOO OFTEN, THE delights of a meal play second fiddle to some other activity—multitasking at our desks or chatting with a friend. But food can awaken dulled senses and insert new pleasures into a day or a love affair. Try these savoring techniques.

- Close your eyes and chew slowly. With distractions gone, flavors become more succulent and textures more sensual.
- Try to identify the various spices in a new dish. Focusing on distinct flavors helps you taste more intensely.
- Combine foods adventurously—cantaloupe with peanut butter, pork with grapes. Surprise releases endorphins and adrenaline, making you feel happy and satisfied.
- Press soft, creamy foods between your tongue and the roof of your mouth, putting them in touch with the maximum number of taste buds and increasing the yum factor.
- Smell and hear your food. Sort through the scents of a sauce for a preview of what's to come. Notice how biting into a carrot sounds different than chewing on toast. Adding more senses enriches the experience.
- Feed, and be fed by, your lover. A berry in another's hand becomes a love offering, a sex toy, an adventure.

Salt

Let there be such oneness between us, that when one cries, the other tastes salt.

—ANONYMOUS

THE SALT OF our tears or sweat is what lets us know we're human—creatures that need the small, tangy rocks of the earth to survive. We eat it. We use it to preserve meat and to consecrate altars. The Romans even paid their soldiers with it. But it was the ancient Chinese who discovered that rubbing salt on skin will soothe and burnish the flesh. And so began the tradition of using salt for pleasure.

You Make your own scrub by combining ½ cup sea salt with 2 tablespoons olive or almond oil and 2 tablespoons white vinegar. Before leaving your bath, rub the mixture on arms and legs, leave it on for five minutes, then rinse with cool water. Your skin will feel luxuriously softened and moisturized.

You Two Invite him into the shower, then buff each other with scented salt scrub. The magic mineral, together with your hot rubbing, wakes up nerve endings and opens pores so that your bodies feel steamy with wanting when you hop into bed afterward.

Strawberry

Upon the nipples of Julia's Breast:
Have ye beheld (with much delight)
A red rose peeping through a white? . . .
Or ever marked the pretty beam
A strawberry shows half drowned in cream?

—ROBERT HERRICK

BECAUSE OF ITS heart shape and nipple-red color, the strawberry has long been associated with sensuality. The favorite fruit of Venus, the goddess of love, a strawberry in your dreams means you are ripe with desire—and sex is in the offing. And legend says that if you share a double berry with a man, you will soon fall in love with each other.

You Newlyweds in provincial France were always served cold strawberry soup as an aphrodisiac. Turns out this folklore has scientific underpinnings. The fruit's seeds are rich in zinc, which boosts testosterone—the hormone that fuels libido in both sexes. So when you want to get in the mood for love, eat a handful of strawberries.

You Two Put a strawberry in his belly button. Lick it, and then, holding it with your lips, glide the nubbly fruit up his body to caress his nipples (a quite unusual sensation) and then down to his erection (even more titillating). Variation: Insert the berry in your vagina. *Then* move it over his body with your fingers, finally offering it to him to eat.

A Day Off

An old Hungarian adage says that coffee should be black like the devil, hot like hell, and sweet like a kiss. Find all those elements in today's cup of java. Then discover something else new about coffee's character—something that makes you feel devilish, hot, and sweet all day.

Movin' & Groovin'

Stretching Yourself

The beauty is that people often come here for the stretch, and leave with a lot more.

—LIZA CIANO, CO-OWNER OF YOGA VERMONT

WHEN YOU SLEEP, or sit for a long time, muscles get tight and blood pools in your smallest veins. When you get up and stretch, what you're *actually* doing is moving that pooled blood through your veins so that nutrients and oxygen perk up and unkink those tight muscles. But what it *feels* like you're doing, as any cat can tell you, is opening your body so pleasure can flow through.

You After sitting in front of a computer for hours, a stretch break is like a mini massage. By improving circulation to your brain, you can think faster. By loosening muscles, you ease stress and even relieve menstrual cramps. And by becoming more flexible, you're better able to reach back for a kiss and, later, try some fancy new positions.

You Two When doing the dog, make like a cat. On all fours, stretch your back by rounding and then arching it as he thrusts. These moves tilt your pelvis forward and back, constantly changing the angles and sensations of penetration. It ups the excitement like crazy.

DAY 239

Swirling Spirals

More than thirty-five thousand years ago . . . [we] became aware of the pulsating rhythm that infuses all life, the dance of the double spiral, of whirling into being, and whirling out again.

—STARHAWK, *THE SPIRAL DANCE*

THE SPIRAL IS one of life's most basic patterns. Shells and sunflowers grow in spirals. Galaxies, strings of DNA, and eddies of water whirl in spirals. An ancient symbol found on every civilized continent, the spiral signified the cycle of life — we are born, we die, we are reborn to the same place but with new wisdom. And because they're curved and eternally giving life, the spiral also became the perfect symbol for Woman.

You Spirals are mesmerizing and sexy. They're what make curls appealing and Slinkies slinky. But spirals also make thinking creative. When you're stuck in a mind rut, find the familiar pattern, and then look from a new perspective, a little higher on the spiral. Does your usual way of kissing belong to an old, shy you? If a kiss were wet communication, would you lick your lips first, like a siren? Same mouth, new smooch. Spiral thinking.

You Two You've probably already made the leap to spiral sex. Yes, swirl your tongue around his erection and you'll drive him mad with pleasure. But try it this way. Spiral from the tip to the base of the bulb, then suddenly take all of him in your mouth. Same lips, new spirals, hotter outcome.

Motion of the Ocean

Roll on, thou deep and dark blue Ocean—roll!

—LORD BYRON

THERE'S A MOVE in hula where your feet stay still but your hips rotate in a complete circle. It's meant to make both dancer and audience feel the rolling of the ocean, one of nature's most powerful forces. In the same way that the moon pulls on the sea, your female self pulls on you from the center of your hips. If you give yourself to it, you'll feel an erotic force rolling through you, connecting you to everything female and juicy, and causing swells in your labia.

You A great way to connect with this energy is to do that hula step. Without moving your feet, draw a circle around them with your hips. First clockwise a few times, then counterclockwise. Keep your knees bent. It looks and feels sexy, but it also strengthens your center of balance and exercises your abs and PCs.

You Two Do this same ocean move when you're on top of your man. Keep your knees close to his hips—so he stays still and you have more range of motion. Alternate between clockwise and counterclockwise circles to roll onto all sides of your vaginal canal and all surfaces of his lucky penis.

Sexy Moves

FROM TIME IMMEMORIAL, wise women have known that certain motions or stances make you feel juicy. You'll see them in many goddess figurines and women's dances. To get the full effect, hold a *pose* for at least a minute; or continue a *motion* for at least fifteen.

Bring energy and sensation to pelvis

- Do African dance
- Practice Kegel squeezes
- Squat with open legs
- Put hands on pelvis and "breathe" through your vagina
- Stand with hands on hips, one hip cocked, then the other
- Perform the hula
- Use a hula hoop

Widen labia and sensitize clitoris

- Sit in half Lotus; one leg bent so foot touches crotch, other hangs off chair
- Sit in chair, one foot on chair seat, toes and knee pointing out, elbow resting on knee
- Cross alternate legs repeatedly, spreading your thighs each time

Make breasts tingle

- Do slow shoulder rolls
- Pushing from above the nipples, press breasts down
- With arms out, shake breasts like a samba dancer
- Hold your breasts high with your hands
- Twist to one side from waist up; raise arms to hold hair out

Make your body feel like sex

- Slither like a snake
- Tilt pelvis forward and back, arms raised in joy
- Belly dance
- Soak and massage your feet

Edwarda Scissorlegs

A girl's legs are her best friends, but the best of friends must part.

—REDD FOXX

IN ANCIENT EGYPT, scissors were often inlaid with the image of a man on one blade and a woman on the other, their bodies constantly squeezing together and drawing apart. In the age of courtly love, suitors sometimes gave their ladies a love box containing scissors (considered a feminine tool, perhaps representing her parted legs) housed in a manly leather sheath. When you see even a common instrument like a pair of scissors as a symbol of erotic love, how rich is the rest of your life!

You In the position described in the following You Two, your scissoring legs either shield your vulva or open your labia wide and expose your clitoris. So your sensations, which seesaw from muted to intense, build delicious pressure. But you can create the same orgasmic effect in almost any position simply by sliding your thighs one-up/one-down, or open and closed.

You Two Sit on the edge of the bed (maybe a table would be a better height) and lie back with your legs pointing straight up. He stands and enters. Holding your calves, he spreads your legs wide and then brings them together in rhythm with his pumping. This scissoring action constantly changes how deep he can go—with legs together, you're tight and shallow; with legs apart, he can plunge way in. He's always on the tantalizing scissors' edge.

Alternatin' Rhythm

Some people tap their feet, some people snap their fingers, and some people sway back and forth. I just sorta do 'em all together, I guess.

—ELVIS PRESLEY

DAY

244

HAVING YOUR VAGINA around his penis is great stuff for a guy. And having your mouth around it is fabulous too—but different. Your vulva surrounds him constantly, while your lips are more unpredictable. The inside of your mouth is harder and toothier against his skin, but it feels more like an intimate caress or kiss. Since a guy's senses can be dulled by one continuous type of touch, sometimes it's *alternating* sensations—or sorta doin' 'em all together—that sends him over the moon.

You We women like variety too, of course, but we don't seem to need as much as men do. Some of us have been known to scream bloody murder when he gets just the right speed and pressure going, and then he *changes* it! So don't try to apply your sensations to his body. This is one of those cases where he's just plain different.

You Two You might work him up to a moderate level of hysteria with your hands first. Then hop on top and raise the roof a little higher. Now switch to oral. (DO NOT be squeamish. They're your own juices, for goodness' sake!) Keep alternating between mouth and vagina. The varied rhythms and pressures will make him last longer and scream louder.

A Day Off

Try inline skating, racewalking, climbing a tree, or walking backward—something that makes you use your legs and hips in a way you're not used to. What "new" parts of your body do you feel? What do these motions remind you of? Think about how to incorporate those moves into your lovemaking.

DAY

245

Drama Queen

Only the Shadow Knows

For she was beautiful—her beauty made
The bright world dim, and everything beside
Seemed like the fleeting image of a shade.

—PERCY BYSSHE SHELLEY

THE FAMOUS CHINESE shadow puppets originated about 100 B.C., when one of Emperor Wu's concubines died. The royal minions fashioned the lady's likeness out of donkey leather, and made her silhouette dance behind an illuminated backdrop. Since a person's shadow was considered part of their soul, it seemed to the delighted emperor that his beloved had returned to sensuous life.

You Italian cameo makers, who carve the jewels from real carnelian shell, know about the sexy appeal of a silhouette. Curvy profiles are revealed, while flaws—and true identities—are concealed. If you stand in shadowed light, in profile, you will appear mysterious, enchanting, and more perfect than you already are.

You Two Cut a four-inch round hole in a sheet, three feet from the bottom, and hang it from an open door frame. He stands on the opposite side while you turn on a light behind you. Run your hands over your darkened silhouette and strip—slowly. He can't see your cellulite or your embarrassed grin, so wriggle it, girl. Bring his erection through the hole and let your naughty shadow have its way with the disembodied appendage.

Milkmaid

Honey and milk are under your tongue,
And the fragrance of your garments is like
the fragrance of Lebanon.

—SONG OF SONGS 4:11

IN ANCIENT EGYPT and Sumer, where the burning sun scorched people and plants alike, the moisture left by cool lunar rays was considered a life-giving boon from the Goddess. Portrayed as the Great Cow, she offered her nourishing milk in the form of dew, rain, and especially fluids that were white like the moon—cow and goat's milk, semen, and the lubricant of aroused women.

You Cleopatra and even Queen Elizabeth I bathed in milky water to beautify their skin. The lactic acid in milk helps slough off dead skin cells; its amino acids moisturize; and its glycerine promotes elasticity. Simply add 1 cup powdered (or 2 cups fluid) milk to your bathwater, with a drizzle of sweet almond oil for scent or seaweed extract for thickening, and luxuriate in the creamy nourishment of the goddess.

You Two Have your man lie in a tub with just a little water in it. Kneel between his legs and pour whole milk over his nipples and penis. This will feel soft and voluptuous in the extreme—and will remind him of suckling at your breasts. Then have him pour while you try to lap up the cream as it flows down his body. Worthy of a yummy encore.

R-Rated

They are doing things on the screen these days that the French don't even put on postcards.

—BOB HOPE

I DON'T KNOW about you, but I never thought of standing on the hood of a car in spike heels, hiking my pencil skirt up to *there*, and making a guy crawl over broken glass to reach my cootchy. But when Madonna does just that in *Body of Evidence*, you want to rush out to the parking lot and leap atop the nearest Chevy. Always trying to outdo itself with over-the-top action, Hollywood can still inspire us to bring out the "full tilt" in our lovemaking.

You When you imagine you're someone else, you can bypass inhibitions and go directly to the brazen hussy you were meant to be. Rent *The Last Seduction* to borrow Linda Fiorentino's "I want sex right now; let's go" chutzpah; *White Palace* to channel Susan Sarandon's tiger-mauling, life-restoring sex technique; and *Sex and Lucia* to absorb by osmosis Paz Vega's artfulness with a blindfold and elbow.

You Two For raw, unvarnished sex, re-create the pivotal scene in *Sea of Love*. Like Ellen Barkin, don't just push your man against a wall, *slam* him there. Don't cuddle; press into him like you're ironing on a decal. Pull away and stalk around like a panther in heat before returning to your prey, then yank him down on top of you. Like a skilled actor, you'll be adding the juicy details that make any scene intense and searing.

10 Dramatic (and Fun!) Things to Do

1. Rent a convertible for the weekend.
2. Snap up a last-minute getaway to Cancun.
   (Visit *www.lastminute.com* or *www.lastminutetravel.com*)
3. Accessorize your business suit with a studded patent leather belt.
4. Take salsa or belly-dancing lessons.
5. Dab on a robust perfume that exudes power and oomph—like Missoni's *Profumi Missoni*, Susanne Lang's *Midnight Orchid*, or *Gaultier 2*.
6. Rent a Japanese tatami room for a secluded, one-on-one dinner.
7. Wear a hat with a twelve-inch brim—like Rene Russo's beach chapeau in *The Thomas Crown Affair*.
8. Dramatize your bathroom with piles of black or flower-print towels.
9. Get a radically different hair cut.
10. Make a grand entrance. Renowned soprano Renée Fleming recommends sweeping into a room with a sense of adventure.

May the Force Be with You

I see the mutual seduction between them, I see the currents that pass between his body and hers. . . . They are throbbing before they even touch each other.

—ANAÏS NIN

DAY
250

THANKS TO NEW instruments like the SQUID (Superconducting Quantum Interference Device), scientists can finally measure the electromagnetic pulsations that constantly radiate from our bodies. These force fields grow bigger and stronger when our brains or emotions are active, or when we get near a "sympathetic" electromagnetic field—like the body of a lover. So put head, heart, and proximity together and you've got major electricity, baby.

You Clap a few times, then rub your hands together briskly to increase their electromagnetic charge. You'll feel tingling or heat. Place your hands over tired eyes to refresh them, atop sore muscles to soothe them, or all over your body to add zing to your self-pleasuring routine.

You Two Embrace your man by pressing your entire body into his. Then back away. Move in to hold him close again, then step back. This game of close-and-apart draws him into the chase and builds an erotic force field that actually magnetizes his body to yours. One man I know said it was the hottest come-on he'd ever experienced.

The Grand Exit

What matters isn't being applauded when you arrive—for that is common—but being missed when you leave.

—BALTASAR GRACIAN

A STYLISH, WELL-TIMED exit can leave the thought of you hanging in the air like a waft of Arpège. The person left behind still feels, even smells, your presence but can cling only to mystery (*Where is she going?*), expectation (*What will happen when . . . if . . . she returns?*), and desire (*I want her back now!*). Like a pregnant pause, this fertile emptiness makes whatever you do next terribly exciting. Or poignant. Maybe even brilliant.

You With some basic acting techniques, you can make a power exit from your next business or PTA meeting. Watch for the moment when you're on a high note and your audience craves more. Generate presence by holding your rib cage high and making eye contact with a few key players. Then leave the room radiating intensity. Your ideas will stay etched in their minds.

You Two Sometimes you get more sex by leaving. After a hot session, stand, turn, and look right into his eyes. With a tarty expression, slip one finger into your vagina, wink, and bring the finger to your mouth. Then suck on it. Remove the wet finger and sashay out of the room. When you return, he'll be hard again, and probably salivating.

A Day Off

Today, whenever you think of it, laugh at absolutely nothing. Laughter releases endorphins, which among other things ease heartache and bring joy. It captures the best kind of attention, because there's nothing sexier than sharing your pleasure with others.

DAY
252

Magic

The Kiss

Such kisses as belong to early days,
Where heart, and soul, and sense in concert move,
And the blood's lava, and the pulse a blaze,
Each kiss a heart-quake.

—LORD BYRON

REMEMBER THOSE EARLY kisses? Full of urgency and wonder, we came to them with mouths open, eyes crossed, and hearts pounding. Even our brains contributed by growing special neurons to help us find each other's lips in the dark. We can still produce those electric, knee-wobbling, soul-piercing kisses by approaching each one as if it were the first.

You To find new magic in a kiss, try *receiving* it. Instead of pressing or puckering, let his lips *penetrate* yours. What new ripples, edges, and wet curves can you discover? How warm, how rough, how expressive is his mouth? By the way, an exploratory one-minute kiss burns twenty-six calories — enough to work off a glass of pink champagne.

You Two Want intensity? Try licking *around* his mouth — over the Cupid's bow, into the corners, and just beneath the lower lip. Then pull back and wait. According to the *Kama Sutra*, these tertiary nerves are directly connected to the penis, so you shouldn't have to wait long. If necessary, apply logic. Studies show men who kiss their wives every morning — with feeling — earn more money and live five years longer than those who don't.

Spinal Tap

He is simply a shiver looking for a spine to run up.

— PAUL KEATING

COILED IN THE lower back, five to nine inches above the tailbone, lie the sensitive nerves that branch out to clitoris or penis. Push firmly along the spine there, and you will produce subtle tingles and luscious swellings in your genitals—or his. Without understanding why, he will feel harder, stronger, almost bursting with sensation when you're around. Are you magic?

You If you have a tennis ball, you can get a great back rub without having to beg him to do it. Sit in a chair, put the tennis ball next to your spine at the lower curve of your back, and lean into the chair. Slide up and down to roll the ball. You'll ease stress and increase blood flow to your genital tissues all at the same time.

You Two Because the primary nerves in the spine are deeply buried, they require vigorous handling. A trail of spirited bites up and down his backbone will send electric shocks through every nerve. But, for the sexual coup de grâce, wait until he's cresting into orgasm; then pulse your fingertips—firmly, insistently, like you're never gonna stop the sweet torture—into the secret erogenous zones in his lower back. Fireworks will ensue.

Between Your Legs

*The place where all of us come from, the very place of our birth . . .
is the most important, the most powerful, the most beautiful place
on earth. Worship it with all your heart, or you will be lost!*

—RUFUS C. CAMPHAUSEN, *THE YONI*

WE WORRY ABOUT cellulite, sagging breasts, and pouchy tummies. But, for a man, the sight, smell, feel, and even just the idea of a woman's "secret triangle" is the real Holy Grail. He fantasizes about nestling his head on this mysterious mound. He yearns to touch it, penetrate its depths, or even catch the tiniest glimpse as a woman crosses her legs. We have long forgotten it, but this dark cave is the true home of our female power.

You Hawaiian shamans say, "Energy flows where attention goes." You'd be surprised how sensations magnify when you put your attention on your vulva. During foreplay, orgasm, or even while showering, close your eyes and notice how supple, warm, and versatile that part of you is. Your thoughts will increase blood flow and vibrate nerve endings in places you never knew you had.

You Two Those ubiquitous crotch shots in *Penthouse* and *Playboy* may be sleazy, but they're there for a reason. Men *love* to feast their eyes on what a woman has between her legs. Really rivet his attention by holding your sex lips wide open — a sight men find intensely erotic and beautiful. You'll not only raise his temperature several degrees, but by stretching that delicate flesh, you'll make your labia and clitoris throb with sensitivity.

20 Quick Ways to Feel the Magic

1. Eat hot Mexican or Thai cuisine. Spicy foods release endorphins into your bloodstream.
2. Laugh for one full minute.
3. Wear soft, figure-hugging leather. It feels like liquid against your skin.
4. Visit an online art treasury (e.g. *www.metmuseum.org*; *www.naturephotosonline.com*; *www.okeeffemuseum.org*).
5. Breakfast by a sunny window. First-thing-in-the-morning light balances circadian rhythms.
6. Walk barefoot on fur, grass, or in a stream of water.
7. Listen to the music of the Buena Vista Social Club, Rachmaninoff, or a conch shell.
8. Inspect a patch of dappled light.
9. Try something new. It stimulates adrenaline and dopamine.
10. Sleep in the nude—or on 400 thread count sheets.
11. Sniff an essential oil. Peppermint increases brain activity and jasmine reduces anxiety.
12. Eat a mango and let the juices run down your chin.
13. In the shower, buff with sugar scrub. It exfoliates, softens, and indulges.
14. Read Anaïs Nin, Pablo Neruda, or the *Song of Songs*.
15. Sprinkle ground ginger, which wakes up lazy sense receptors, on your chicken or vegetables.
16. Work out. It feeds neurons with oxygen and endorphins.
17. Watch the 1997 movie *Bliss*, or anything with Clive Owen.
18. Meditate for three minutes. Breathe, listen, drift. It cleans the brain's synaptic connections.
19. Have a glass of port with Roquefort and a fresh baguette.
20. Buy new shoes.

Pheromones

A woman's perfume tells more about her than her handwriting.

—CHRISTIAN DIOR

LIKE SNOWFLAKES, NO two people's pheromones are alike. The chemicals we secrete in saliva, sweat, and genital fluids are blueprints of our unique DNA, meant to attract mates with messages about our fertility, health, and genetic compatibility. Ever swooned over a guy's slept-in T-shirt? Clever woman. You were picking up vital clues to his suitability as a breeder — and finding out if his brand of sexuality matches yours.

You According to biologist Dr. Winifred Cutler, regular exposure to male pheromones makes your menstrual cycle more fertile (great if you're trying to conceive) and more regular (great if you're trying not to conceive). And pheromones from Mr. Right stimulate production of oxytocin, a hormone that helps you achieve more orgasms! Maybe that's why Roman women paid handsomely for the sweat collected from gladiators' skin.

You Two Since men's testosterone levels spike in response to female pheromones (especially when the women are ovulating), use your scent to make him greedy for you. Wet a finger in your vagina and circle your own nipples and mouth — to attract him there. Dip in again, then graze *his* upper lip. Your pheromone-rich fluids will send gotta-have-her-now messages directly from nostrils to brain to previously napping penis.

Lingerie

If God wanted us to be naked, why did he invent sexy lingerie?

—SHANNEN DOHERTY

PEOPLE WORE UNDERWEAR as far back as Bronze Age Crete. But lingerie, so frothy, soft, and delicate, was born when 1880s French women began cutting out the constricting mid-riffs of their corsets. Covering the body without actually con-cealing it, sexy undergarments allow us to express our feminine style without revealing more than we want. Instead, they beckon a man—promising just a hint of the curves, shadows, and secret places that lie in wait.

You For *your* pleasure, not anyone else's, wear a silk camisole under your business suit. It's the perfect combination of femi-ninity and power. More fun than a blouse or tank, a cami can peek out from your blazer to make naughty insinuations by day—and, sans jacket, become the focus of attention that eve-ning. And your skin will love the luxurious change of pace.

You Two 1) When he's in the shower, jump in wearing your camisole and panties. Lather his hands and slide them under the soaked, see-through fabric. 2) Leave your panties on dur-ing sex. Besides the thrill of your hard-to-get routine, he'll get extra stimulation along the side of his penis.

A Day Off

Smile. Pull your shoulders back. Stand tall by imagining a string being pulled out the top of your head.

Like magic, the muscular feedback you give your brain makes you feel and appear *more self-confident and more beautiful.*

Love in the Kitchen

The Kitchen Table

I'm at the age where food has taken the place of sex in my life.
In fact, I've just had a mirror put over my kitchen table.

—RODNEY DANGERFIELD

DAY
260

IN THE FILM *The Postman Always Rings Twice*, Jack Nicholson and Jessica Lange make love atop a kitchen table, in a coupling so intense many believed the two were having real sex. The spur-of-the-moment tryst would have been hot anywhere, but the kitchen table added a taste of shameless lust and fevered urgency that sent people racing home to their own dinette sets.

You Sex in the kitchen is an automatic pulse-pounder. Your only job is deciding whether you want to open your legs to his *kisses* (sit on the high countertop) or his *thrusts* (choose the lower table). Hint: If you give him something tasty to aim for, like fruit juice on your labia, he'll stay in one spot even longer.

You Two The next time he goes to the refrigerator for beer, grab his belt loop and guide him to the kitchen table. Sit near the edge, so your pelvis is positioned at the perfect height to parry his standing thrusts. If you're near a countertop or wall, plant your feet there and let your bottom slide off the table edge. That way, your hips can gyrate more freely—and so can his.

The Spatula

You usually associate sex toys with things you buy in places with names like The Pink Pussycat Boutique. But that ignores all the stuff you already have lying around the house.

— STEFAN BECHTEL AND LAURENCE ROY STAINS, *SEX: A MAN'S GUIDE*

SPATULAS WEREN'T ALWAYS confined to the kitchen. In pre-Colombian culture, spatulas were the sign of a shaman, for he alone used the handy tool to mix herbs and insect scrapings for healing ceremonies. In ancient Rome, palette-like broadswords called *spathas* were the sign of a soldier. Today, a spatula is the sign not only of a good cook but also a witty, ingenious, and epicurean lover.

You The women of ancient Egypt used bone spatulas to scoop out kohl and apply lip gloss (made from fat and red ochre). Rubber spatulas are ideal for scraping every ounce of moisturizing cream from the jar or mixing loose powder colors to arrive at the perfect shade. Wooden ones can remove gum or candle wax from carpet — soak the glob with cleaning solution, break it up a little, then "shave" the rug with the spatula.

You Two Arrive in the bedroom with a spatula, and your man is instantly intrigued. Spank him with it, and you wake up hundreds of neglected nerve endings. But top the spatula with a leather glove, and you make him feel buffed like the paint on a vintage Rolls-Royce. Or, simply use the spatula to apply frosting to his nipples and inner thighs and lick it off like the icing on a cake.

Ice

A woman at 20 is like ice, at 30 she is warm and at 40 she is hot.

—GINA LOLLOBRIGIDA

IN A FUNNY way, ice is very female. Like a woman's multi-faceted personality, ice is composed of jewel-like crystals (think of a snowflake). Like a woman, it can be cold and dangerous, yet delicately transparent. Ice can even be "steamy" when it gets too hot. But with just the right amount of warmth, it melts—caressing a lover's skin with startling chills of delight.

DAY
262

You Silky, bracing, and ripe—like us—"Sex on Ice" is a cock-tail of sensual celebration. Combine equal parts vodka, rum, and raspberry- and melon-flavored liqueurs with two straw-berries and a dash each of strawberry and cherry schnapps. Blend with crushed ice, pour into a martini glass, and garnish with whipped cream and a cherry.

You Two Caress not his penis, but his *inner thigh* with a piece of ice during oral sex. Match the pace of your hand to that of your lips so the two movements flow as one—hot and cold melting together in seamless, shivery bliss.

Food—The Original Aphrodisiac

FOOD AND SEX are a perfectly matched pair. We even use similar words to describe them—hunger, juicy, spice, appetite, yum. But here are seven things you may not know about the items in your pantry:

- Apples—In medieval Germany, an apple infused with the sweat of a lover was thought to be a potent aphrodisiac.
- Avocado—Derived from the Aztec word *ahuacati*, meaning "testicle." Aztecs considered the fruit so sexually potent, virgins were restricted from handling it.
- Cherries—According to sex shop owners, cherry is the most popular flavor of edible underwear.
- Coriander—Increases libido, especially in women.
- Garlic—Scientists claim it contains the same chemical as the hormones of a sexually aroused female.
- Graham crackers—Once believed to *reduce* arousal.
- Oysters—Rich in phosphorus, which aids in muscle contractions. Casanova ate at least twenty every day as "a spur to the spirit and to love."

The Apron

*With her pretty hair tucked into a little cap, arms bared to
the elbow, and a checked apron which had a coquettish look in
spite of the bib, the young housewife fell to work, feeling no doubts
about her success.*

—LOUISA MAY ALCOTT, *LITTLE WOMEN*

**DAY
264**

THE APRON REACHES all the way back to Adam and Eve,
who "sewed fig leaves together, and made themselves aprons"
(Gen. 3:7). Since then, bibbed smocks have been used to protect blacksmiths from sparks, butchers from gore, and sitcom
housewives from cookie dough. Though 1950s homemakers
wore them as a mark of pride, vintage and designer aprons are
so sexy-chic today they make even sports-besotted lunkheads
turn off the TV and whistle.

You Made from vampy animal prints, red satin, and black
Ultrasuede, aprons are a "now" fashion accessory. Plus, the
pockets are handy for carrying lipstick, spanking tools, and
Astroglide. Earn big points with your fella by giving *him* one
of the new manly aprons, designed to make him feel like "King
of the Barbecue."

You Two Serve dinner clad only in a bibbed, pink gingham
apron and high heels. No further inducements are necessary,
but you *could*: 1) lean your breast into his mouth so he'll lick
you through the thin fabric; 2) turn around to give him the
backside view, then sit with your bare bum in the curve of his
crotch; 3) use the apron to blindfold him, then feed him by
hand.

Plastic Wrap

Nudity is who people are at the most interesting point of the evening, when they take off their protective layer, when no one is watching.

—BRIDGET FONDA

MOSTLY, WE WANT to bare ourselves to a lover, to press against his flesh and penetrate his soul. But a little insulation can make things interesting. It can beguile. Protect. Make body heat even hotter. In 1913, when a Swiss textile engineer invented cellophane to shield his tablecloths from wine spills, did he imagine that plastic—made into sheer nylons, eye-riveting Lycra, kinky PVC, and even kitchen wrap—would also become sexy?

You If you want oral sex during your period but have a squeamish lover, cover your vulva with a large square of cellophane. While remaining tidy, both of you can still see and feel everything. Okay, not *everything*, but close enough.

You Two In *302 Advanced Techniques for Driving a Man Wild in Bed*, I suggested giving your man a tin foil hum job. But plastic wrap is way better—it eliminates the sharp edges and holds in more heat. Apply water-based lube to his testicles and wrap them with cellophane. Then put your lips around the whole package and hum. The hot, kinky, buzzing sensation is absolutely outrageous.

A Day Off

Simmer apple cider, cloves, and cinnamon on the stove. Not only does this brew create a lush, homey environment, but also all three ingredients are considered natural aphrodisiacs.

Later on, to make cider even sexier, add rum, cinnamon, and allspice.

Secret Moan Zones

Ears

How silver-sweet sound lovers' tongues by night,
Like softest music to attending ears!

—WILLIAM SHAKESPEARE

CHINESE ACUPUNCTURISTS SAY that all meridians meet in the ear—which means you can affect almost any part of the body by touching someone there. And Western medicine tells us that gentle pressure on the ear floods the body with endorphins, the feel-good brain chemicals. No wonder a "sweet nothing" whispered in the ear not only sounds good but also *feels* so yummy!

DAY
267

You Try easing a headache by massaging your ear lobe. Find the sorest point there and press it firmly between thumb and index finger. For a sore throat, squeeze all around the outer rim of your ear. To amp up sexy feelings, pinch the upper part of the rim that's actually attached to your head—the root.

You Two During a kiss, massage both his ears. Grasp the rims firmly and tweak with a scissoring motion. Then fondle the "seat of his desire"—where the rim starts at the inside top of the ear. Finish off by sliding your lips along his jaw line to take the earlobe (which swells and becomes sensitive during arousal) between your teeth. Pull until it releases from your mouth. He'll be putty in your hands.

The Humble Knee

He went down on his knee before her, on the poor mean stairs,
and put an end of her shawl to his lips.

—CHARLES DICKENS, *HARD TIMES*

FOR A GUY, knees have special meaning. A knight got down on one knee to surrender to or receive honors from a king. A man might bend his knee to pray, giving himself over to something greater. Or he might propose marriage on bended knee, committing himself to the relationship. With the flex of a knee, he finds the very best in himself and offers it to service or spirit or love. It's the place on his body that has a lot of "give."

You Knee massage is very comforting. Stroking your own knees can remind you of times you felt safe and loved, sitting on a parent's knee. Rubbing your man's knee can put him in touch with a sense of commitment, honor, and trust. It can help you both be flexible and willing to give up unnecessary defenses. The knee, it seems, is very close to the heart.

You Two And then there's the *back* of the knee, with skin so thin you can feel a pulse and nerves so near the surface they tickle. Run your tongue along the crease, then blow on that skin. As the moisture evaporates, he'll feel first hot, then cold. And the intimacy of feeling your breath in such a vulnerable place will make him melt into you.

The He-Spot

There are mysteries, secret zones in each individual.

—KRZYSZTOF KIESLOWSKI

DID YOU KNOW that a man's prostate comes from the same embryonic tissue as a woman's G-spot? Hidden deep inside, they both produce milky fluids that seep out during orgasm, and they both cause tremors that feel like they come from the center of the earth. The ancient Tantrics made an art of male G-spot play, but it regained popularity in the late 1800s when a steel massager came on the market that wives could use to pleasure their man's "innermost being."

You Does your man batter into you like a pile driver? The vibrations of thrusting are carried to a guy's prostate, which nestles inside right below his penis. Those pulsations feel really, really good to the small gland, all swollen and ready to spasm with orgasm. He's not trying to pound you into submission, he's just going crazy with pleasure. So don't throw him out of bed yet. Use this information to your advantage. See the following.

You Two Besides the part the prostate plays in orgasm, it's also the emotional nerve center of a man's sexuality. Yet this erogenous zone supreme rarely gets any attention. In missionary, you can easily reach between his legs and press the area between testicles and anus. Use your knuckle or the ball of your thumb to move in circles, and when he's near the brink, pulse inward about once per second. His earth will definitely move.

DAY
269

Locating His Secret Spots

YOU'VE GOT HIS main erogenous zones well covered, but every guy has private hot spots. Explore with fingertips and tongue to find—and awaken—the unexpected places that make your man moan. For starters, try these.

Pulse Points—where skin is thin and throbbing

- temples
- side of neck
- inside of elbows
- inside of arm, just below armpit
- groin crease
- back of knees
- inside of ankle

"Lay" Lines—analogous to the ridge of the penis

- from chin to collarbone
- down sternum, between pecs
- from navel to penis
- inner thigh from knee to groin
- spine

Untouched Territories— protected/neglected areas where touch feels new

- scalp and ears
- nape
- underarm
- area covered by pubic hair
- perineum/prostate
- lower inside quadrant of buttocks
- butt crease
- between toes and fingers
- palm
- arch of foot

The Sensitive Inner Thigh

No matter what any newspaper says about me, I am one of the most sensitive human beings on earth.

—JEAN-CLAUDE VAN DAMME

EVEN A MACHO man can be very sensitive about his inner thighs. For one thing, the thighs help protect his family jewels, so it's sacred territory. For another, skin is thin there, and someone could catch him off guard by tickling him silly. And, according to the Tao, the inner thigh contains all the meridians that bring life energy to his penis. For him, the situation could not get more serious — or more loaded with erotic possibilities.

You Of course, we women can be obsessed with our inner thighs too. But did you know that developing strong thigh muscles does more than help you look good in a bikini? When you contract your hip adductors during sex, you bring heat and blood to your vulva and increase friction on your clitoris, even making it stand out a little more. Who knew you could have better sex through leg lifts!

You Two Imagine a runway going from his knee to his perineum — the actual path of his genital meridians and an area rich with nerves. Travel it with your lips, starting with a grazing kiss at the knee, then pressing harder and nibbling as you go. Tease him by working up his leg slowly without touching his penis. Repeat on the other leg. And don't come in for the real landing till he actually shivers with sensitive anticipation.

The Scalp

Forget not that the earth delights to feel your bare feet and the winds long to play with your hair.

— KAHLIL GIBRAN

PRACTITIONERS OF AYURVEDIC medicine have been running their fingers through clients' hair for over a thousand years. Originally, Indian women developed the techniques of scalp massage to make their hair strong and lustrous, but barbers quickly adapted them to stop men from losing hair and to stimulate their brains. Noticing that a good head massage also released endorphins and lulled the body into bliss, lovers soon made the skill an important part of long, artful foreplay.

You Massaging your head when you shampoo can strengthen hair and relieve stress and headaches. But rub your scalp with essential oil when it's dry, and you've added a beautifying therapy. Ayurvedics say that almond oil aids split ends and tangles, coconut oil helps stop premature graying, and olive oil keeps pores open so natural hair oils can circulate.

You Two With his head in your lap, use your fingertips to make tight circles on his scalp, beginning at the hairline and moving toward his crown and nape. Press firmly enough to slide skin over skull. Cup his head, and make circles with your thumb from the base of his cranium out to his ears. Repeat everything. When he's reached nirvana, slide your hands down his face, chest, and belly to move the lush energy to his genitals.

A Day Off

Slowly go over your body with feathery fingertips to discover new erotic territory of your own. Don't forget places like the valleys on the back of your hand or the inside of your cheek. Where does this light touch make you feel like sighing? A sex goddess is a woman who knows the secrets of her own body—and then reveals them to her lover.

Trees

Alder — Tree of Resurrection

She hoped he would be asleep that she might arouse him with her caresses.

— KATE CHOPIN

LIKE A WOMAN, the wood of an alder burns slow but hot. So hot that medieval warriors used alder fires to forge their swords — believing they imbued the shaft with magical staying power. Because heat wafts up from its core, alder wood is used to make charcoal and even gunpowder. It was this feminine power to make things flame and rise — seeming miraculous to men — that inspired Homer to name alder the Tree of Resurrection.

You Alder burns slowly because it's very close-grained, so fire takes a while to burn through each layer. If, like the alder, you gather your feminine power and hold it closely to your heart, it becomes more intense and layered. It simmers.

You Two Use your female fire to resurrect him. Make sure he orgasms with you on top, then raise yourself to a kneeling position. Guide his hands to your nipples. Hold the base of his penis in place as you lift up so only the tip remains inside. With one hand, massage his shaft. With the other, pet his belly and thighs. Occasionally, tighten your PCs and think of your inner heat. Soon, the dead will rise again.

Baobab — The Hole-y Tree

A woman who cannot be ugly is not beautiful.

— KARL KRAUS

BECAUSE THEY'RE HUGE and gnarly, some call the baobab trees of Africa grotesque. But their dented branches hold big pools of water, allowing the trees to outlive everything on the dry savannah — often surviving for more than 2,000 years. And their massive, gaping trunks have served as lairs for cheetahs, cozy settings for pubs, and lodges for fertility rites. It's the potholes that make a baobab exuberant and beautiful.

You Hollows are where the body is most tender. There, skin is thin and unprotected by hair or bone — "imperfections" that make you want to touch. For that melting feeling (on him or you), caress the dip between collarbones, the crevice between tendon and bone under the wrist, the indentations around the ankle, or the crease above the lip.

You Two The most sensitive spot on his body is the frenulum — the small, wrinkled hollow on the underside of the penis, where there's a break in the rim of his glans (the head of his penis). Rub your thumbs there, alternating gently — or tap with the nubby *underside* of your tongue. Increase pressure until he skyrockets to orgasm.

Ponderosa Pine—
It Knows How to Wow

Everything has its beauty, but not everyone sees it.

—CONFUCIUS

WHEN IT COMES to sexy, you might not think of a pine tree. But a ponderosa stands tall and mighty, like the best of erections. Its long needles are soft, feathery, even tasty, while its umber trunk has the cozy roughness of a three-day beard. When the wind blows, its branches sigh like a lover. And its bark even gives off the delicious scent of vanilla. The ponderosa is a tree, but because it gives you something for all the senses, it's got the kind of charisma we all "pine" for.

You As far back as ancient Assyria, pinecones were used in ornamental art to symbolize testes, especially when paired with the feminine lotus. But most pinecones, *true* pinecones, are ovaries. So . . . a guy's "cones" may be more obvious, but it doesn't mean he's the one with the balls.

You Two Glide your tongue down the crease that separates his two testicles—a not-so-obvious but very hot spot. Give him a great view by sitting on his chest, facing his feet and leaning forward. Meanwhile, you can press against him for clitoral pleasure.

What Trees Say about You

THE CELTS HAD an alphabet of trees, each symbol representing a similarity between Nature and personality. So, the tree that appeals to you is one that can reveal your hidden self:

- Oak — If you love oaks, you probably have their strength and largess. You might even be a crusader. Nurture your soul by creating a nest for lazy, eternal afternoons in bed.
- Birch — Birches stand tall and white with few branches. Like them, you love elegance and simplicity. Explore your wild sexual imagination, as multilayered as birch bark.
- Ash — Ash wood makes strong baseball bats but flexible archery bows. You too are steadfast but like to tempt fate. Try crazy positions and kinky scenarios. Inside, you'll remain solid and secure.
- Fir — Like the forest primeval, you are a mysterious woman of moods. In your mossy depths, you harbor many forms of life. Your best sex has variety, drama, and earthiness.
- Willow — Graceful willow branches bend with the wind. You too are sensitive and intuitive. Feathery touches and dreamy fantasies will turn your lovemaking into magic.
- Cedar — Like the cedar, you are an old soul. You know how to wait beautifully. Take your time in love. Let him anticipate, wonder, crave. You hold eternity.

Hawthorn—The May Tree

It was the month of May. . . . When lovers, subject to the same force which reawakens the plants, feel their hearts open again . . . and yearn for a renewal of the magical awareness which is love.

—SIR THOMAS MALORY

FOR THE ANCIENT Celts, May 1 was a time to celebrate. Flowers and love were back in bloom. On Mayday morning, they rose early and bathed in the dew of hawthorn blossoms to bring luck and beauty. Then they adorned the maypole (representing the male) with a wreath of hawthorn blossoms (the encircling female) and danced around it, finally pairing off for some lusty loving in the woods. Yay, spring!

You Young Celtic women could hardly wait for the hawthorn tree to bloom. Finally, they could bring home a sprig as a charm to attract the perfect husband. Just having the fragrant, lacy blossoms around makes a girl feel beautiful and ripe. Could be *that's* what attracted those sexy Irish men.

You Two In lieu of flowers around the base of his "maypole," use a knotted stocking. Tie it just tight enough to cause some pressure, just as you did with the scrunchy on Day 212. But this time, climb on top and let the three or four clumps rub against your most sensitive spots—and his—with your every thrust.

Aspen — The Quaking Tree

And the wind, full of wantonness, wooes like a lover
The young aspen-trees till they tremble all over.

— THOMAS MOORE, "LALLA ROOKH," FROM *THE LIGHT OF THE HAREM*

EVEN IN THE barest breeze, aspen trees quiver and rustle like an eager lover between the sheets. They can do this because their sleek leaves, curved into a near round, are attached to long, flat stems that twist and turn — producing the music of a babbling brook. If your man's stem knew how to twist and flutter inside your curves, wouldn't you quiver, maybe even babble, too?

You During intense sex, if you are able to keep moving but relax and feel a sense of stillness, you'll give your sensations a new outlet. Instead of dissipating in the air, your heat and excitement will stream through your legs, arms, and spine, as if your body is dancing from within.

You Two For your next sex-capade, sit atop the washer or dryer while it's running. He stands in front, maybe on a phone book or footstool to make him the right height. Both the machine — and your sex — will have kink, hum, and quiver.

A Day Off

Trees are always making sap, seeds, and often flowers — the tools of their sexuality. Yet they do it with incredible stillness.

Rest under a tree and learn about the sensual, still place within you.

You've Got Rhythm

Full-Length Love

His finest hour lasted a minute and a half.

—PHYLLIS DILLER

BY THE TIME you get in the groove, is he already finished, rolled over, and snoring? The sexy men from Brazil hold the record for longest roll in the sack, with an average of thirty minutes. And American guys follow closely behind at twenty-eight minutes—I guess they leave time for commercials. Quickies are fun, and sitcom-length sex can feed a need, but what about when you want a luxurious, three-bags-of-popcorn, epic-length love movie?

You There's always the do-it-yourself option. One way to make even *that* last longer is to use a scalp massager (it straps on and pulses your whole hand) or apply your wand vibrator to the back of your hand. Then insert one throbbing finger in your vagina and hold it there. Suffused vibrations travel through your entire pelvis for as many hours as you can stand it.

You Two The squeeze technique will do the trick, but guys often respond better to action. Let him thrust up a storm, but then slow your hips to about half-full speed for the length of sixty heartbeats. Resume the fast pace, then throttle down to a quarter speed for about thirty heartbeats. Alternate repeatedly. This releases his accelerating pressure but keeps his engine hot enough for a full-length marathon.

Stillness

Learning how to be still, to really be still and let life happen — that stillness becomes a radiance.

— MORGAN FREEMAN

IRONICALLY, THE WAY to put more zing in your life is to become more still. When you take a few moments to stop and breathe, you see deeper colors, feel softer touches, and think clearer thoughts. Now you can see the solution to a vexing problem and hear the love in a friend's voice. In the stillness, you feel waves of life energy move through your body — invigorating you and turning into whole-body orgasm when you make love.

You New Age dance guru Gabrielle Roth says the best way to still the mind is to move the body. It keeps you from being bored as your mind empties. As you walk around your office or home, be aware of how your feet feel as they roll from heel to toe. Let a smile start in your eyes, then spread to your mouth, shoulders, pelvis, and knees. Your body will come alive with inner stillness — and radiate.

You Two With that same, still awareness, lie on the bed with your feet on the floor. Invite him to position himself between your legs, then wrap them round his waist. He should lift your thighs high and tight against him, tilting your body so it rests only on your shoulders. Keep still as a pond while he thrusts. It makes for more pressure on your G-spot and his penis tip, while creating an unbeatable view.

Delayed Rhythm

She knew how to allure by denying, and to make the gift rich by delaying it.

—ANTHONY TROLLOPE

WHEN IT COMES to food and money, delayed gratification isn't fun. But in music, a delayed rhythm makes a song poignant. When the beat of a tune is interrupted by an extra long note (usually just before the finale), it makes you stop and pay attention. You hang on the edge of a tonal cliff, savoring the suspended sweetness and hungering for resolution. When the last few bars finally arrive, the expected sound is so much yummier.

You Delaying an orgasm makes the sensations sweeter and more intense. But guys usually don't get the concept. They're on a speeding train that wants to pull into the station. *You* are the one who has to postpone arrival. The secret is switching tracks—taking another direction with a different kind of treat. Read on.

You Two When the rhythm of thrusting gets a little tiresome, but you're still really hot, nudge him off. Quickly put your nipple in his mouth and his hand on your vulva, guiding him to give you multiples. While his peak is postponed, he gets to suck on his favorite candy and relish the power of making you come. Then hop on top and bring him to what will now be an even more intense climax. Clever girl.

Sexy Playlist

RHYTHMS MOVE YOUR body and evoke moods. Design a playlist that sets the tempo for romantic cuddling, slow steamy sex, or hot nookie. Here are some ideas to mix and match.

Romantic Rhythms
Rachmaninoff — *Rhapsody on a Theme of Paganini*
Boyz II Men — *I'll Make Love to You*
Delibes — *Flower Duet* (from *Lakmé*)
Etta James — *Sunday Kind of Love*
Van Morrison — *I'll Be Your Lover, Too*
Chris Isaak — *Wicked Game*

Sexy Tempo Changers
Ravel — *Bolero*
Bizet — *Overture to Carmen*
Orff — *Fortune plango vulnera*, then *Dulcissime* (from *Carmina Burana*)

Slow and Steamy
Marvin Gaye — *Sexual Healing* or *Let's Get It On*
Prince — *Pink Cashmere*
Miles Davis — *Moon Dreams*
Peggy Lee — *Fever*
Jimi Hendrix — *Foxy Lady*
Barry White — *Can't Get Enough of Your Love, Babe*
Herbie Mann — *Summertime*

Fast and Hot
Rolling Stones — *Let It Loose*
Miles Davis — *Honky Tonk*
Bruce Springsteen — *I'm on Fire*
Nelly Furtado — *Maneater*
Santana — *Migra*

The Tempo of a Kiss

Give me one of your most savory kisses
Give me one of your most passionate kisses:
I will return four that are hotter than fire . . .
And mixing our happiest kisses
we'll enjoy one and then the other at our leisure.

—LOUISE LABÉ (TRANS. THE AUTHOR)

THE BEST KISSES have rhythm—a shared symphony of slow and swift, silky and rough, probing and retreating. They crescendo to passionate peaks, then fall into pauses of empty eternity. They alternate between wet and dry, laughter and tears. When a kiss is performed just right, it brings the pulse of your heartbeat into his lips—and the throb of his wanting into your soul.

You A study at the University of Albany revealed that men prefer a greater proportion of wet to dry in their kisses—probably because saliva exchange provides clues about fertility and allows him to pass on stimulating testosterone. So if his kissing rhythm has more slobber than elegance, he's probably just trying to get to know you—and well, yes, turn you on.

You Two Heat up a kiss by cycling. Alternate putting your tongue in his mouth with sucking his lower lip. According to the *Kama Sutra*, a man's bottom lip is directly connected to the penis (for women, the *upper* lip is connected to the clitoris). And your in/out, push/pull, softer/sharper tempo transfers from mouth to genitals, making him throb and swell with the beat.

Breathe with Me

*Ancient lovers believed a kiss would literally unite their souls,
because the spirit was said to be carried in one's breath.*

— EVE GLICKSMAN

BREATHING IS ONE of your most natural and intimate rhythms. When you breathe slow and deep, it's as though you can feel the *insides* of your brain, arms, and vulva. If you pant, your heart beats faster and you get excited. If you breathe slowly, your heart rate decreases and you feel relaxed. Breathe in through your skin and your senses open wide. Inhale through your belly and you ignite sexual fires.

You In both Tantra and Quodoshka (a Cherokee sexual tradition), women use rhythmic breathing to control their orgasms. Slow inhalation delays a climax, and fast brings it on. And you know how your clitoris gets too tender to touch after orgasm? Panting *through* your climax cures the problem.

You Two During sex, try panting together in rhythm. Blood and heat will flow into your genitals and his. But as you near orgasm, change your breathing to slow and deep. This spreads arousal through your bodies and makes the buildup last oh so long. With your rhythmic breathing, sensation intensifies. Hearts synchronize. Worlds rock.

A Day Off

Slow the tempo of your day. Bathe instead of show-ering. Stroll to work. Don't e-mail until after lunch. Save sex for times when you're at peak energy (you'll sync with his rhythms better that way).

DAY

287

Les Femmes

Coco Chanel

A girl should be two things: classy and fabulous.

—COCO CHANEL

UNTIL THE EARLY 1900s, women's bodies were trapped beneath voluminous skirts and restricting corsets. Then came Chanel. A woman who rode horses and worked for a living, Coco invented the little black dress so a woman could go seamlessly from her new work life to parties, designed practical suits that kept their shape when the wearer raised her arm, and accessorized with ropes of faux pearls every woman could afford. At last, women could be stylish and sexy while doing *whatever the heck they wanted!*

You Chanel No. 5 is what made Coco a millionaire. Made up mostly of sandalwood, musk, jasmine, rose, and ylang-ylang, it's what she called "a woman's perfume with the scent of a woman." If you can't afford the real thing, use essential oils to put together your own combo of these age-old scents of passion and sex—the real scent of a woman.

You Two A Chanel kind of woman takes charge in the clothes department. Tonight, strip *him*. Slowly begin shirt removal, licking chest and belly as every inch is bared. Kneel to remove footwear, massaging and finally sucking his toes. Tickle his rump as you slide off trousers. Fondle and lick *through* his briefs before at last freeing his manhood. Meantime you, "classy and fabulous," wear only a rope of pearls.

Catherine Deneuve

I need uncertainty in everything.

—CATHERINE DENEUVE

FAMED FOR HER many roles as an Ice Maiden, the impossibly beautiful Deneuve seems almost frigid. Untouchable. The opposite of hot. But what makes her irresistible is the sense that the right man could crack that icy glaze. She *wants* to expose herself, to be completely in a man's hands, even if it's dangerous. What man could resist that fragile, fire-and-ice dare?

You Always a paradox, Deneuve had her children out of wedlock when it was not considered respectable. Yet, France chose her to model Marianne, the admirable Spirit of the Revolution, whose face adorns stamps and statues. Like Deneuve, you might find it useful—and fascinating—to reveal the "madonna" *and* the "whore" we all have within.

You Two Trail an ice cube along the back of his neck, across his nipples and inner thighs, behind his knees, and across his rump. Then lick the frosty nerve endings with your hot tongue. But don't let him touch you till all the ice is melted. He'll love your incarnation as a come-hither Ice Queen.

Madame de Pompadour

So impertinent a question so early in the conversation!
How promising.

—CHARACTER OF MADAME DE POMPADOUR
FROM THE 1927 FILM *MADAME POMPADOUR*

DAY
290

EDUCATED AND WITTY, Madame de Pompadour became the chief mistress of Louis XV because she made him feel she *knew* the powerful, sexy man inside—the man he longed to be. When he masqueraded as a yew tree, she became Diana, goddess of the hunt, praising him for his rugged strength. Even when they no longer shared a bed, Pompadour advised Louis on "his" brilliant political moves, retaining her influential position for nearly twenty years.

You Pompadour put on plays, studied botany, inspired a new technique of porcelain-making, and planned buildings such as the Place de la Concorde—filling Louis's life with beauty and verve. When you are adept at the art of living, like Pompadour, you become an irreplaceable treasure.

You Two The Pompadours, a British army unit, lined their uniforms with purple, in honor of the great courtesan's lilac underthings. Oddly, men seem to make icons of women's undies—especially if they're an ensemble. Simply wear a *matching* bra and panties to bed and he'll not only attack you, he may also idolize you.

How to Develop Je Ne Sais Quoi

FRENCH WOMEN HAVE it in spades — that certain something that makes a woman seem extra feminine, extra mysterious, extra sexy. Here's what they learn at their mothers' knees:

- Focus on who *you* are, not who *he* is or who he wants you to be. *Femme fatales* sway to the beat of their own drum.
- Wear lacy camisoles that show. Under a suit. Partnered with a little sweater and jeans. Juxtaposed with suede boots.
- Develop a unique, personal style. Wear your grandmother's cameo. Cook with vodka instead of sherry. Use pale blue stationery to send notes.
- Never leave the house — or give oral sex — without wearing lipstick.
- Choose feminine over sporty — heels over sneakers, loose curls over functional ponytails, sashaying over striding.
- Invite a man to caress your hair by decorating it first yourself. With wisps and curls, tortoiseshell pins, scarves, flowers, and soft cloches.
- Use your eyes to talk and your lips to kiss.

George Sand

Once my heart was captured, reason was shown the door, deliberately and with a sort of frantic joy. I accepted everything, I believed everything, without struggle, without suffering, without regret, without false shame. How can one blush for what one adores?

—GEORGE SAND

PASSIONATE AND OPINIONATED, Aurore Dupin was born in the early 1800s, when only men were allowed to write professionally. So she put on trousers and top hat, took the pen name George Sand, and published eighty novels full of sexual feelings and fervent social views. Her lovers were prominent poets and composers—Musset, Mérimée, Chopin—yet she was not beautiful. Instead, she challenged and inspired, taking her paramours on an adventure to becoming freer artists and greater men.

You George believed you should "try to keep your soul young and quivering right up to old age." How exciting it must have been to live with her, to *be* her. Do something that inspires you every day, and you'll keep that nourishing—and alluring—gift alive.

You Two Like George, take the dominant role that would usually be played by a man. Command him to stand with his hands behind his head, legs spread. He must stay that way while you caress him everywhere, play with his erection, and bring him close to the brink with your mouth. Because of his upright position and the long delay, his eventual orgasm will be earth-moving.

Juliette Binoche

Forty is really the best age for a woman. That's when we hit our peak and become this ripe fruit.

—JULIETTE BINOCHE

AT AGE FORTY-THREE, "La Binoche" appeared in her first *Playboy* spread. At forty-four, she became the new face of Lancôme. How does she do it? According to one of her film directors, her "tears and laughter are never far away," giving her a radiant, goddess-like aura. She's sexy, says Askmen.com, because she carries her 5'6" frame like she *knows* she's hot. Either way, it's what's *inside* that gives her the ageless, other-worldly beauty that still makes men swoon.

You In midlife, Juliette has embarked on a new career — directing and performing in a new dance show with a top British choreographer. Saying that "normal is very dangerous for the soul," she stays young by constantly stretching herself. Try something new every day. Okay, every other day. It makes you grow and glow.

You Two Behave like the eternal goddess you are. Get on top but face his toes and arch your back, like a proud queen. Pick up his hands and place them exactly where you want them. Rotate your hips just enough to keep him hard. He gets to watch your magnificent rump, nestle in your deepest recesses, and get off on your *très* sexy self-confidence.

A Day Off

Watch the film Amélie *(Audrey Tautou)*, Jules et Jim *(Jeanne Moreau)*, or Casque D'Or *(Simone Signoret)* to see ces femmes *at their most alluring. Just looking at them gives your attitude a sexy French accent.*

Little Things That Mean a Lot

Finger Yoga

I have occasionally had the exquisite thrill of putting my finger on a little capsule of truth.

—E. B. WHITE

HAVE YOU SEEN pictures of the Buddha touching his forefinger to his thumb? Or noticed Hindus greeting each other with palms pressed together at the heart? These hand postures are *mudras*, gestures used to guide energy flow in the body. Yogis teach that because all 4,000 nerve endings in our fingertips connect to specific organs, you can talk to your body and mind by curling and touching fingers together. This yoga of the fingers can relax, heal, and even stimulate your libido.

You To perform the Kundalini Mudra, which awakens sexual energies, rub your hands together briskly for ten seconds. Then curl the fingers of your right hand around your left forefinger, placing your right thumb atop the enclosed finger. Hold your hands close to your belly and sit quietly for about fifteen minutes. It may help you warm up for a quickie!

You Two Try inserting your forefinger alongside his penis while he's thrusting. Although it's not an official mudra, I find this little move helps to form a circuit from vagina to heart, across to his heart and penis. Besides, it provides extra ridges for him to rub against and lets you experience what your vagina feels like when it's making love.

Good Tension

The world is all gates, all opportunities, strings of tension waiting to be struck.

—RALPH WALDO EMERSON

MOST OF THE time, we think of tension as a bad thing. But tension makes a film exciting, a drum create sound, and a tennis racket generate power. When you stretch something tight, it makes more intense vibrations—like a guitar string resonating to make music or the anticipation of a tryst making your body quiver. By making skin taut, you expose the nerves to more sensation, and voilà, you've created flesh with more intense *feelings*.

You One way to bring on orgasm is to put tension into the muscles around and inside your vulva. Squeeze your anus, which tightens all the surrounding tissues. Press down, as if birthing a baby, which broadens and stretches your inner muscles. Pull the loose skin atop your pubic mound away from your clitoris, exposing more of its sensitive flesh. Simple moves. Deeper, more complex vibrations.

You Two When giving oral sex, pinch the tiny fold of skin at the bottom of his underside ridge. Then pull down to make the skin of his entire shaft taut and tingly. His naked nerves will tremble with the lightest lick, and he'll feel literally on the edge of his seat.

Pleasure Plus

Pleasure is the beginning and the end of living happily.

— EPICURUS

THE PART OF your vagina that generates the most pleasure is the opening and the first third of the inner canal. Likewise, a man is most responsive at the upper third of his penis — the glans and coronal ridge. Yet, during regular sex, his tip spends most of its time rubbing against the deeper, looser, less sensitive part of you. That's perfect when you want slower arousal and longer lovemaking. But when maximum zing at warp speed is your goal, things may need to be rearranged.

You For self-pleasure, try thrusting your vibrating dildo only partway in and out of your vagina. Then turn it to lowest speed and hold it steady, one-third of the way in, angling it onto your G-spot. Since this is your deepest well of womanly pleasure, you'll be unlocking your full potential for all kinds of happiness — orgasms, creativity, love, and outrageous female magnetism.

You Two During sex, hold the base of his shaft as he strokes in and out. This little addition keeps the sensitive glans at the tightest, most sensory-rich part of you — creating more sensation for you both. Plus, your hand provides *even more* friction for his penis and your clitoris. It's a win-win-*win* situation.

Mirroring

HAVE YOU NOTICED that when someone smiles, your mouth automatically smiles back? Or that being around a friend who's nervous makes you act jumpy too? That's because your mirror neurons have been activated. Special nerves that reflect back and mimic the actions of those you're close to, mirror neurons are designed to help you connect in an intimate way. They even allow you to read other people's intentions and emotions, to feel their joy or doubt or desire. Without consciously thinking about it, your body then mimics those emotions or actions. Now, you're both on the same wavelength.

You can create that feeling of rapport — or perhaps get him to kiss the way you want — by mirroring intentionally. Like dancing, first you follow his lead. *But then you take over*:

- Maybe he approaches you with tilted head. You tilt yours. He may put his hand on your arm. You do the same. His toes turn out? So should yours. You're getting in sync.
- But now you take the lead. Look at his lips; he'll look at yours. Open your mouth for a deep kiss. So will he. Pause for a moment of pre-smooch rapture and, without knowing why, he will too.
- He begins to sense your rhythm, even your feelings. They seem like his own. It appears that, miraculously, you know what he wants to do before he does. It's like the perfect mind-reading tease.
- Kissing synchronization has been achieved.

All Thumbs

The fingers must be educated, the thumb is born knowing.

—MARC CHAGALL

YOU CAN TELL so much about a man by his thumbs. In palmistry, the length of a thumb tells you if a guy is governed more by logic or willpower. Its width reveals how aggressive he is. Its shape, how much he tends toward the uncouth or the poetic. And the way it angles off his hand shows if he's gentle and romantic or more interested in other women. Do these indicators sound like they apply to any other male organ?

You A guy uses his thumb to control things—TV remotes, beer pop-tops, car wax. Ask him to insert his first two fingers in your vagina and rest his thumb on your clitoris. He will naturally start to manipulate your flesh by rubbing fingers and thumb together—which angles his fingers onto your G-spot and smooshes your clitoris into the mix. This kind of "control" works out well for both of you.

You Two When things have warmed up nicely in doggie position, have him rest his weight on his elbows so you can pick up his hand and suck his thumb. This small gesture brings in new tactile territory and connects the thumb, the root of his personality, with the penis, root of his manhood—giving him a double whammy of ego and sexual stroking.

His Lower Locks

Those curious locks so aptly twin'd,
Whose every hair a soul doth bind.

—THOMAS CAREW

IF YOU'VE EVER had a pubic hair caught in your teeth, you've probably wondered why he needs them. Since they don't start growing until the androgens of puberty kick in, pubic hairs are a visual signal of sexual maturity. They're nature's way of saying, "*Now* you can come and get it!" Pubes also reduce friction during sex and release the pheromones that attract us. But most important for lovers to know, those locks transmit and magnify sensation.

You Some ways to avoid the hair-in-teeth problem might be: 1) Shave him. See Day 204 for a sexy session. 2) Smooth him down with a warm, wet washcloth first. Oh so sensual. 3) Hold the base with one hand to give your lips elevation from the surface. 4) Flatten your hands on both sides of his erection, which also increases his sensation.

You Two When you're on top, reach back and grab a little tuft of pubes. Tug in rhythm with your strokes. You're stimulating the base of the hair follicle, much deeper beneath the skin than you could normally get. Besides, when fully aroused, he hungers for more savage sensations.

A Day Off

Make a list of twenty things starting with "c" (or any letter) that give you pleasure. It might include; chocolate, camellias, Clooney (George), caresses, cashmere, Chopin études, convertibles, cuddling, clandestine meetings, curry, Casablanca, etc.

With one letter, you rediscover many yummy things.

Fun with Furniture

The Gallant Armchair

A house that does not have one warm, comfy chair in it is soulless.

— MAY SARTON

BECAUSE OF ITS comfort and support, the armchair was once reserved for royalty. The rest of us sat on hard stools or dirt floors. Today, an overstuffed chair is the perfect nesting companion for every sensual woman. Offering itself as a spooning partner for long lazy afternoons, a cozy chair is inviting, tasteful, and comfortably protective—even when your hair is in curlers. If it could take you to Paris for the weekend, your easy chair would be the perfect date.

You Want more kisses down there? Your armchair can help. Sit on the back of the chair, legs dangling behind it and spread wide. Raising your legs for balance, lean back till your shoulders rest on the chair seat. No man can resist such a brazen and beautiful invitation. Meanwhile, your slight dizziness doubles your pleasure.

You Two This one's for him because, basically, you'll be pretty helpless. Stand in front of a soft armchair, facing the chair, elbows propped on the chair back. Then mount the chair arms with your knees. You provide a wide open, freely accessible target at the *perfect* height for his deep-sunk, hard thrusts. Did I mention *you'll* be having a great time?

The Uplifting Footstool

Only passions, great passions can elevate the soul to great things.

—DENIS DIDEROT

IN ANCIENT TIMES, a footstool often elevated a person to greatness. Egyptian pharaohs mounted their loftier-than-thou thrones via golden hassocks. In Mesopotamia, priestesses stood atop footstools, naked, to make royal decrees—showing that the law came from a higher place. If we climbed atop an ottoman in the buff to ask our men to kiss us where it counts, might we elevate them to greater passion or greater performance?

You You can help prevent tension headaches by propping your feet on an ottoman (for better blood flow), but it's even more uplifting to get your vibrator involved. By squatting on the *edge* of a low footstool, you tilt your pelvis down and spread your labia wider, so sensations are increased. And the space below leaves plenty of room for the ups and downs of a dildo.

You Two Try the Elevated, Reverse Power Missionary. Have him lie on his back, butt propped on a low, cushioned footstool, legs in the air as if to do bicycle exercises. Keeping your legs outside of his, push his thighs toward his chest, sit on his rump, and insert. Now you can bounce with as much force as you both can stand. Penetration is canyon-deep, and because blood flows *away* from his pelvis, he gets prickly, "light-headed" sensations in his penis. Most uplifting.

The Dance of the Hanging Chair

To swing or not to swing? Swing.

—BRENDAN FRASER, SPEAKING AS GEORGE
IN *GEORGE OF THE JUNGLE*

DAY 304

KALYANA MALLA, A twelfth-century Indian poet, believed that sexual imagination helped couples stay close and loyal. So in the *Ananga Ranga*, he offered scores of positions designed to absolutely amaze. Trouble was, you had to be limber as a yogi and stronger than Atlas to pull them off. The answer? A concoction of ropes, pulleys, and cloth that made swinging from the raja's chandeliers easy. It was the first love swing.

You A simple hanging chair, available from most hammock vendors, can rock you to sleep or to solo nirvana. The gentle downswing produces lovely pressure in the pelvis, and if you insert ben wa balls, every swoop will feel like a jiggly inner skydive.

You Two Sit in a love swing and spread your legs brazenly around the upper supports. He stands in front of you, hard as a steel beam, and swings you weightlessly on and off his erection. For him, it's about the stunning visuals, the blood-rush to his penis, and the feel of absolute power. For you, it's G-spot heaven. And because it's effortless, this delirium can go on for hours—feeling something like sex on ball bearings.

A Day at the Office

ALL WORK AND no sex makes Clive a dull boy. Visit his office, or invite him to yours, and save him from a life without luster. The furnishings are perfect:

- Desk — The perfect height for you to sit on, and for him to stand and insert. If convenient, hang your rump off the edge and brace your feet on a nearby wall or filing cabinet. Allows you to rock your pelvis all over the place.
- Coat rack — Grab on, straddle it, and rub your pelvis against it as you squat up and down. A pole dance that arouses both of you. Then use the rack for support as he sneaks in from behind.
- Swivel chair — Sit in it while he kneels before you. With tongue between your legs and hands on the chair arms, he can move the whole shebang side to side. A swimmy sensation for you; less work and a lot of play for him.
- Window frame — Using it for support, do the stand-up doggie while enjoying the view from the forty-third floor. If you stay clothed, no one out there will have a clue.
- Copy machine — Afterward, photocopy a body part or a kiss and leave it behind as a keepsake.

The Naughty Chaise

Marriage is the deep, deep peace of the double bed after the hurly-burly of the chaise lounge.

—MRS. PATRICK CAMPBELL

HOOTCHY-KOOTCHY ON THE chaise actually began 5,000 years ago in the ziggurats of Babylon. At the top of these pyramidal structures sat an ornate golden daybed where a priestess lay, awaiting the touch of a god. At 650 feet in the air, it's hard to know who actually arrived, but these wild nights seemed to result in the birth of many unexpected, "holy" children.

You Billboards for the 1978 movie *Sextette* showed Mae West reclining on a chaise with the caption "Mae West Is Coming." Lie on a chaise and you instantly feel decadent—like a movie star with nothing to do but eat chocolate and seduce men. A chaise can provide you with moxie, lush reverie, or a place to have out-of-your-mind motel sex.

You Two A chaise is a bed you can *straddle*. 1) Sit on top of him, rest your feet on the floor for bounce-ability, and ride him hard. If you need high heels to reach the floor, all the better. 2) Get into missionary position but have him drop his feet to the floor on both sides of the chaise. With freed hands, he can grab your rump and toss you at will. A very forceful and free-flowing experience.

The Halcyon Rocking Chair

Worry is like a rocking chair: It gives you something to do, but it doesn't get you anywhere.

— ERMA BOMBECK

EVEN BEFORE BIRTH, we were rocking—the sway of our mothers' wombs making us feel blissfully safe and at one with our private universe. No wonder a cradle or rocking horse could instantly change us from irascible tots into zoned-out Buddhas. So why did we wait till the 1700s to invent the rocking chair? Is "getting somewhere" more important than feeling serenely, sensually at home?

You Studies show rocking chairs actually reduce stress and lower blood pressure. Because they keep posterior muscles contracting and relaxing, they also ease back pain (with his bad back, President Kennedy ran the country from a prescription rocker in the Oval Office). But savvy women know too that rocking with a lover promotes feelings of primal oneness. A useful tool for the skittish fiancé.

You Two A rocking chair can really move you. 1) Kneel in front of a rocker, forearms resting on the chair seat. He stands behind you, grabs your thighs, and lifts you onto his erection. As he thrusts, the chair rocks your entire body up and down his pelvis. 2) He sits in the chair. You get on top and rock. Feels like love on a train.

A Day Off

Lounge in a hammock.

For extra luxury, add a cashmere throw, Cathleen Schine's The Love Letter, *a glass of port, and a bonbon.*

DAY
308

Gems

Diamond

This diamond has so many carats it's almost a turnip.

—RICHARD BURTON

FOR ELIZABETH TAYLOR'S fortieth birthday, Richard Burton gave her a 69.4-carat pear-shaped diamond. The gem (approximately 1½ inches long) might have looked ostentatious on some. But on Taylor, who was, at the time, flabbergasting the world with an übersexy Cleopatra, it seemed natural. After they divorced, Liz sold the jewel for $5 million and funded a hospital in Botswana—a woman who knew her own value, flaunted it, and used it to make the world a better place.

DAY

309

You Unlike other carbons, a diamond uses *all* its bonding electrons to link with neighboring atoms. These pair bonds are what give the gem unsurpassable hardness and fire. Could it be that we too gain strength and brilliance by connecting deeply with—and even depending on—others?

You Two Diamond molecules refract light because they're shaped like pyramids. Try making a three-cornered pyramid on your man. While licking his erection, rub both his feet; or kiss his mouth while tweaking both his nipples. As with diamonds, the three points create a chemical connection that will make any guy see stars.

Ruby

She took him to her ruby palace and used all her magic powers to make him as strong and good and lovely as any woman could wish.

—FRANK L. BAUM, *THE WONDERFUL WIZARD OF OZ*

DAY

310

BECAUSE OF THE ruby's rich red color, Oriental legends say it contains a "deep drop of the heart's blood of Mother Earth." Maybe that's why the gem symbolizes devotion and generosity—but also the kind of red-hot passion that upends people's lives. When Prince Andrew gave Fergie a ruby engagement ring, did he know he was playing with such wild fire?

You Until about 1800, red stones like garnet and spinel were called rubies—allowing them to fetch the gem's handsome price. In Arabia, these stones were identified by putting them to a flame. The lesser rocks burned, but the rubies became even more lustrous. Likewise a man, subjected to the heat of your passion, will either crumple or become a better man. That's how you'll know if he's the real thing.

You Two The sight of a woman's nipples will heat up a man's desire. But when made to look like rubies, your little gems will put fire in his veins. Rouge them. They'll seem ripe, love-bitten, hot. Then see how he becomes "strong and good and lovely as any woman could wish."

Emerald

These gems have life in them: their colors speak, say what words fail of.

— GEORGE ELIOT

DID YOU KNOW that, carat for carat, emeralds are the most expensive gems in the world? First discovered in Cleopatra's Mines, they were the foundation for ancient Egypt's vast wealth. Why? Well, they're rarer than diamonds, but long ago the green jewels' real value came from their desperately coveted ability to heighten a woman's sexual desire.

You Clear emeralds are extremely rare, but it's the inclusions found in most that make them startlingly beautiful. These flaws, which reflect and deepen light, are actually growth tubes. As with emeralds, it's a woman's crow's-feet and laugh lines—marks of her struggles, triumphs, and hard-earned wisdom—that make her truly incandescent.

You Two The gift of an emerald may heighten desire, but here's something even better. When he's on top, have him skooch higher so his pubic bone presses on your clitoris. Wrap your legs around him and pull his torso down to yours. Locked together, you rock up and down, instead of thrusting in and out. With insistent pressure and body weight, placed right where it counts, you both get more power per square inch. In fact, 60 percent of women who've tried it felt much hornier, and 90 percent had more intense orgasms.

Gems for Life

FOR THOUSANDS OF years, people have associated gems with moods, qualities, and cycles—the passion of a ruby, the mystical aura of an amethyst, the eternity of a diamond. Wearing the right jewel for a job interview or love tryst might give you the extra confidence or sexy swagger that makes all the difference.

Stone	Garnet	Amethyst	Aquamarine
Birthstone Month	January	February	March
Anniversary Year	2nd	6th, 9th	19th
Numerology	2—Diplomacy/ patience	7—Introspection/ analysis	5—Enthusiasm/ sensuality
Love	Deep love; ensure meeting again	Gentle, spiritual love	Unconditional love
Stone	Diamond	Emerald	Pearl
Birthstone Month	April	May	June
Anniversary Year	10th, 60th	20th, 35th	1st, 3rd
Numerology	6—Responsibility/ wisdom	4—Practicality/ loyalty	2—Diplomacy/ patience
Love	Marriage/eternal love	Contentment; harmony	Purity/marital bliss
Stone	Ruby	Peridot	Sapphire
Birthstone Month	July	August	September
Anniversary Year	15th, 40th	1st, 16th	5th, 7th
Numerology	1—Leadership/ self-reliance	5—Enthusiasm/ sensuality	6—Responsibility/ wisdom
Love	Passion	Attraction; drives away troubles	Devotion/loyalty
Stone	Opal	Topaz	Turquoise
Birthstone Month	October	November	December
Anniversary Year	14th	4th	11th
Numerology	9—Compassion/ artistry	3—Optimism/ imagination	6—Responsibility/ wisdom
Love	Faithfulness	Forgiveness	Friendship

Sapphire

Kissing your hand may make you feel very very good but a diamond and sapphire bracelet lasts forever.

—ANITA LOOS

THE BLUE SAPPHIRE, like the deep sea or sky, seems to contain the mystery and eternity of the universe. The ancient Persians believed the Earth rested on a giant sapphire, and its reflection colored the heavens. For the Buddhists, the stone meant eternal loyalty. And questing knights carried sapphires to help them find that which was elusive—truth, faith, and steadfast love.

You Perhaps because of its bottomless blue, the sapphire (even a much less pricey, lab-grown gem) seems to bring serenity and peace of mind. Try looking into one when you feel tense, when you need a little help meditating, or when you want to recapture lost hope or childhood joy.

You Two This may sound weird, but how can you knock something so simple and effective? In the middle of a kiss, softly suck some air out his mouth. Very slowly. Like the sapphire, this little move has depth and fire, yet it seems somehow innocent and eternal—as if you're inhaling his soul right into you.

DAY

313

Amber

Here we are . . . trapped in the amber of the moment.
There is no why.

—KURT VONNEGUT, JR., *SLAUGHTERHOUSE-FIVE*

IF YOU SAW the film *Jurassic Park*, you know amber is hardened tree resin that may hold trapped insects or leaves from 30 million years ago. But the organic gem also ensnared many an ancient shopper. One of the first commercial products, amber was made into pendants as far back as 12,000 B.C. Prussian King Frederick I even had an entire room made of it, as honeyed and irresistible as a woman's womb.

You The perfume made from melted amber has a velvety, succulent fragrance that lingers on the skin for hours. It's healing, too. Biofeedback studies show that amber oil relaxes brain waves, strengthens heart energy, and increases sensual pleasure. When you want to be carried away by euphoric delight, dab on a little "Northern gold."

You Two The smell of amber evokes spices, gold dust, and tented harems. Put on a CD of Sting's *Desert Rose*, drape yourself head-to-toe in sheer scarves, and slather on amber oil. Glide up and say, "Your love slave is here to serve you." If he needs encouragement, touch only the tip of your tongue to his lips—a *Kama Sutra* kiss.

A Day Off

Wear a gem—even if it's only imitation. Every now and then, take time to admire its sparkle, knowing it reflects your much more magnificent womanly fire.

DAY
315

Slap & Tickle

The Thump

Sometimes a little jolt like that does one good.

—WILLA CATHER, *ALEXANDER'S BRIDGE*

GENTLE TOUCHES ARE like chocolate pudding—delicious, soft, and comforting. But with too much comfort, sensations are lulled to sleep. That's when a few thumps add just the right spice. With every quick tap, skin and nerves come zinging to attention. Not knowing when the next little thwack might come, nerve fibers start to relax but also tingle with anticipation. The feeling's as electric as lightning.

You When you want to feel instantly alert and *in* your body, thump your legs and shoulders by alternating with the sides of both fists, like a slow drum roll. Percuss lightly over your breastbone to release tension and evoke joy. The slight fizzing sensation that follows may even make you laugh.

You Two Oil your hands and massage his equipment with smooth, flowing motions. Up, down, all around. But every once in a while, hold the base firmly and thump the sensitive tip against your palm. Or your belly. Or, better yet, your clitoris. His happy little organ will get the shock of its life. And so will yours.

Eyelashes

Thine eyes are springs in whose serene
And silent waters heaven is seen.
Their lashes are the herbs that look
On their young figures in the brook.

—WILLIAM C. BRYANT

WAY BACK IN ancient Egypt, women caught on to the allure of a fluttering eyelash. They applied kohl (a black powder made from soot, sandalwood, and clarified butter) to make lashes dark and thick—and to keep away dust, glare, and bugs. Centuries later, when Greta Garbo transformed her white lashes with layers of black mascara, eyelashes became the symbol of not just beauty, but of heavy-lidded, sultry sex.

DAY
317

You Make your eyelashes longer, thicker, and silkier by brushing them. Dip an eyelash brush or clean mascara wand in olive oil (or even rose oil to add delicious fragrance) and wiggle it through your lashes twice a day. You'll soon have thick, smoky curtains of love.

You Two Eyelashes on flesh tickle and whet the skin's appetite for more. Bat your lashes against his lips, tummy, and penis. Alternate between fast and slow flicks as you travel up and down the shaft and all around the head. Your close, warm breath will add heat, and soon he'll tingle, glow, and feel like laughing and coming all at the same time.

The Sweet Spot

It is certainly a soft spot to fall on and a sweet spot to look at.

—GILBERT K. CHESTERTON, *THE WISDOM OF FATHER BROWN*

BEFORE MEN AND women began ogling each others' chests, it was the rump that got us humans all hot and bothered — plump, squeezable, and rewardingly sensitive. Blood pools there during arousal, tenderizing the skin. And the nerve endings in the derrière use the same pathways to the brain as do the ones in the genitals, turning the area into a mixed-up hotbed of pleasure. Especially in the thinner-skinned, lower inside corner of each cheek — the sweet spot.

You Find something to rub your butt against as he pounds into you — the bedsheet, the car seat, the wall during a standing quickie. Or put your hands beneath your rump when in missionary. You'll add the extra stimulation that puts you over the top.

You Two Slowly slide his pants down, cupping his cheeks along the way. Lick and massage the sweet spot to warm it up, then spank one time. Perhaps lick him up front before repeating the shocking cycle. The jolt will crack open your lovemaking.

Accoutrements for the Hand

TO SOFTEN, DEEPEN, or sharpen the sensation of your slaps and tickles, wear or wield some of these:

- Leather gloves—delicious aroma, slinky feel, softens a playful blow
- Velvet gloves—a luxurious, "teddy bear" tickle
- Ostrich plume—for a light-as-air, wake-up-the-fine-hairs tease . . . and super-soft slap
- Toe or heel of your stilettos—stylish kink, pointy sensations
- Panties over your hand—smooth as silk, call-girl sexy
- Ping-pong paddle—the bumps vary sensation, the threat adds adrenaline
- Fur—fine fibers provide millions of elegant little tickles
- Garters—the ends skim along saucily or sting sharply
- Hairbrush—the bristle side for soft prickles, the back side for rousing love taps
- Tassel—for soft, quivery shivers, and subliminal visions of you as a go-go dancer
- Leather c**k strap—need I say more?

A Grown-Up Tickle

Those who tickle themselves may laugh when they please.

—GERMAN PROVERB

PHYSIOLOGISTS TELLS US that tickling occurs when we excite the receptors for both touch and pain at the same time. Our skin doesn't know whether to pull away or cuddle up for more—that delicious I love it!/Stop it! sensation. Why then can't we tickle ourselves? Because tickling is not only physical. Like really hot sex, tickling requires a tension, a level of not knowing but wanting to, that can only be created by two.

You Charles Darwin, who studied tickling extensively, concluded that it's a vital ingredient in bonding. When someone stimulates you to laugh and feel merry, you feel closer to them. And, conveniently, men are usually slightly more ticklish than women. So if you want to bond with your guy, tickle him more.

You Two Very sensitive nerves extend from his genitals, out along the groin crease, and up the sides of his torso. Make circles with your fingernails, just barely grazing the skin, from the sides of his rib cage down this line. Occasionally stray to his inner thighs or backs of his knees, so he doesn't know where you'll strike next. You'll send shivers of electricity to his equipment without even touching it.

Little Drummer Girl

But hark! My pulse like a soft drum
Beats my approach, tells thee I come.

—HENRY KING

WE HUMANS HAVE been drumming since 6000 B.C. Women, in fact, led most of the ancient drumming circles, calling others to worship, healing with pulsation and chant, and helping everyone resonate more deeply with the rhythmic energy of life. They understood that the beat of the drum opens our hearts to joy—while at the same time awakening something primal in our psyche.

You The vibrations produced by thrumming on skin can be very soothing. Drum your fingers on the area around your heart to release tension, on your skull to induce a peaceful trance, and on your pelvis to relieve menstrual cramps.

You Two With one hand, tap lightly under your guy's eyes, sending him into a state of bliss. With the other, drum softly on his testicles. It's like using a very low-wattage vibrator on his privates. The two rhythms meld and resonate through his entire body, opening his heart and making his genitals pulse with deep, throbbing excitement.

A Day Off

Fantasize about a man with slow hands. Hands that caress and lull. Hands that tickle and arouse. Hands that know exactly where to go.

DAY
322

Argentina Is for Lovers

Tango

Tango is not in the feet. It is in the heart.

—ANONYMOUS

THOUGH THE TANGO may have originated with gauchos, whose sweat-hardened chaps forced them to walk with flexed knees, soon everyone wanted to "wrestle with passion." To tango, you simply walk as elegantly as possible, while pressed close enough to feel the flush of your partner's cheek and the beat of his heart, and while he invades your most secret spaces with his legs. In this dance, as with sex, intense feelings are more important than technique—and if you do it right, your ankles and your souls become one.

You What makes a great tango dancer is the same thing that makes a superb lover. The *tangueros* say you must open a space inside and let the music of your partner fill it. Listen to his body language, imagine what he is experiencing, and then simply enjoy the feel of your arms around him.

You Two The simple steps of the tango are often decorated by slides, wraps, and long stretches of the leg—again, also good for sex. Stand facing each other, his hands supporting your lower back, your hands on his shoulders. Glide your foot up his leg and arm to rest on his shoulder. He inserts; you straighten into a near split by continuing the upward progress of your foot over the top of his shoulder. It's astonishing, beautiful, and hits all kinds of below-the-border angles.

DAY
323

Patagonia—The Vast Wild

We simply need that wild country available to us. . . . For it can be a means of reassuring ourselves of our sanity as creatures, a part of the geography of hope.

—WALLACE STEGNER

THE VERY NAME "Patagonia" conjures up images of raw, remote wilderness—the kind of place a man longs to cut his teeth against and a woman feels on her skin like a ravishing bite. At the very bottom of Argentina, Patagonia is a land of snarly windswept grasslands, emerald fjords, and crackling glaciers. Butch Cassidy and the Sundance Kid fled there because it was isolated and impenetrable. But stayed there probably because, like most, they were seduced by the way the challenges and wild freedom of the place re-enchanted their souls.

You Skies riddled with stars, grasses taller than a horse, places where no one has trod for a hundred years are necessary for the spirit. They leave us bare to our senses. Get thee to the wilderness—but if you can't, read *The Call of the Wild*, don't speak for a day, or drink the starlit air on your rooftop. It'll make you a wilder woman.

You Two On the vast plain of his chest lies undiscovered territory. Zigzag your tongue or hair up and down the crevice between his pecs—some of the most sensitive skin on his body. It's connected to his nipples, yet remote. It challenges him to explore delicate feelings. And it will make his chest hairs—and more southerly regions—quiver.

A Sense of Place

You can't know who you are until you know where you are.

— WENDELL BERRY

FOR THE PEOPLE of Buenos Aires, a café is not just a place to eat. It's a hearth where you meet a friend for a heart-to-heart, take a daily sabbatical with a game of dominos, or dissect matters of political import. The walls of the famous Café Tortino (established in 1858) exude an almost spiritual air—thick with the conversations of writers like Lorca and Neruda, the reminiscences of lonely immigrants, and the whispers of lovers who understood that the place you meet holds memories that will feed you later.

You You can give a room a sense of place by adding memorabilia (birthday photos, grandma's quilt, a basket from your trip to the Southwest), doing soulful things there every day (meditate, write letters, kiss your lover), and naming it (the Goddess Room, My Cave, the Inner Sanctum). You've set the stage for things sensual and deep to occur.

You Two Before having guests over (in the South Parlor, perhaps), make love on the coffee table. It will fill the room with electricity, and the two of you will remember delicious kisses and moans every time someone sets a cup of coffee there.

Evita

I have one thing that counts, and that is my heart; it burns in my soul, it aches in my flesh, and it ignites my nerves: that is my love for the people and Perón.

—EVA PERÓN

AN ILLEGITIMATE CHILD born into a poor family, Eva Perón rose to become the first lady of Argentina (1945 to 1952) and one of the most powerful women of our time.

Even as a child, her passion for expressing the deepest ideas of her heart guided her—first to become an actress and radio star, then to, as she put it, "raise the volume of people's lives" by righting social injustices. As Argentina's first lady, dressed in furs and jewels, Eva helped build hundreds of schools and hospitals, get fair pay and respect for exploited workers, and enact laws that gave women the right to vote. As lyricist Tim Rice wrote, all through her wild days, she did indeed keep her promise.

Part of what drove her was love for Juan Perón—a man she truly felt was next to a living god. But because she believed that "A man of action is one who triumphs over the rest. A woman of action is one who triumphs for the rest," she tied her causes to his with a crucial difference in motivation.

When she died of cervical cancer at thirty-two, thousands mourned her as a saintly friend to women and the poor, while others reviled her as a social-climbing tart. No matter how you see her, Evita was a woman of power who made her own and thousands of other's dreams come true by following her heart's passion. For me, that is her true legacy.

Waterfall Wet

I feel like a wet seed wild in the hot blind earth.

— WILLIAM FAULKNER

PLAYING AN IMMENSE and thunderous role in *Indiana Jones and the Kingdom of the Crystal Skull*, Iguazú Falls (straddling the border between Argentina and Brazil) are almost twice as big as Niagara. The raging curtain of water plummets out of an intensely green and steaming jungle, surrounding you in a magnificent, drenching womb. Underneath its civilized bikini wax, this is how your vulva appears to the aroused male — wild, powerful, and gushing with sex.

You Wetness is your erotic advantage. It doesn't depend on beauty, muscle tone, or technique. You're devastatingly sexy simply because you're wet — and he isn't. Don't keep this hidden. Before he enters you, let him see your moistness. He thinks it's mysterious and wonderful that "he" made you that way.

You Two Bring a glass of wine to bed, perhaps a spicy Argentine Syrah. Half-reclining, let a few drops dribble into your pubic hair. Then open your thighs and let him watch as you pour a small cascade over your pubic bone. He will simply have to lick your wine-soaked clitoris and labia. Cool wine, hot tongue, a waterfall of bliss.

Gaucho

A man on a horse is spiritually as well as physically bigger than a man on foot.

—JOHN STEINBECK

IN ARGENTINA, IF you see a leathery-faced god galloping by on a horse, long hair flying, and wearing a wide-brimmed hat, dashing scarf, and baggy trousers cinched with a huge studded leather belt—out of which sticks a fierce, sharply polished knife—he's a gaucho. These hard-working horsemen who wander the Pampas are known for their kindness to travelers and have become a national symbol for a proud and free way of life.

You I'm not suggesting wearing gaucho pants, though there's something about the way they sway that makes almost anyone's ass look fabulous. But I am suggesting walking with a certain swagger, gaucho-style—as if you're on a steed, sitting atop the world, subtly wagging your behind like fine horse flesh. Feels great, looks smokin' hot.

You Two Kneel near the edge of the bed and lean forward, resting your hands and forehead on the bed. When he comes in from behind, clamp your feet around his thighs, as if hanging onto a horse. He lays against your back and goes for a very snug, deep ride.

A Day Off

Argentina's vibrancy comes from contrast—remote places and sophisticated cities; gruff gauchos and romantic tangos; still-supressed yet powerful women. Revel in contrast. Feast on peasant stew and Godiva chocolate, wear zebra flats with a business suit, go hiking and to the opera. Do you feel more alive?

DAY

329

Sugar & Spice

A Rose Is a Rose

O rose garden of the beauty, open your face.
Even the moon became ashamed after seeing your face.
I want that rose garden.

—RUMI (TRANS. NEVIT O. ERGIN)

DAY
330

DIZZYING AROMAS. RED-HOT colors. Plush petals that lay themselves open for touch. No wonder medieval anatomists likened the rose to female genitalia—and believed it could cure drunkenness and insomnia. Cleopatra used the bloom's power to beguile Marc Antony, leading him to bed through knee-deep carpets of rose petals and lying with him on blossom-stuffed cushions.

You Designer Carolyne Roehm says, "A room with a bouquet becomes a room with a soul." Cluster red roses together with ripe berries for a lush earthy look, or with lilies to create a feminine presence. Make a romantic potpourri from rose petals given you by lovers. Or add a drop of rose oil to your bathwater—it's a superb anti-ager.

You Two Send a brawny bouquet of Red Magic roses and chocolate cosmos to your man, as Maria Shriver once did for Arnold. Or sprinkle rose petals on his body and lick around each one. Then make love. The petals, smooshed between you, create creamy textures during sex and fascinating patterns to admire in the afterglow.

Operating Instructions

Few men know how to kiss well; fortunately, I've always had time to teach them.

MEN *WANT* TO be great lovers. Legendary, if possible. But faced with female equipment and desires that seem vastly more complex—and ten times touchier—than a jet propulsion engine, they're baffled. Should he put his tongue in your mouth? Is it important to find that darn G-spot, or does his probing hurt? How long do you *really* want him to do that zigzag thing? The poor darlings need direction.

DAY

331

You You won't come off like a nag if you seduce him with sexy-siren moves. Put your hand atop his and glide it over your inner thighs—as soft or roughly as you like. Brazenly insert your nipple in his mouth, and moan when he licks it. Soon he'll be *looking forward* to your next revealing exploits.

You Two Precise, step-by-step instruction can be titillating if delivered with a purring voice and a well-timed moan. "Nibble on my neck, would you, baby? Then run your tongue down my breast and into my belly button. Yes, now in circles. Oooh, even bite me there. Now put your fingers inside my pussy, real slow and . . . mmmm . . . stroke me like when we . . ." The combination of your sexual confidence and racy verbiage will make him long to be ordered around.

Cinnamon

I have perfumed my bed with myrrh, aloes, and cinnamon,
Come, let's take our fill of loving until the morning.

—PROVERBS 7:17–18

IN THE ANCIENT world, cinnamon was more precious than gold. Derived from the bark of Asian evergreens, it preserved meat, embalmed bodies, and acted as a sweet-and-woody aphrodisiac. Medieval physicians treated coughs and sore throats with cinnamon, but the Emperor Nero simply burned it. In one extravagant gesture, he threw a year's supply of cinnamon onto his wife's funeral pyre—to atone for murdering her.

You Get healthier—and more seductive—by baking a few cinnamon rolls. The U.S. Department of Agriculture discovered that a little cinnamon every day can reduce blood sugar and cholesterol by 20 percent. The Smell & Taste Treatment & Research Foundation in Chicago tested 200 aromas and found that cinnamon was one of the most arousing scents for men.

You Two Dab some cinnamon-vanilla perfume between your breasts or slip a cinnamon stick under his pillow. A few whiffs will increase blood flow to his penis and keep him erect longer. Or apply cinnamon leaf oil (a milder version of super-tangy, plain cinnamon oil) to his nipples. When you blow on them, his skin will feel pleasantly afire.

The Test of a Real Man

HE MAY BE a hottie, but is he a mensch? You can tell if a guy has the right balance of sweetness and machismo if he:

1. Has plants in his apartment—real ones, that are still alive
2. Offers to leave and get condoms when, on the way to the bedroom, you tell him you don't have any
3. Shares a bubble bath with you
4. Dresses his bed with 100 percent cotton sheets, and maybe even a comforter
5. Asks for your advice—and takes it
6. Looks deeply into your eyes while he's coming
7. Cooks you an omelet the morning after
8. Has Michael Bublé in his CD collection
9. Gives you a massage that doesn't turn into sex
10. Compliments you on how you park a car, cook a meal, or make a dress look elegant

Blindfolded

As he had guessed, with her hands bound and eyes covered, she felt no sense of responsibility for whatever might occur.

—ANNE-MARIE VILLEFRANCHE, *PLAISIR D'AMOUR*

COVER YOUR EYES and you're in another world—private, vulnerable, immediate. Only the fine hairs on the back of your neck know what's coming next. And only your nose, ears, tongue, and fingers experience it. You *smell* your lover's anticipation, *feel* his lustful glance, *hear* his silent disrobing. Or is that the swish of a necktie he's about to wrap around your wrists?

You When you can't see what he's doing, anything he does— even if it's clumsy or clichéd—feels thrilling. He's an unknown lover with a new touch, a tangier kiss, someone you have to discover all over again. And finding your way to his chest or foot or penis is so much more exciting when you're forced to use your other senses to get there.

You Two Hand him a silky scarf and say "I want you to blindfold me tonight and have your way with me." Then let yourself go. The gift of your trust is a huge turn-on for any man. And, under cover of darkness, you find the bravado you need to touch yourself for his pleasure, or lick parts of him you "couldn't know" you're devouring with your tongue.

Fruitflesh

*Awake, O north wind; and come, thou south; blow on my garden,
that the spices thereof may flow out. Let my beloved come into his
garden, and eat his pleasant fruits.*

—SONG OF SONGS 4:16

WE CAN LEARN things from fruit. Take a peach. It's firm and
round on the outside, a little squishy in spots, but deep-settled
in its skin. Inside, it goes wild with tropical colors, sexy-soft
caverns, and honeyed nectars. Yet it's centered and confident — knowing it contains the seed of creation. Be like a peach.
Gritty. Boldly sensual. An unashamed feast.

You To be healthier, younger, and more beautiful, eat — and
wear — more fruit. Raspberries are high in vitamin C (aids in
collagen formation), apricots in beta carotene (fights cancer
and heart disease), and apples in phytochemicals (delays
aging). Bananas contain bufotenine, which increases self-confidence and libido. And mashed strawberries, applied like a
mask, perform super-deep cleansing.

You Two Halve an orange. Squeeze the juice of one half all
over his erection and slowly lick it clean. Then chisel a hole in
the other section of orange and set it atop his stalk like a cap.
Squeeze and swivel the fruit (the twisting motion drives men
wild), while you siphon off the mushy nectars that dribble
down from above.

DAY
335

A Day Off

Savor one Godiva Passion Truffle. Well, maybe two.

The Chocolate Soufflé version is airy and delicate, while Passion Fruit is refreshingly tart. You have to try several to find just the right flavor of passion for you, right?

DAY

336

Creatures of a Sexy Imagination

Two Heads Are Better than One

Separate, she wants his force of body and strength of reason; he, her softness, sensibility, and acute discernment. Together they are more likely to succeed in the world.

—BENJAMIN FRANKLIN

THE ANCIENT EGYPTIANS had a two-headed sphinx that guarded the gates of sunset and sunrise. Between the two manes lay the passage where the sun traveled from yesterday to today, creating the mystery of time. Like the lions, when we combine two opposing views—intellect and intuition, giving and receiving, hard line and soft touch—we get the magic of human chemistry and insight.

You Anne Morrow Lindbergh expressed the wisdom of the two-headed sphinx when she said, "Security in a relationship lies neither in looking back to what it was, nor forward to what it might be, but living in the present relationship and accepting it as it is now."

You Two Kiss him exactly the way you want to be kissed, and ask him *not* to kiss back. Then switch. You get the thrill of being in control, while he learns to tingle with restraint and anticipation. Meanwhile, you both get vital clues to the kind of smooching that drives the other wild. Not to mention the magic of the two kisses you're in right now.

DAY 337

Fairyland

Faeries, come take me out of this dull world,
For I would ride with you upon the wind . . .
And dance upon the mountains like a flame!

—WILLIAM BUTLER YEATS, *THE LAND OF HEART'S DESIRE*

DAY

338

FAIRIES MAY HAVE gotten their tiny image from the Greek goddess Psyche, whose name means "butterfly," but originally, they were thought to be real, life-sized women. Their power to transform a man into an animal or turn him to stone—which, really, any ordinary sex goddess can do—must indeed have seemed so fantastic as to give them the appearance of magical, ethereal beauty.

You We've all seen women who are not classically beautiful but who can light up any room—or any man. Like them, your fairy dust is not made of good looks or special charms and has nothing to do with being tiny. Your power comes from knowing you can make a man's organ rise at will—just by standing around with a twinkle in your eye.

You Two Further control is easy and, to him, miraculous. I've suggested ways of squeezing his penis to delay orgasm (Day 101) and to make him "tower" (Day 163). But if, during missionary for example, you squeeze the base for only five seconds and release, right before his moment of no return, he'll practically erupt. Go, Twinkletoes!

Giantess

I should have loved to live near a young giant girl,
Like a voluptuous cat at the feet of a queen.
To watch her body flower with her soul . . .
To guess if her heart brewed some smoldering flame;
To roam at leisure over her magnificent form . . .

—CHARLES BAUDELAIRE,
THE GIANTESS (TRANS. THE AUTHOR)

ODIN, THE TOP god of Norse mythology, became divine by marrying one of the ancient race of giantesses. Known for their wild natures and great wisdom, these big goddesses were coveted because, by centering his life around a giantess, a man could gain strength and long life. Still true today. Men married to us passionate, wise women (giantesses in the field of being human) live about ten years longer than their single brethren.

You Science tells us that our bodies generate an electromagnetic field that can be felt by others and that can be expanded with thought. Breathe deeply for a few minutes and imagine your glow extending further into the room with each exhale. You will make a giant impression on everyone who comes near.

You Like the ancient giantesses, try engulfing your man with sexy slowness. When he lies on his back with knees drawn up, stand astride and lower your rear to rest on his knees. Then glide down his thighs, oh so slowly, as he watches your gorgeous twat swallow his erection. You can also use his thighs (and your feet) as a springboard to bob and weave all over him.

Vampire Love

DON'T WE LOVE those dark, dangerous, bad boys? So tortured, so wild, so . . . ravishing. How fabulous if, occasionally, your guy were just a bit "vampiric" in bed. The best way to transform him is to bite with your own fangs.

- The Eyes — Intensify your gaze by trying to pierce his body with your eyes. Let his gaze pierce you back. You'll discover secrets about his skin, hands, nipples. And all that ferocity builds up heat.
- The Kiss — Imagine you're going to drink his soul. Approach his neck (the line from chin to collarbone is as sensitive as the ridge of his penis) and breathe hotly. Close your bite by slowly scraping teeth over skin. Lick in circles. Suck. Offer your own neck.
- The Other Kiss — Dart your tongue between his lips. When he does the same, clamp onto his tongue with your teeth. Gently. Then pull back, letting his tongue slide out between your teeth. Keep this up as you caress his erection.
- The Growl — Think hungry. Think primal. Think vampire. Do it while your mouth is over his belly, neck, or genitals so he can feel the hot rumble of it.
- The Power of Surrender — Fall into your sensations and let them lead you. Slide all over him, using every part of your body to excite him, move him around, dominate him. Grab his penis and rub it on your breasts. Then put it where you want it and devour him.

The Three Graces

For in that place where Love's reports are laid . . .
He saith that this so gracious and fair maid
Hath to herself all graces gathered.

—GUIDO CAVALCANTI (TRANS. EZRA POUND)

IN GREEK ART, you'll see many carvings of three gorgeous damsels—all naked, one with her back to the viewer. Representing the triple aspect of the goddess, they give the gifts of Brilliance (beauty, charm, sensuality), Flowering (creativity and pleasure), and Heart's Joy (tenderness and love). Seemingly too much for one body to contain, these graces were personified as three. And yet, we human women manage to be beautiful, creative, and tender all at the same time. Naturally.

You Single-minded creatures, men are mystified by a woman's ability to think about and do many things at once. If you multitask on him—say, cook him breakfast, caress him, and tell him where you're gonna "take" him later, all the while standing at the stove—you'll dazzle the pants right off him.

You Two Tackle three erogenous zones at once. Simply smooth your lips over his erection while one hand tweaks his nipple and the other tickles his anus or perineum. If this doesn't blow his mind, there's something wrong with him.

Siren Song

Once I sat upon a promontory,
And heard a mermaid on a dolphin's back
Uttering such dulcet and harmonious breath
That the rude sea grew civil at her song
And certain stars shot madly from their spheres,
To hear the sea-maid's music.

—WILLIAM SHAKESPEARE, *A MIDSUMMER NIGHT'S DREAM*

REMEMBER THE DOUBLE-TAILED mermaid on the original Starbucks logo? Too suggestive for most, her spread-eagled pose had to be toned down, but her mystique still lures millions into the Sea of Java. The siren, an audacious mermaid holding her two tails wide is actually an ancient symbol for female sexuality—a mystery men find as baffling and terrifying as the ocean's deep, and even more enticing.

You We're taught that ladies keep their legs together. But in the bedroom, you may find it advantageous to be a siren. The pose described in the following You Two tilts your hips up, forcing his thrusts to hit your G-spot and his pelvis to caress your bottom. It also spreads your labia wide, exposing your clitoris to more pelvis-slaps. An erogenous zone bonanza!

You Two Lie on your back, and then grasp your feet and hold them high in the air, spreading your legs wide. No man can resist this siren's call. Something primal in him will ache to plumb your depths—and when he does, the new angles will give him an oceanic orgasm.

A Day Off

Pretend that you are larger than life, can fit on the head of a pin, or own two heads or two tails.

How do you walk, feel, and think differently? What new tricks can you perform? What comes to your sexy imagination? Use your supernatural powers in the bedroom.

What Color Is Your Love?

Paint Your Town Red

When in doubt, wear red.

—BILL BLASS

LIKE SALSA, FRESHLY kissed lips, and firemen, red is *hot*. Just looking at it can make your heart beat faster and your breath ragged. Why is red so sexy? It's a lot of energy crammed into a small space, like nuclear power. If you want to pack that kind of wallop, draw all your energy inside, hold it tight, and warm it with a dash of love. Your movements, your voice, and your eyes will seem to simmer with explosive power.

You According to a study by Dr. Andrew Elliot, a psychology professor at the University of Rochester, men find women sexier when they're wearing crimson. When out with a woman in a red dress, a man is even willing to spend more money, says the *Journal of Personality and Social Psychology*. Best of all, red attracts the kind of guy who likes powerful women—so all that sex, spending, and sizzle won't scare him off!

You Two For some sassy loving, insert "red." When he's thrusting away and getting nowhere, spank him once on the fullest part of his butt. Caress the area tenderly while his nerve endings wake up. Then, as he gets into a deeper rhythm, apply three sudden, sharp whacks. His fanny, his lust, and your libido will be red, spanking hot.

Oceanic Blue

*Can ye fathom the ocean, dark and deep, where the mighty waves
and the grandeur sweep?*

— FANNY CROSBY

IN THE TRANQUILITY of a vast blue sea lies the potential
for a tidal wave. That's how it is with the color blue. It produces
body chemicals that are calming as the ocean (great for bed-
rooms and hospitals) but, in its brighter shades, becomes electric as a storm. Like slow, penetrating foreplay, blue goes deep,
lulling you into a trance while all the time it's building explosive, surging passions.

You Blue has benefits. Studies show that exercising in a blue
gym or in blue sweats can help you lift heavier weights and do
more reps. Wear true blue to a job interview and you'll appear
loyal and focused. Find a guy who likes blue — because he likes
to explore sex with a one-and-only and stay around for a long,
long time.

You Two For the penetrating "blue" foreplay mentioned
above, sit between your man's inner thighs and massage from
knee to groin with the heels of your oiled hands. Use deep,
rolling strokes like sea waves, building the pressure in his erection slowly, inevitably. Stay away from his penis until you are
ready for an oceanic orgasm.

Royal Purple

In the past, people were born royal. Nowadays, royalty comes from what you do.

—GIANNI VERSACE

COMBINING THE HOT power of red with the cool depth of blue, purple has an air of rich sophistication. Cleopatra, famous for her complex beauty, loved it, and kings and queens of nearly every country have worn purple robes to impart an almost mystical authority. But you don't have to be royal to feel—and look—like a million bucks. Either wear violet, or make purple in your soul by mixing fire (red) with meaning (blue). Isn't that the mystery, the "purpleness," of passion?

You Purple stimulates the brain and boosts creativity, probably because it calms nerves (that's the blue part of it) while also creating excitement (that's the red). Wear purple when you want to turn on your imagination or feel uplifted. Considered the most spiritual of all colors, it will even deepen your yoga or meditation practice.

You Two Instead of purple robes, you can use modern technology to make your man feel like an emperor. Get one of those remote-controlled, egg-shaped vibrators (a purple one, perhaps?) that you can insert. Give him the controls. With power over when, where, and how long you remain exquisitely close to orgasm, he'll have a passionate love slave at his kingly command. And oh what fun for you.

His Favorite Color

COLOR PSYCHOLOGISTS TELL us that color choices can reveal the man behind the myth. Here's what your guy's favorite hue says about his personality and sexual proclivities.

Blue — Mr. Commitment is loyal, trustworthy, and affectionate. In bed, he's willing to spend hours bringing you to sexual nirvana.

Red — Mr. Excitement loves power, speed, and risk. He'll want to grab a quickie on the park bench, then go home for some hard, long loving on top of the washing machine.

Yellow — Mr. Brainiac is creative, adaptable, and optimistic. He likes to laugh in bed and try complex positions. A good bawdy joke or a sex factoid gets him in the mood.

Green — Mr. Nature loves the outdoors and will give you the shirt off his back. In bed, he's generous and endearingly simple. No fancy toys, just plenty of skin on skin.

Purple — Mr. Complicated is deep and mysterious. If you're willing to explore erotic boundaries and treat him like a sex god, he'll take you places you didn't know existed.

Orange — Mr. Rock Star is flashy and outrageous, like Prince at the Super Bowl. He loves sexual fantasies — talking about them, acting them out, and playing kinky fantasy roles.

Black — Mr. McDracula is into authority and power. He likes his emotions strong and his sex a little bit rough. Give him some Velcro handcuffs and he's good to go.

Brown — Mr. Snugglebunny likes to walk on the beach and say those three little words. For him, sex is a private, all-day cuddlefest where he satisfies your every romantic need.

Tangy Orange

If you aren't going all the way, why go at all?

—JOE NAMATH

ORANGE IS FLAMBOYANT and controversial. By stimulating emotions and appetites, it demands attention and gets people talking. To be orange is to be a star. Why? Because it combines the fling-yourself-into-the-sun passion of red with the cheer and braininess of yellow—the same mixture that makes sassy, smart women so completely irresistible.

You In nature, orange is associated with transition—ocher autumn leaves and tangerine sunsets. Wear orange when you want to change someone's mind or when you need to build a bridge between his desire for football and your preference for a romantic dinner.

You Two The edgy boldness of orange is like a shot of espresso for the libido. Have him sit with his back against the headboard and slip a long scarf (cadmium-colored!) behind him, loose ends facing you. Stand tall astride his thighs, grabbing the scarf ends for support. Display your naked self. Then lower your hips slowly and insert him. Using the scarf ends like a lever, swivel and hoist yourself up and down. Besides the brash and kink of it, this position hits all the zingiest spots in both of you.

Hothouse Green

Colette wrote of vegetables as if they were love objects and of sex as if it were an especially delightful department of gardening.

—BRIGID BROPHY

YOU KNOW HOW the snap of a pea pod or the scoring of a cucumber seems to *smell* green—bursting with life and freshness? It makes you want to sink your fingers into the soil or tumble through new-mown grass. Wanting to appear that juicy and fertile, like a spring garden covered with dew, brides in the Middle Ages wore green. It's a color that can make you look pure as a virgin but also earthy, ripe, and good enough to eat.

You In feng shui, green means renewal. Refresh your spirits and vitalize your body by sprinkling different shades of green (varied shades are important) throughout your home—apple green curtains in the kitchen, forest green towels in the bath, emerald pillows for couch or bed, and live plants with lush green foliage everywhere.

You Two Cooling greens mix perfectly with the heat of a body. Insert a mint deep in your vagina an hour before you have sex. It tingles your insides and makes you grin at the thought of his taste surprise. You'll be extra hot, but with a touch of ice, when he finally enters you.

A Day Off

All day, surround yourself with blue for calm or yellow for good cheer. In the evening, switch to red for sex. Notice the difference in your moods and actions. Think about how you could use color to build inner strength, optimism, and sensuality.

DAY

350

Portals

The Open Door

Doorways are sacred to women for we are the doorways of life and we must choose what comes in and what goes out.

—MARGE PIERCY

IN FENG SHUI, your front door is a gateway between the outside world and your inner sanctum—a place where you take off the cloaks of businesswoman and carpooler to relax into your true self. Sex, too, is a doorway, where you fling off convention and open your body and soul to the wild ecstasies within.

You Practitioners of feng shui advise keeping your front door clear of obstructions so opportunities can find their way in. Likewise, when you want love to enter your life, keep your mind free of thoughts like "There are no good men out there," or "If only I were skinnier." Invite romance in with the open door of a sexy smile.

You Two A doorway can also support you. Lean over and grasp a door frame, while your man braces himself against the other side of the frame. It gives the doggie a fresh location, a new posture, and extra push.

DAY
351

The Golden Gate

And the doorway of the mysterious female
is the base from which heaven and earth sprang.
It is there within us all the while;
draw upon it as you will, it never runs dry.

— *TAO-TE CHING*

DAY

352

FULL OF PERFUMES and magic, the vulva is the portal to bliss for any man—and the gateway of life for every person. So venerated has it been in almost every culture, from Asia to the Americas, that you'll still see *Sheela-na-gigs* (carved vulvas) at the entrance to many medieval churches in Europe. People still touch them as a blessing and as a means of passing through from worldly cares to heavenly paradise.

You Through centuries of rubbing, the vulval lips that formed the gates to many ancient temples became silky smooth. So, too, the skin all over our bodies develops a patina with age. We may get laugh lines, we may plump, we may sag—but we are rubbed to a glow by the hands of our beloved.

You Two Have him sit with his back against the headboard, while you stand facing him, straddling his legs. He'll be wowed and then compelled to kiss that magical gateway. Gravity increases blood flow and sensitivity in your vulva—and your stance of command sends extra shivers through both of you.

Mouth

*Theres nothing like a kiss long and hot down to your soul almost
paralyses you . . .*

—MOLLY BLOOM IN *ULYSSES*, BY JAMES JOYCE

THE *KAMA SUTRA* says a woman's mouth mirrors her genitals—the lips like the labia, the cleft in the upper lip like the
clitoris, and the soft palate just above the front teeth like the
G-spot. As a replica of her womb, this upper erogenous zone
is one of the main gates to a woman's intimate self. Perhaps
that's why we feel deliciously ravished and touched to the very
core of our being by a deep, slow kiss.

DAY

353

You Test out the connection between lip cleft and clitoris by
rubbing or scratching above your mouth. Or try smoothing
your tongue over the top of your mouth to see if you are more
sensitive to the soft palate/G-spot connection. Use these sensual channels to catch up to your man's speedy arousal or
deepen your own orgasm.

You Two While the roof of the mouth connects to a woman's
G-spot, in a man it's a conduit to the perineum—the really
sensitive spot between his testicles and anus. During a kiss,
run your tongue over his palate. It's unexpected, ticklish, and
earth-moving.

Sexy Chakras

IN EASTERN THOUGHT, the chakras (energy centers in the body) are portals to expanded consciousness. Focusing on these areas during sex can make new senses blossom and provide a portal to erotic bliss. Rest your attention lightly in one of these spots—even throughout the day—and see if something new opens up for you.

Location	Body/Mind Sense	Sexual Sense
Pelvic floor	Voluptuousness, smell	Lusty, undulating earthiness
Belly	Creativity, sensation	Adventurous sex, romance, sensuality
Diaphragm	Confidence, power, touch	Sex as life force, being *in* your body
Heart	Harmony, love, hearing	Erotic love, sharing affection
Throat	Communication, taste	Sex as communion, honeyed words
Between brows	Inner vision, knowing, sight	Intuiting what your partner wants
Top of head	Completeness, all senses	Merging with partner and cosmos

Penis Portal

Anybody who believes that the way to a man's heart is through his stomach flunked geography.

—ROBERT BYRNE

CONSIDER THE SLIT in a man's penis. Like any opening, it's an exit—for his life-giving seed; but also an entrance—to his fertile virility. It's a place where he's receptive and vulnerable, yet all man. Without it, his organ would be lifeless, literally; and the poor man wouldn't be able to pass on his genes. But also, his penis wouldn't have nearly the same personality, the same insouciance. That small hatch gives a guy—and an embryo—real character.

You To get an idea of its extreme sensitivity, think of the skin surrounding his slit as similar to your labia, and the slit itself like the opening of your vulva. If you imagine that connection when you lick him there, you'll feel the sensation deep in your *own* genitals.

You Two While your mouth is covering him, lick with upward strokes right in the glans slit. Then remove your lips, hold the furrow open and make butterfly flicks with a hard tongue. Oral dynamite.

The Inside Passage

Intercourse is not primarily an experience of personal love . . . but of the gods. The partner is no longer felt to be limited to the familiar conscious personality, but has become also the gateway to the infinite mystery of life.

— ELEANOR BERTINE

THE TAOIST MASTERS say there is an invisible channel running from the perineum up through the top of the head—a tube that follows nerve pathways connecting endocrine glands in both locations. Because these glands regulate vitality, if you imagine sexual energy moving through this inner channel, you actually rejuvenate your body and sexuality. If you *both* feel the flow in a circle (e.g. out the top of your head, down through his inner passage and out his perineum, in through yours), it becomes a gateway to full-body orgasm and even enlightenment.

You Some women say that, when they focus on this inner channel during sex, their hips undulate more hypnotically; others that their nipples tremble; still others that they feel an orgasm all the way up to their eyebrows. Why not test your own reaction?

You Two The best way to feel this energy flow during sex is to sit up, with legs wrapped around each other's behinds. Imagine a river of sexual sensation coursing from genitals to head. Lock eyes or hug close enough to feel his breath. Have him cup your butt cheeks and lift you up and down. That way, even if you don't ride the hidden inside passage, your rocking stimulates new points for you both. And the grip of his palms feels outrageous.

A Day Off

When you walk through your bedroom door, think
of it as a portal to another, more sensual, world.
How is it different from your regular world? How
are you different?

DAY
357

Inner Beauty

The Flower That Is You

When you take a flower in your hand and really look at it, it's your world for the moment.

—GEORGIA O'KEEFFE

ACCORDING TO STUDIES done at Rutgers University, a flower bouquet almost *always* elicits the Duchenne smile, the kind that makes your eyes crinkle and produces measurable changes in the brain. Why? Scientists believe flowers speak to us in an ancient chemical language—both colorful and primal—that unlocks the brain's mechanism for pleasure, memory, and transcendent wonder.

You Walk through a garden and learn about yourself. Like a flower, you are curvy, soft, and smell like sex in tropical places. You brighten any room just by being in it. But more than that, you inspire hope in those around you by showing them how to make something gorgeous out of life's mud.

You Two Just before he enters you, inhale and tighten your PCs. As he crosses your threshold, exhale and release the muscles, creating the sensation that you are blooming for him. On his next in-stroke, inhale and tighten again—which stretches his penile skin back and pulls him in like a honey-drunk bee. As a bonus, the contractions and breaths help to engorge your genitals for more powerful orgasms.

Take It S-l-o-w

Anything worth doing well is worth doing slowly.

—GYPSY ROSE LEE

SOMETIMES OUR LIVES seem a headlong rush of text messages on the run, lipstick applied while driving, and fast food. Not so for the Italians. When a McDonald's opened at Rome's Spanish Steps, the masters of *la dolce vita* reacted by starting the Slow Food movement. Now, in seventy Slow Cities, people garden instead of buying freeze-dried food, park their cars to enjoy the view, and reconnect with taste buds and friends over three-hour lunches.

You When you slow down to savor life, you gain depth, dimension, and earthiness. Slow-paced living even helps your skin retain collagen. So on your next trip to the bank, bag your cell phone and throttle down. Ogle handsome passersby, stop for a frappucino, admire flirty skirts in The Gap's windows. Get there — but enjoy the journey.

You Two During full-throttle sex, grab his hips to slow the action, then grind against him. The contrast wakes up dulled senses. Or get on top and thrust so slowly you can hear . . . every . . . slippery . . . slurp. This snail's pace builds anticipation and makes him focus on each twinge of your inner muscles. That exquisite moment just before climax will seem to last forever.

A Secret Journal

When your heart speaks, take good notes.

— SUSAN BORKIN

SOME OF THE first journal keepers were the ladies of the tenth-century Japanese court. Hidden under the bed cushions, their "pillow books" gave the women a place free of the men's iron control to explore their innermost thoughts and dish over juicy court gossip. Intrigued by the new secrets in their eyes, the men could only wonder why the royal women had become so much more fascinating.

You Journaling is like good therapy, but cheaper. Pick up a diary so pretty or striking it makes your heart sing. Then ramble. What happened to you only once? What does a favorite lyric say to you? If passion were a person, what would she do? When you crawl into yourself, you may discover something beautiful and strong hiding there.

You Two Write out your erotic dreams, detailing exactly how James Bond rips off your blouse and licks the rim of your left nipple for three hours. When you arrive at a scenario you really like, let your man find the pages "accidentally" or read them to him as foreplay. He'll be aroused by your naughty thoughts — and will probably act out your most "secret" fantasy.

Beautiful Despite Their Looks

YOU'VE HEARD OFTEN enough that true beauty comes from within, but sometimes a girl needs *evidence*. Here are only a few of the many not-so-purty women who became icons of sex and beauty.

Cleopatra — According to Guy Weill Goudchaux in his article *Was Cleopatra Beautiful?*, she had "the features of a bird of prey." But she captivated Julius Caesar and Marc Antony, the most powerful men of her time, with her intelligence and sensuality.

Anne Boleyn — Too thin and olive-skinned for her time, she won hearts with her vivaciousness and quick wit. A besotted Henry VIII changed laws and religions to marry her.

Josephine Baker — In 1920s America, black was not yet beautiful. But because of her no-holds-barred dancing, sophistication, and raw female power, she was idolized as the Black Venus.

Wallis Simpson — Edward VIII gave up the English throne for her. She had a horsy face and string-bean body but "could make a matchstick seem like a Havana cigar." (Unknown)

Janis Joplin — She was plain to the point of homely but so charismatic that millions dreamed of bedding the sexy High Priestess of Rock. She had soul — big-time.

Helen Mirren — She's sixty-four, with a big nose and no face-lift. But at the 2007 Academy Awards, *she* was the one men slavered over. Her espoused beauty secret is happiness.

Dancing

To dance is to be out of yourself. Larger, more beautiful, more powerful. This is power, it is glory on earth and it is yours for the taking.

—AGNES DE MILLE

IN ANCIENT CRETE, respectable matrons often spent entire nights dancing naked under the olive trees, inviting sensual ecstasy into their bodies. Intuitively, they understood what dance therapists now tell us—movement not only *reflects* feelings, but, by releasing memories from our muscles, it *causes* them. Clench your fist and you start to feel angry. Dance the samba and you feel sultry. Your movements connect the inner and outer you.

You If you'd never seen Patrick Swayze in *Dirty Dancing*, would he still seem quite so handsome? Dancing moves sexual energy through your body and reveals it to the world. Shimmy and shake to some Tito Puente or Babatunde Olatunji. You'll burn fat, stimulate hormones, and unlock your sexual charisma.

You Two Professional lap dancers say these two moves earn the biggest tips. 1) He sits in a chair; you stand facing away, legs shoulder-width apart. Roll your pelvis, look back at him, smile, bend forward, and slap your derrière. 2) Face him, put your hands on the chair back, straddle his upper leg with your knees and use one of them to caress his inner thigh. Simple. Beautiful. Powerful.

The Spirit of Adventure

Dive into the fountain of life.
Dive, so the piece of soil you step on
Gives rubies and scatters pearls.

—RUMI (TRANS. NEVIT O. ERGIN)

QUANTUM PHYSICISTS TELLS us we're composed of sub-atomic particles of energy that vibrate at different speeds, depending on whether we think exciting or dull thoughts. Per-haps that's why some women light up a room—and some don't. Women who are alive to adventure, who have a fierce spirit, make the air electric. Through the dazzle they project, we per-ceive them as beautiful, fascinating, profoundly sexy.

You According to the Salk Institute for Biological Studies, brain cells without a job to do will die. But challenged to learn, the brain grows new cells—which nourishes the cardiovascu-lar system, which makes skin glow and eyes sparkle. Become beautiful by learning a new word, venturing out on a new route to work, tackling a Sudoku puzzle. It's cheaper, better—and longer-lasting—than Botox.

You Two Oil your hands and take a penis adventure. Grasp the base and, with one finger, inscribe small circles on the underside ridge, bottom to top. Work *slowly*, finally sliding all around the tip and deeply into the tender slit. When he moans or writhes, you've found a hot spot. These new discoveries will make his equipment seem lovelier to you. And you will look absolutely luminous to him!

DAY
363

A Day Off

Find a photo of yourself as a happy little girl.
What is it about her that's cute, endearing, lively?
Keep the photo by your mirror and know that you
still have that wide smile, those sparkly eyes, the
quirky chin tilt that screams out vulnerability and
optimism at the same time. You are beautiful.

DAY
364

The Secret

BY NOW, I hope you've picked up the idea that sensual inspiration is everywhere—in a pine tree, an old-time movie star, or a pinch of cinnamon. All you have to do is see through passion-colored glasses. Look at a chair or a leaf, for instance, and notice its curves and textures. See what it reminds you of. Be in love with it. Because when you love something, it tells you its secrets. Here's how it might work:

- Kitchen mitt—You handle your pop-tarts. The mitt is padded. It works like a hand. It protects. How would that feel on a rump? Softer and nicer than a slap? Hmmm.
- Shell—It's delicate but open. Could I let myself be vulnerable and open too? What else looks like this—my vulva? How beautiful. Maybe I could display myself *that* way.
- Green—How does green feel? Cool? Earthy? Cucumbers. Even juicier and colder from the fridge? Inside me . . . or rolling on his skin . . . or squishing between us, or . . .

You get the idea. Let the world become your erotic oyster. Make passion your daily habit and you will be happier, smarter, sexier. You will connect to the center of who you really are. And you will find yourself in a new world, one where you are aroused by all that you touch, and where all that you touch—every peach, every project, every lover—comes alive with the power of your desire.

Credits

Index

373